The Oral History Manual

AMERICAN ASSOCIATION
FOR STATE AND LOCAL HISTORY
BOOK SERIES

SERIES EDITOR

Rebekah Beaulieu, Taft Museum of Art

MANAGING EDITOR

Aja Bain, AASLH

EDITORIAL BOARD

Jessica Dorman, The Historic New Orleans Collection
Harry Klinkhamer, Venice Museum & Archives
Anne Lindsay, California State University–Sacramento
Steven Lubar, Brown University
Laura A. Macaluso, York County History Center
Ann McCleary, University of West Georgia
Debra Reid, The Henry Ford
Laura Roberts, Roberts Consulting
Zachary Stocks, Oregon Black Pioneers
Jamie Simek, Eiteljorg Museum
William Stoutamire, University of Nebraska–Kearney
William S. Walker, Cooperstown Graduate Program SUNY Oneonta

ABOUT THE SERIES

The American Association for State and Local History Book Series addresses issues critical to the field of state and local history through interpretive, intellectual, scholarly, and educational texts. To submit a proposal or manuscript to the series, please request proposal guidelines from AASLH headquarters: AASLH Editorial Board, 2021 21st Ave. South, Suite 320, Nashville, Tennessee 37212. Telephone: (615) 320-3203. Website: www.aaslh.org.

ABOUT THE ORGANIZATION

The American Association for State and Local History (AASLH) is a national history membership association headquartered in Nashville, Tennessee, that provides leadership and support for its members who preserve and interpret state and local history in order to make the past more meaningful to all people. AASLH members are leaders in preserving, researching, and interpreting traces of the American past to connect the people, thoughts, and events of yesterday with the creative memories and abiding concerns of people, communities, and our nation today. In addition to sponsorship of this book series, AASLH publishes History News magazine, a newsletter, technical leaflets and reports, and other materials; confers prizes and awards in recognition of outstanding achievement in the field; supports a broad education program and other activities designed to help members work more effectively; and advocates on behalf of the discipline of history. To join AASLH, go to www.aaslh.org or contact Membership Services, AASLH, 2021 21st Ave. South, Suite 320, Nashville, TN 37212.

The Oral History Manual

Fourth Edition

Barbara W. Sommer and Mary Kay Quinlan

ROWMAN & LITTLEFIELD
Lanham • Boulder • New York • London

Published by Rowman & Littlefield
An imprint of The Rowman & Littlefield Publishing Group, Inc.
4501 Forbes Boulevard, Suite 200, Lanham, Maryland 20706
www.rowman.com

86-90 Paul Street, London EC2A 4NE

British Library Cataloguing in Publication Information Available

Library of Congress Cataloging-in-Publication Data

Names: Sommer, Barbara W., author. | Quinlan, Mary Kay, author.
Title: The oral history manual / Barbara W. Sommer and Mary Kay Quinlan.
Description: Fourth edition. | Lanham : Rowman & Littlefield, [2024] |
    Series: American Association for State and Local History book series |
    Includes bibliographical references and index.
Identifiers: LCCN 2024014749 (print) | LCCN 2024014750 (ebook) | ISBN
    9781538181683 (cloth) | ISBN 9781538181690 (paperback) | ISBN
    9781538181706 (epub)
Subjects: LCSH: Oral history—Handbooks, manuals, etc. | Oral
    history—Methodology. | Interviewing—Handbooks, manuals, etc. |
    Historiography.
Classification: LCC D16.14 .S69 2024 (print) | LCC D16.14 (ebook) | DDC
    907.2—dc23/eng/20240613
LC record available at https://lccn.loc.gov/2024014749
LC ebook record available at https://lccn.loc.gov/2024014750

♾️™ The paper used in this publication meets the minimum requirements of American National Standard for Information Sciences—Permanence of Paper for Printed Library Materials, ANSI/NISO Z39.48-1992.

Contents

Preface

Stories are everywhere:

- Advertisers create mini-stories to sell stuff.
- Celebrities bare their deepest secrets in stories told to entertainment magazines.
- Everyday people turn to social media to share stories of their lives, from banal to bizarre.

In fact, stories and storytelling, defined in myriad ways and sometimes called by the more scholarly sounding term *narratives*, have become ubiquitous in contemporary Western culture. And some story performances, like the produced excerpts from StoryCorps recordings broadcast on NPR, have loyal followers who relish the often tear-jerking moments.[1]

If learning how to capture those kinds of stories has drawn you to *The Oral History Manual*, you'll be disappointed. But if you want to document information about people's lives and uncover new information and insights about past times and places, you've come to the right place. Oral history, of course, is not solely concerned with documenting historical facts. Nor is it necessarily limited to documenting lived experiences in the distant past. Rather, oral historians seek to explore and document narrators' understanding or interpretation of their experiences in past times, places, and ways of life. It is that sort of information that offers deeper insights about the past for those who encounter oral history interviews now and for many years into the future. As authors, this is what we hope you will take away from this manual.

Books have stories, too, even books about history and oral history. This book is no exception. The idea for this book began with a small grant from the Nebraska Humanities Council, now Humanities Nebraska, to Barbara Sommer more than two decades ago. Its purpose was to support development of an oral history project. Sommer, having recently met Mary Kay Quinlan, invited her to join the project.

Based on the results of the Nebraska Humanities Council project, which focused on oral history project development, interview guidelines, and information about interview preservation and access, Sommer and Quinlan began to be asked to present training workshops. They presented the workshops in Nebraska, throughout the Upper Midwest, and at national conferences including the 1998 American Association for State and Local History (AASLH) conference in Sacramento, California. The next year, at the AASLH conference in Baltimore, Maryland, Sommer was approached by Mitch Allen, founder of AltaMira Press (now Rowman & Littlefield, the publisher of the AASLH Book Series). What about writing a book on how to do oral history based on information presented in the workshop? She said yes, but the book would have another author, Mary Kay Quinlan. After discussions among Allen, Sommer, and Quinlan, they decided to move ahead with what became *The Oral History Manual*. The first edition came out in 2002, introduced at the AASLH conference and the Oral History Association meeting that year.

We, Barb Sommer and Mary Kay Quinlan, are proud now to present the fourth edition of this manual. In it, we have updated information about oral history ethics and technology, oral history and social justice, remote interviewing options, and preservation and access steps. But, importantly, we have not changed the basics: the steps included in each edition that define the practice of oral history and help guide oral historians to meet national standards.

When we discussed the book with Mitch Allen, he suggested that it should follow and build on the publications of Willa Baum, pioneering oral historian and former director of the University of California Berkeley's Regional Oral History Office. As co-authors, we have been true to this goal. Each edition of *The Oral History Manual* retains its ties to Baum's ground-breaking work, especially *Oral History for the Local Historical Society* (first edition, 1969) and *Transcribing and Editing Oral History* (1977), as well as Baum's work with David K. Dunaway, *Oral History: An Interdisciplinary Anthology* (1984). In addition, Quinlan brought the teachings of Martha Ross, under whom she studied, to the book, and we drew, and continue to draw, on publications and anthologies from Donald A. Ritchie, Valerie Raleigh Yow, Alistair Thomson, and Robert Perks; works in excellent oral history series including Practicing Oral History (Routledge, Taylor & Francis Group), Palgrave Studies in Oral History, the Oxford (University) Oral History Series, The Columbia (University) Oral History Series, the *Oral History Review*—the journal of the Oral History Association—and the wonderful and exciting body of work by ground-breaking oral history authors. But the basics began with Willa Baum, and we, as co-authors, are committed to continuing to draw inspiration from her work in the fourth edition of *The Oral History Manual*.

This manual, from its first edition to its fourth edition, is designed to present and explain oral history fundamentals. These are the basics: careful and thoughtful planning that supports community engagement and involvement of narrator and interviewer, interview preparation that reflects respect for the narrator, thoughtful interviews that help capture the knowledge of the narrator, preservation of interview information in the context in which it was spoken, and ongoing access to the oral history. When mastered, they can be applied to projects across the spectrum, from archival-based projects to work in social justice settings and in the community, and to its use in podcasts and blogs. The basics lay the common groundwork for excellence in the practice of oral history and for effective ongoing use of this primary source material.

The Oral History Manual aims to enable students, communities, families, businesses, interest groups, and anyone else who perceives that history lives in the memories of men and women. It focuses on firsthand knowledge of past times and places and the systematic documentation of that information in ways that will stand the test of time. As eminent oral historian Ronald J. Grele often advocated, oral historians should not merely pursue "little stories" but the *history* that sets the stage for the present.

In this fourth edition of *The Oral History Manual*, you will find:

- an expanded introduction to oral history research methodology;
- added information about social justice, community engagement, narrator compensation, and many other new and relevant topics for oral historians;
- a description of the life cycle of an oral history interview;
- more details on planning and administering oral history projects;
- additional discussion of legal and ethical issues, particularly as they affect potentially vulnerable narrators or involve social justice considerations;

- updated information on digital technology for oral history interviewing;
- expanded discussion of preparing for oral history interviews;
- more details on processing oral histories and making them accessible; and
- a chapter on creating tangible outcomes from oral history materials.

Throughout this fourth edition of *The Oral History Manual*, as with its predecessors, the focus is on oral history fundamentals. But, and we want to stress this even more than in earlier editions, the focus also is on the importance of documenting the context of all decisions made in relation to planning and carrying out an oral history project, including fully contextualizing the interviews themselves. The use of oral history methodology is more widespread than ever, with projects that document homelessness, aim at community organizing, explore real-time interviewing of people caught up in traumatic experiences, and record the lives of immigrants, refugees, and marginalized people of all sorts. The dizzying array of environments where oral history has found a home makes it imperative that projects carefully document the circumstances of their work. Only then will those who explore such oral histories in the future be able to make sense of the multiple pasts those oral histories record.

The proliferation of digital technology and ease of online publication of oral history materials has been the focus of change in much of the oral history community in recent years and has sparked lively and thought-provoking discussions among oral history practitioners. Like people involved in all endeavors closely tied to rapidly changing technology, oral historians face ongoing challenges of adopting and adapting to new tools that will serve their needs. Indeed, the pace of change underlies this manual's focus on oral history *fundamentals* and on the *process* of oral history planning and execution. We hope readers using this manual will see both the opportunities and challenges the digital age has created and will find herein information to guide them as they analyze their goals and make decisions about their own oral history work.

Just as a successful oral history project is the result of a dedicated team effort, so also is this fourth edition of *The Oral History Manual* a reflection of the countless hours of support and exploration of ideas with our oral history colleagues and friends.

We thank the Nebraska Humanities Council/Humanities Nebraska for giving us the grant that supported initial research for this book, Mitch Allen for coming to us and encouraging us to write the first edition of this book, and the support of many others through the decades who have read it and used it in the classroom and the community. Thank you to Lu Ann Jones, National Park Service historian (retired), for her careful reading of the manuscript and to students who reviewed the third edition: the students in Spring 2023 HIS 300: Doing History in Public History at Augsburg University, Minneapolis, Minnesota; Adam Negri, student in the History of Medicine PhD program, University of Minnesota Medical School, Minneapolis, Minnesota; Matt Jones and the oral history class at Eastern Michigan University Archives, Ypsilanti, Michigan; and Carson Tomony, history graduate, Augsburg University, Minneapolis, Minnesota. Thank you to Christopher Welter, archivist at the Iron Range Research Center in Chisholm, Minnesota, for his help with access to several oral history collections. Thank you to Tracey Williams-Dillard, chief executive officer and publisher of the *Minnesota Spokesman-Recorder*, and *Minnesota Spokesman-Recorder* staff photographer Chris Juhm for their work on the photograph of the interview setting. Thank you to Matt Waite, professor of practice at the University of Nebraska-Lincoln College of Journalism and Mass Communications, for helping us understand artificial intelligence. Thank you, also, to those who contributed photographs and examples of work cited throughout the book and to those who continue to use the book. As a reviewer said of the first edition, we hope it continues to help its readers "learn to think like oral historians."

Mary Kay especially wishes to thank her family, which, for many generations, has cherished the value of ordinary people's lives and stories; her Oral History Association colleagues, who have challenged and informed her understanding of this intensely human endeavor; and co-author Barb Sommer. Our paths crossed serendipitously many years ago, and the result is a professional and personal friendship that, like the best oral histories, has stood the test of time.

Barb wishes to thank her family for their ongoing support and her Oral History Association colleagues, including Nancy MacKay, for many thoughtful oral history conversations and support. Thank you also to members of the AASLH Book Series, through which this book is published. And she wishes to especially thank Mary Kay for her friendship and for thoughtful discussions through the years that have improved each edition of this manual, including this fourth edition.

Barb and Mary Kay thank our editor, Charles Harmon, for his support of this project and his care in moving it toward publication.

—Barb Sommer and Mary Kay Quinlan

NOTE

1. Oral historian Alexander Freund of the University of Winnipeg has written extensively and thoughtfully about the story and storytelling phenomenon and what he calls "the mass culture of confession" that has emerged in the early twenty-first century. "While humans have always told stories, never before have people told so many stories about themselves." See Freund's thought-provoking discussion in "'Confessing Animals': Toward a *Longue Duree* of the Oral History Interview," *Oral History Review*, 41 (Winter/Spring 2014).

1

Introduction to Oral History

This edition of *The Oral History Manual* is not a one-size-fits-all book for how to do oral history. The unique experience of creating oral history interviews—and oral history projects—is inevitably a dynamic, not a fixed, process. But it is one that can be based on fundamental guidelines that can ground oral history work, even as individual projects may require modifications to meet a project's particular needs.

In this book, you'll find information about oral history—what it is and what it isn't—and the basics about planning, recording, and preserving an interview to make it accessible on an ongoing basis. Oral history is used in many areas of study. They include history, ethnography, anthropology, ethnic studies, public history, and museum studies. Oral history also can be used in many ways, including recording first-person information with people of all backgrounds and ethnicities; incorporating quotes from interviews into books and articles and other uses; using first-person interviews to document US, state, regional, and local history; developing exhibits in historical organizations; teaching oral history in the classroom; designing and developing projects used by undergraduates and graduates in their studies including master's theses and doctoral dissertations; documenting community; and recording interviews for social justice purposes. These are common descriptions of oral history, although the categories are somewhat artificial and can overlap both in purpose and action. What is at their core are the steps that define oral history and the work of oral historians. The steps are a universal guide to recording first-person information.

Oral history is a methodology that is used across and within disciplines. David K. Dunaway and Willa K. Baum, editors of *Oral History: An Interdisciplinary Anthology*, published in 1984 and updated in 1996, recognized this, and

it continues to be recognized today. While disciplines exist in separate, discrete homes within academia, the lines between them are far from clear cut. Thus oral history is a research methodology that readily can be used to further collaborative interdisciplinary and cross-disciplinary work in higher education.

As Dunaway and Baum suggested so well, oral history can be used in the study of social history, women's history, ethnic history, Indigenous history, LGBTQ history, public history, and local history; in related disciplines such as anthropology, museum studies, the work of historical organizations (museums, historic sites, libraries, archives), folklore, educational studies, journalism, and gerontology; and in any area that involves an interest in first-person information about the past. Practitioners in these disciplines are wide-ranging: academics in post-secondary institutions including faculty and undergraduate and graduate students; independent oral historians; communities, defined as "any group of people bound together by a shared identity"[1]; international, national, state, and local historical/humanities and arts organizations; public and private librarians; and educators (often focusing on grades nine through twelve).

With this in mind, let's begin by taking a look at what oral history is and then move to a brief introductory discussion of its many uses in various disciplines. As we move through the chapters, we'll examine and discuss the methodology; the last chapter examines in more detail uses of oral history as primary source information across disciplines.

WHAT IS ORAL HISTORY?

What do you think when you hear the words "oral history"? Many define oral history as spoken stories about things that happened in the past. But confusion creeps in when we begin to examine the definition. Are family reminiscences oral history? What about oral traditions? Or journalists' stories about past events? What is the difference between each of these types of narratives and oral history? Is there a difference? Yes, there is, and this manual will help you learn about those differences and how to master oral history methodology.

So what is oral history, and how did this term come to be applied to the collection of first-person information? In 1980 and 1984, Charles T. Morrissey wrote articles published in the *Oral History Review* describing the origins of the term.[2] What is "oral" and what is "history," and when the words are used together, what exactly does "oral history" mean? He concluded that, although it is a generic term that may be interpreted in a variety of ways, it refers to a basic structured collection of spoken firsthand memories in an interview setting. Since the introduction of oral history as a name for the spoken memory interviews that Allan Nevins began collecting at Columbia University in the late 1940s, the term has been identified with the process of collecting oral information about the past.

Oral history is primary source material created in an interview setting with a witness to or a participant in an event or a way of life for the purpose of preserving the information and making it available to others. The term refers both to the process and the product.

Because the spoken firsthand memories given in an interview are from a witness to or a participant in an event or time period, they are primary source material, "the material by which history is known."[3] In previous times, information now collected by oral historians might only have been part of a written record such as letters, diaries, or other "substantive and meaningful documents"; it is now widely recorded, adding this information to the record and broadening our understanding of primary source documents.[4]

Oral history interviews generally are grouped into two categories: life interviews and project interviews. Life interviews involve multiple interview sessions with one person to create a collection of autobiographical materials. Oral history projects encompass a series of interviews with a variety of individuals about a specific historical topic, place, or event of interest. Projects can be one-time tasks or ongoing, multiyear programs that regularly add interviews to their collections. In either case,

care in planning and adherence to the oral history process help support interviews that have depth and nuance.

Who participates in an oral history interview? An interviewer, often working with a community or representatives from a community, develops the interview structure. This includes doing background research, developing questions, scheduling the interview, conducting the interview, and taking care of follow-up tasks. Narrators are chosen for their firsthand knowledge about the interview topic and ability to communicate this information.

WHAT DO WE MEAN BY THE TERM ORAL HISTORY?

Oral history means many things to people. To some, its meaning can be as broad as any discussion about the past, while to others, it is a defined research methodology. As a result, in the years since the term first began to be used, oral history has come to have a popular (vernacular) and an archival meaning.[5]

The vernacular or popular use of the term oral history is perhaps the most common. It often refers to recorded discussions about the past in whatever form they may occur. The term shows up in magazine articles and newspapers in references to memories of events. It can be a part of family reunions and get-togethers. A quick review of the oral history listserv brings up many questions about various approaches based on the vernacular use; the growing number of blog-based references are among the most recent examples. The vernacular meaning is an illustration of what has been called "oral history's particular power" to connect people to the past and is part of the power and popularity of its use.[6]

The archival meaning is more precise. It is based on the use of oral history as a research methodology. In this use, the term is described by basic benchmarks. Each benchmark is a point of reference that helps identify an interview as an oral history:

Oral history benchmarks are the essential framework that guides oral history practitioners.

- Evidence of thoughtful planning, laying the groundwork for full documentation of interview context
- Careful attention to copyright and other legal and ethical issues
- Use of a structured, well-researched, clearly documented question or topic guide and probing follow-up questions to collect firsthand information
- Clear identification of participants and their relationship to the interview purpose

- Controlled interview setting
- Use of high-quality recording equipment
- Recorded interviews
- Adherence to careful processing techniques
- Preservation in a designated repository
- Access to interview information[7]

Oral historians use the benchmarks as guides to help meet Oral History Association standards, summed up as follows:

- Informing narrators about the purpose of an interview
- Being aware of and respecting legal and ethical needs
- Recording an interview with respect for the narrator and full documentation of purpose and context
- Being aware of needs related to social justice and trauma interviewing
- Using equipment that helps a recorded interview stand the test of time
- Preserving an interview and making it accessible on an ongoing basis[8]

Pioneering oral historian Willa Baum summed up the importance of understanding what oral history is when she wrote: "The goal is a good historical account, firsthand, preserved, and available."[9]

INTRODUCTION TO THE ORAL HISTORY LIFE CYCLE

Oral historians often credit the use of the oral history benchmarks and standards as a help in learning to "think like an oral historian." Learning to think like an oral historian is a somewhat subjective act, or perhaps an art. It involves more than doing an interview or leading a discussion about the past. For oral historians, it includes the full process of creating an interview, including the steps it takes to curate it and document the details, the context, and how and why it was created. The process applies to all oral histories, whether a single interview, a life history involving a number of interviews with one person, or a project resulting in a set of interrelated interviews with a number of people about a defined subject.

The oral history life cycle illustrates how to think like an oral historian. It has five stages: idea, plan, interview, preservation, access/use. The first three guide the creation of an interview. The final two cover its curation. The circular pattern illustrates the interconnectedness of all stages.[10]

The life cycle is not a hard-and-fast rule, but a guide. It can lead the way for current practitioners to more fully document why interviews are being recorded and the circumstances of their preservation. It can help future users of interviews to understand and honor the full context

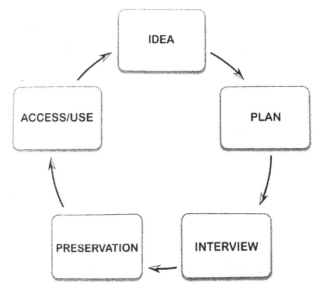

Oral History Life Cycle. *Adapted by William J. Lux. Used with permission.*

of the meaning of the interviews. These guidelines can be especially important for interviews that may involve sensitive topics or narrators who may be vulnerable or in jeopardy in any way; they can help make the difference in preserving voices that could otherwise be lost.

IDEA

Oral history begins with an idea. It often is triggered by an awareness of information in people's memories. For example, it may come from an interest in documenting neighborhood gentrification or changing businesses on a local main street. Or it could be an interest in documenting care for people living with HIV/AIDS or how teachers coped with online teaching caused by the COVID-19 pandemic. It could be to do interviews about contributions of recent immigrants to a community's arts and culture, or about trauma that immigrants face. It could be an idea that will help push ahead a social justice agenda or further other community goals. Oral history ideas are wide-ranging and innovative.

Ideas are exciting and often help draw people to oral history. But they also raise questions. Examples of questions to consider when thinking about how to do oral history are: Is oral history an effective tool for documenting an idea? What types of information are already on the historical record? Is information about the idea, or about part of it, missing from the historical record? Is there access to narrators who have undocumented first-person information about the idea? Are there suggested topics that can help focus it? If answers to preliminary questions are yes, it is time to move to the planning stage.

PLAN

The plan is a critical stage in the oral history life cycle. It is the blueprint for the idea. Planning steps, often incorporating active outreach through community engagement, focus the idea, identify the purpose of the interviews, determine who will be interviewed, identify the types of recording equipment to be used, list the topics expected to be covered in the interviews, and establish how and where the oral histories will be cared for when recorded. Each of these steps is critical to oral historians.

Planning steps lead to decisions that have an impact on the interview stage. For example, a decision about a repository provides information planners need when deciding on and developing a donor form. Decisions about topics to cover in an interview help keep a project, and its interviews, focused. Overall, the excitement of an idea draws people in, but developing a plan helps provide the structure to move it forward.

INTERVIEW

The interview is the center of oral history and the oral history process. The two stages preceding it help define its purpose and content; the two stages following it help define its ongoing preservation and access. It is the product of a careful plan and, as oral historian Donald A. Ritchie has stated, a well-prepared interviewer asking questions of a narrator.[11]

Oral historians often think of interviewing as an art and a science. The art is in doing an interview; the science is in the methodology that supports the interview. Together, the art and science of interviewing can result in interviews that capture the full meaning and messages in the recorded memories.

PRESERVATION

Preservation begins the curatorial part of the oral history process. There are hundreds of thousands of oral history interviews in the United States and many more throughout the world. New interviews are recorded regularly. The recordings offer unprecedented access to information about the past, putting previously unheard voices and information on the record.

Preservation begins as soon as recording ends. For oral historians, preservation of intact, complete interview recordings sets oral histories apart from other types of interviews. But, as oral historian and archivist Nancy MacKay has noted, the period between turning off the recorder and turning in the recording is when any oral history is at its most vulnerable. This is when the plan helps again. Designation of a place to hold and care for the recordings is a key step in the life cycle.[12]

ACCESS/USE

Oral historians record oral histories to document and preserve memories of events or ways of life and make the information available to others. The interview is the active collecting stage of the oral history process, but it is done for the purpose of documenting information for future access and use.

Access is the last stage of the oral history life cycle. Steps in access can protect oral histories, document their context, and make them available to researchers and others. When cared for, oral histories can provide ongoing access to first-person information for decades.

ORAL HISTORY AND OTHER FORMS OF RECORDED FIRST-PERSON INFORMATION

Oral history shares some of the basic benchmarks with other first-person collecting techniques. What are some of the differences, and why are they important? Each use is discipline-based and adheres to the standards of its discipline. While all collect valuable information about the past, research preparation, interviewing techniques, and copyright control may vary.

Many academic historians whose work focuses on twentieth- and twenty-first-century history conduct interviews as part of their research. Often, historians call such research oral history. But unless their narrators have signed donor forms and the interviews are somehow available to others, such interviews do not, strictly speaking, meet the standard definition of oral history.

Interviewers sometimes record interviews with groups of people. The groups can be large, such as at high school or college reunions, or smaller, but if a recording session does not include recognition and use of oral history benchmarks, it also does not meet the standard definition of oral history.

Oral history is sometimes confused with recorded speeches or with someone reading historical documents into a recorder. This is not oral history. Audio or video reminiscences collected by turning on a recorder and asking Grandma to talk about the olden days or recording conversations at family reunions also are often confused with oral history.[13]

Finally, some written materials, such as notes from unrecorded interviews or discussions and transcripts of recorded meetings, are sometimes referred to as oral histories. However, information in these documents, though of interest as original sources, may lack the exact documentation and full context that oral history recordings offer; these materials should not be labeled as oral histories.

What, then, is oral history? Oral history is a research methodology that supports and defines the interview as the active collecting stage.

> Oral history as a research methodology is guided by life cycle steps that support the interview.

ORAL HISTORY AND RELATED DISCIPLINES

As a research-based methodology, oral history has clear ties to the discipline of history. The "Principles and Best Practices" of the Oral History Association recognize the ties, reminding us that oral history interviews are historical documents. The British Oral History Society recognizes the tie through the early and ongoing contribution of oral history as a "key component in community histories."[14]

In addition to these ties, oral history has links to other disciplines and memory-based telling of stories. Several of the most well-known are journalism, folklore, public history, ethnography, and oral traditions. The ties strengthen and support the creation, preservation, and use of memory-based information.

ORAL HISTORY AND JOURNALISM

People sometimes think of journalistic interviews about historical topics as oral histories. Differences between journalistic interviews and oral histories can include the purpose for which the materials are collected, their immediate intended use, control of copyright, preservation of the complete recordings, and plans made for disposition and long-term availability of original interview materials. The purpose of journalism is to collect, write, and publish news and information through various media, drawing from all sources including interviews to produce a statement that is then identified as a primary source document. The journalistic sound bite is not part of the oral history process. Oral historians use and benefit from journalistic techniques, but application and use of oral history benchmarks set oral history apart from journalism.

ORAL HISTORY AND FOLKLORE

Oral history and folklore are closely related and often are described as being on "opposite ends of a continuum."[15] The American Folklore Society defines folklore as traditional art, literature, knowledge, and practice disseminated largely through oral communication and behavioral examples. It includes the study of these materials and, through public folklore, their use in public programming, documentaries, festivals, exhibitions, publications, and sound recordings.

Even with the close ties between oral history and folklore, first-person information recorded by folklorists can have subtle differences from oral history. Oral historian Donald A. Ritchie provided an example: "An oral historian would most likely interview a husband and wife separately, seeking to identify the unique perspective of each spouse. A folklorist, being as interested in the way a story is told as in its substance, would interview the couple together to observe the interplay as one begins a story and the other finishes it."[16] A thorough understanding of these differences provides a helpful context when creating and using first-person recordings. For more information on the collection and use of folklore interviews, see the American Folklore Society and the American Folklife Center.[17]

ORAL HISTORY AND PUBLIC HISTORY

The National Council on Public History describes public history as the "many and different ways history is put to work in the world." With its reach outside the academic classroom and its use of non-traditional information sources to reframe questions that can help public audiences make personal connections to the past, public history often is characterized as the democratization of history or as people's history. Although the work of public historians dates back decades in public institutions and historical organizations such as the Smithsonian Institution and the National Park Service, the field began to be recognized more formally in the 1970s through establishment of college and university public history programs and public organizations and commissions.[18]

Oral historians have long recognized the ties between public history and oral history. Enid H. Douglass, whose work was largely responsible for development of the oral history program at the Claremont Graduate Program in California, wrote in 1980 about early connections between oral history and public history in the *Oral History Review*, the journal of the Oral History Association. Citing examples of the inclusion of oral history in early public history programs, she discussed the "emergence of Public History and the inclusion of oral history as an essential tool of its trade." Ronald J. Grele, former director of the Oral History Research Office at Columbia University, through his commitment to expanding an understanding of oral history as "more than a repository of facts" and of moving oral history into new directions, actively worked with public history organizations during his tenure at the Oral History Research Office. In his classic *Envelopes of Sound: The Art of Oral History*, published in 1991, he emphasized the connection through the importance of the collaborative practice between oral history and public history. In the internationally recognized *Doing Oral History: A Practical Guide*, Donald A. Ritchie, long-time historian and, later, historian emeritus of the US Senate, helped sum up the discussion when he described the connection between public history and oral history as a natural affinity. As he wrote, "The oral history and public history movements share a natural affinity, both having attracted practitioners and audiences different from those of more traditional history writing." The connections recognized by these leading oral historians continues today as public historians in a variety of organizations and institutions create and use oral histories in exhibitions, documentaries, publications, and other works that reach public audiences. Creation and use of oral histories by public historians can include a focus on project-related purposes for doing interviews, less emphasis on creating a set of oral histories as a research or study collection, and use of excerpts from oral histories in producing specific products such as museum exhibits.[19]

ORAL HISTORY AND ORAL TRADITIONS

Much research is now being done on the relationship of Indigenous oral history and oral traditions. The work updates and refocuses past analysis, looking at the information not as different sources but as fields of information that are "one and the same."[20] The information helps document and define the cultures, which can be "as different from one another as Japanese culture is from Polish culture."[21]

Nepia Mahuika, Maori oral historian and educator, in his book, *Rethinking Oral History & Tradition, An Indigenous Perspective*, summed up the interpretation of oral traditions and oral histories when he wrote: "I argue that indigenous oral histories and traditions cannot be adequately defined by non-indigenous peoples."[22] In doing this, he emphasized the need to keep guidelines about the meanings and use of oral traditions and oral history in Indigenous hands.

To Indigenous communities, with a strong and ongoing emphasis on orality, oral traditions are comprehensive, encompassing stories, teachings, songs, chants, ceremonies, and histories. They cover centuries of knowledge that help define the cultures. They may be told in a non-linear fashion, often are supported by mnemonic devices, and are spoken by knowledge keepers, community members in each generation who are taught to learn and tell the community's stories. The use of memory, important in an oral culture, is critical to preserving and communicating oral traditions.

Oral traditions document the past through the "cultural frame of the narrators"[23] rather than the frame of written histories. They do more than provide information about the past; they are an integral part of the lives of the people today. Oral histories, stories told by individuals about personal memories, may, and often do, incorporate information from traditions, illustrating the active and ongoing importance of traditions in providing context for individual stories.

ORAL HISTORY AND ANTHROPOLOGY/ETHNOLOGY

Oral history and studies in anthropology and ethnology both use interviewing techniques to document first-person information. The differences are in the purposes of the interviews and how they are done. Ethnology is the study of culture, and anthropology is the closely related, broader study of what makes us human.[24] This work is immersive, using detailed observations and first-person interviews to document the lives of the people. Such interviews may not always be recorded and often take place in informal settings throughout a study period. Anthropologists work to the standards of the American Anthropological Association.[25] The American Anthropological Association also offers guidelines for the work of ethnographers.[26] Oral historians work in a more formal interview setting, creating primary source documents, and are guided by the "Principles and Best Practices" of the Oral History Association.[27]

NEW FACTORS IN ORAL HISTORY

The use of oral history has grown considerably in size and sophistication since its early beginnings.[28] Aided by the relatively recent definition of the field of public history, the increased interest in history from the bottom up—social history of non-elites—that began among historians in the 1960s, and active recognition of the importance of sensitivity to social justice, the collection of new historical perspectives in the form of first-person information has become an active outreach effort throughout the world. Daniel R. Kerr summed up the impacts of these developments when he wrote in 2016: "[O]ral history can be a source of power, knowledge and strength" and an effective tool to strengthen movements for social change.[29]

Along the way, as the collection and use of oral history has expanded, it has faced some major developments that have helped further define it. Outlined by oral historian Alistair Thomson in a 2007 issue of the *Oral History Review*, they include:

- Increased understanding of the importance of memory as "people's history"
- Clarification of an understanding of the "subjectivity" of memory
- Discussion about the role of the oral historian as interviewer
- The impact of technology through the digital revolution

Serving as a backdrop to the new developments, several other factors have had an influence on oral history. These are:

- Emerging interest in applying social justice principles in oral history practice
- The proliferation of oral history projects that focus on unfolding crises
- A growing significance of political and legal practices in which personal testimony is used as a central resource
- The use of restrictions on interview access and their impact on content
- The increase in interdisciplinary approaches to interviewing
- The proliferation of studies relating to history and memory
- The availability of digital options to increase access to oral histories
- The evolving internationalism of oral history[30]

These points, which trace oral history's evolution, emphasize the importance of understanding its meaning and methodology and the impact of both on recording, defining, and using information in the interviews.

HOW IS ORAL HISTORY USED?

The use of oral history often goes beyond the original collecting scope, giving it a potential for wide applicability. Oral history does much more than document new information. It provides all those who use it a window to the past and, in doing so, makes history come alive. It reminds us that the actors are real people, each with a unique perspective on the past and present. It helps us understand not just what happened, but how those telling the story understood what happened and what they may now think of it. Exploring many sides of an issue through multiple firsthand individual accounts offers the opportunity to uncover layers of meaning embedded in the stories and insights into how people understand and interpret the past and their place in it. The following examples represent a few of its many uses.

Oral history projects help document events in the history of a community. Life interviews, created for family or genealogical purposes, also can be used as community history sources. Although local in focus, the contributions of community-based interviews to greater understanding of related state, national, and international issues should not be overlooked. They can contain valuable information that goes beyond their original purpose. For example, oral history projects that document responses to race relations, reactions to mis-

sile locations during the Cold War, upheaval in the farm economy, or changes in people's perceptions of Main Street or historic urban neighborhoods, while important to an understanding of the history of a particular community, can also provide invaluable grassroots insight into issues of national importance.

Oral history serves people with a history of disenfranchisement. It often is used to support documentation of social justice movements or needs. Those with little or no written record, or for whom the written record is distorted at best, benefit greatly from the use of oral history. Oral history is inclusive, bringing in many voices, not just the more powerful or dominant that have been traditionally included in existing records. Oral historians look at their work as a way to complement and supplement the existing record, as well as a chance to make fundamental changes or additions to it. In many cases, while documenting a community's history is critical in itself, an oral history project or a set of life interviews can become a catalyst for this work. It can provide an avenue to correct long-held misconceptions about individuals, an event, or a time period; help collect information that balances the existing record; and become an impetus for developing community pride through the telling of people's stories in their own words.[31]

Oral history can help preserve languages and dialects. By preserving the sound and cadence of spoken words, it can help keep languages alive. It is used as a tool to save the vernacular or, in the case of Indigenous peoples, rapidly vanishing languages.

Oral history is used in the classroom as a teaching technique. Its interdisciplinary nature, drawing on a variety of research, verbal, writing, and technical skills, and its built-in ability to tie the school to the community bring a unique focus and skill set to a curriculum.[32]

Oral history, with its emphasis on personal outreach, can help benefit an entire community by bringing people together—narrators with interviewers and others interested in the work of the project. Regardless of the role it plays in community organization, it can become a vehicle for documenting not only facts about the past, but also more subjective insights into how people organize their views of their history and how their frames of reference in their own communities affect their firsthand spoken memories of the events discussed in an interview.[33]

PROCESS MATTERS

Do you need to hold a PhD in history to do oral history? No, definitely not. Is a thorough understanding of the methodology important to the collection of substantive oral history? Yes, it is—not just to those who collect the information but to those who will use it. Oral history represents one of many ways to document the past. It brings an immediacy and an ability to explore subjective nuances to a study of the past. It allows researchers to probe beneath the surface of the written record to discover not just what happened but how and why, to explain anomalies, and to provide convincing evidence or tantalizing clues that enhance understanding of a past time and place. Through it, information that otherwise might have been lost can be collected and preserved as primary source material for researchers and others. And it can help pass a sense of the richness of the human experience to future generations. Moreover, a well-planned and -executed oral history project can bring people together as they collectively work to understand more about the past.

The following pages take the reader through a detailed, step-by-step approach to doing oral history. They explain what works and why. And if you get hooked on oral history—as untold numbers of people have—it offers resources for more ideas on creating and using oral histories. Each chapter is devoted to a specific topic, beginning with an application of the oral history life cycle stages through a discussion of planning and budget steps, legal and ethical issues, equipment and technology issues, interview preparation, interviewing guidelines, preserving oral histories and making them accessible, and ending with a discussion of oral history outcomes. The appendices contain sample forms, a list of selected readings, and a reprint of key sections of the Oral History Association "Principles and Best Practices," the statement of professional standards governing the collection and use of oral history.

NOTES

1. Mary Kay Quinlan, Nancy MacKay, and Barbara W. Sommer, *Community Oral History Toolkit* (New York, NY: Routledge, 2013), volume 1, 10.
2. See Charles T. Morrissey, "Why Call It 'Oral History'?" *The Oral History Review* 8 (1980): 20–48; Charles T. Morrissey, "Riding a Mule through the 'Terminological Jungle': Oral History and Problems of Nomenclature," *The Oral History Review* 12 (1984): 13–28.
3. Carol Kammen and Norma Prendergast, eds., *Encyclopedia of Local History*, second edition (Lanham, MD: Rowman & Littlefield, 2012).
4. Kammen and Prendergast, *Encyclopedia of Local History*, 357.
5. For more information, see Linda Shopes, "Mellon Project on Folklore, Musicology, and Oral History in the Academy—Background Paper: Oral History" (unpublished paper, 2006).
6. Linda Shopes, "Insights and Oversights: Reflections on the Documentary Tradition and the Theoretical Turn in Oral History," *The Oral History Review* 41:2 (Summer/Fall 2014): 267.
7. An earlier version of the benchmarks was published in Barbara W. Sommer, *Practicing Oral History in Historical Organizations* (New York, NY: Routledge, 2015), 27–28.
8. Oral History Association, www.oralhistory.org, accessed November 18, 2023.
9. Willa Baum, Reprint of "The Other Uses of Oral History," a paper presented in 1983 in Anchorage, Alaska, in "Tributes to Willa Baum," memorial issue of *The Oral History Review* 34:1 (Winter/Spring 2007): 15.
10. Barbara W. Sommer, *Practicing Oral History in Historical Organizations* (New York, NY: Routledge, 2015), 33–36. For an additional interpretation, see Nancy MacKay, *Curating Oral Histories from Interview to Archive*, second edition (New York, NY: Routledge, 2016), 26. See Anna Bryson and Seán McConville, assisted by Mairead McClean, *The Routledge Guide to Interviewing: Oral History, Social Enquiry and Investigation* (New York, NY: Routledge, 2014), for an application of the concept to the contents page in the book.
11. Oral History Association, "Oral History: Defined," http://www.oralhistory.org/about/do-oral-history/, accessed November 18, 2023.
12. For a detailed discussion of curating oral histories, see Nancy MacKay, *Curating Oral Histories: From Interview to Archive*, second edition (New York, NY: Routledge, 2015).
13. For additional information, see Oral History Association, "Capturing the Living Past: An Oral History Primer," www.oralhistory.org/wp-content/uploads/2018/06/Capturing_the_Living_Past_-_An_Oral_History_Primer-3.pdf, accessed November 28, 2023.
14. Oral History Association, "Principles and Best Practices," https://oralhistory.org/principles-and-best-practices-revised-2018/, accessed November 18, 2023; Institute of Historical Research, "Making History: The Changing Face of the Profession in Britain," 2008, https://archives.history.ac.uk/makinghistory/resources/articles/oral_history.html, accessed November 18, 2023. See also Oral History Society, "The History of Oral History: How Oral History Developed in the UK," https://www.ohs.org.uk/membership-join/, accessed November 18, 2023.
15. Donald A. Ritchie, *Doing Oral History: A Practical Guide*, third edition (New York, NY: Oxford University Press, 2015), 23.
16. Ritchie, *Doing Oral History*, 23. For more information, see American Folklore Society, "What Is Folklore," https://whatisfolklore.org/, accessed November

18, 2023. See also the American Folklore Society, https://americanfolkloresociety.org/, accessed November 18, 2023. Examples of public folklore programs include City Lore, a New York City program focusing on the city's cultural heritage, http://citylore.org/, accessed November 18, 2023; and the Nebraska Folklife Network, the state's public folk and traditional arts program, http://nebraskafolklife.org/, accessed November 18, 2023.

17. The American Folklore Society, founded in 1888, serves the field of folklore studies, http://www.afsnet.org/, accessed November 18, 2023. The American Folklife Center at the Library of Congress was created by the US Congress in 1976 as the national center for folklife documentation and research, https://loc.gov/folklife/aboutafc.html, accessed November 18, 2023.

18. National Council on Public History, "How Do We Define Public History?," http://ncph.org/what-is-public-history/about-the-field/, accessed November 18, 2023; Rose T. Diaz and Andrew B. Russell, "Oral Historians: Community Oral History and the Cooperative Ideal," *Public History: Essays from the Field*, revised edition, edited by James B. Gardiner and Peter S. La Paglia (Malabar, FL: Krieger Publishing Company, 2006), 203–216; David Glassberg, *Sense of History: The Place of the Past in American Life* (Amherst, MA: University of Massachusetts Press, 2001); David E. Kyvig, Myron A. Marty, and Larry Cebula, *Nearby History: Exploring the Past Around You*, fourth edition (Lanham, MD: Rowman & Littlefield Press, 2019); Denise D. Meringolo, *Museums, Monuments, and National Parks: Toward a New Genealogy of Public History* (Amherst, MA: University of Massachusetts Press, 2012); Barbara W. Sommer, *Practicing Oral History in Historical Organizations* (New York, NY: Routledge, 2015); Carol Kammen, "On Doing Local History: The Local Historian as Public Intellectual," *History News*, 71:1 (Winter 2016): 3–4.

19. Enid H. Douglass, "Oral History and Public History," *The Oral History Review*, 8:1 (January 1980): 5; Ronald J. Grele, *Envelopes of Sound: The Art of Oral History* (New York, NY: Praeger, 1991); Ritchie, *Doing Oral History*, 28. See also Barbara W. Sommer, *Practicing Oral History in Historical Organizations* (New York, NY: Routledge, 2015).

20. Winona Wheeler, Charles E. Trimble, Mary Kay Quinlan, and Barbara W. Sommer, *Indigenous Oral History Manual: Canada and the United States*, second edition (New York, NY: Routledge, 2024), 2.

21. Ibid, 4.

22. Nepia Mahuika, *Rethinking Oral History & Tradition: An Indigenous Perspective* (New York, NY: Oxford University Press, 2019), 15.

23. Ibid, 3.

24. American Anthropological Association, "What Is Anthropology," https://americananthro.org/learn-teach/what-is-anthropology/, accessed February 21, 2024.

25. American Anthropological Association, "Anthropological Ethics," https://americananthro.org/about/anthropological-ethics/, accessed February 21, 2024.

26. American Anthropological Association, "AAA Statement on Ethnography and Institutional Review Boards," https://americananthro.org/about/policies/statement-on-ethnography-and-institutional-review-boards/, accessed February 21, 2024.

27. Oral History Association, "Principles for Oral History and Best Practices for Oral History," https://oralhistory.org/principles-and-best-practices-revised-2018/, accessed February 21, 2024.

28. For an example of early oral history interviews, see the description of Forrest C. Pogue as he used a wire recorder to interview injured soldiers being evacuated from the battlefield in the days immediately after D-Day (the invasion of Europe, June 6, 1944, during World War II). Forrest C. Pogue, *Pogue's War: Diaries of a WWII Combat Historian* (Lexington, KY: The University Press of Kentucky, 2001).

29. To put this growth and change in perspective, see Daniel R. Kerr, "Allan Nevins Is Not My Grandfather: The Roots of Radical Oral History Practice in the United States," *Oral History Review* 43/2 (Summer/Fall 2016): 390.

30. For more information, see Alistair Thomson, "Four Paradigm Transformations in Oral History," *The Oral History Review* 34:1 (Winter/Spring 2007): 49–70. Also see Paul Thompson and Joanna Bornat, *The Voice of the Past: Oral History*, fourth edition (New York, NY: Oxford University Press, 2017); Valerie Raleigh Yow, *Recording Oral History: A Guide for the Humanities and Social Sciences*, third edition (Lanham, MD: Rowman & Littlefield, 2015); Michael A. Frisch, *A Shared Authority: Essays on the Craft and Meaning of Oral History and Public History* (Albany, NY: State University of New York Press, 1990); Alessandro Portelli, *The Death of Luigi Trastulli and Other Stories: Form and Meaning in Oral History* (Albany, NY: State University of New York Press, 1991); Ronald J. Grele, *Envelopes of Sound: The Art of Oral History*, second edition (New York, NY: Praeger Publishers, 1991); Anna Bryson and Seán McConville, *The Routledge Guide to Interviewing: Oral History, Social Inquiry and Investigation* (New York, NY: Routledge, 2014); Mary A. Larson, "Steering Clear of the Rocks: A Look at Oral History Ethics in the Digital Age," *Oral History Review*, 40:1 (Winter/Spring 2013): 36–49; Anisa Puri

and Alistair Thomson, *Australian Lives: An Intimate History* (Clayton, Australia: Monash University Publishing, 2017), e-version: http://publishing.monash.edu/books/al-9781922235787.html, accessed November 18, 2023; Linda Shopes and Amy Starecheski, "Disrupting Authority: The Radical Roots and Branches of Oral History," *History at Work: The National Council on Oral History blog*, http://ncph.org/history-at-work/disrupting-authority-the-radical-roots-and-branches-of-oral-history/, accessed November 19, 2023; Douglas A. Boyd and Mary A. Larson, eds., *Oral History and Digital Humanities: Voice, Access, and Engagement* (New York, NY: Palgrave Macmillan, 2014); Nancy MacKay, Mary Kay Quinlan, and Barbara W. Sommer, *Community Oral History Toolkit*, five volumes (New York, NY: Routledge 2013); Tamara Hareven, "The Search for Generational Memory," in *Oral History: An Interdisciplinary Anthology*, second edition, edited by David K. Dunaway and Willa K. Baum (Walnut Creek, CA: AltaMira Press, 1996), 241–56; Christine Anne George, "Archives Beyond the Pale: Negotiating Legal and Ethical Entanglements after the Belfast Project," *The American Archivist*, 76:1 (Spring/Summer 2013): 47–67, https://www.scribd.com/document/135837476/Archives-Beyond-the-Pale, accessed November 18, 2023; *Oral History in the Digital Age*, /https://oralhistory.org/oral-history-in-the-digital-age/, accessed November 18, 2023.

31. For more information about trends in oral history, see Teresa Barnett, "Special Section: Looking Back, Looking Forward: Fifty Years of Oral History," *The Oral History Review*, 43:2 (Summer/Fall 2016): 315–91. Articles in this special section are Mary A. Larson, "'The Medium is the Message': Oral History, Media, and Medication," 318–37; Anna Sheftel and Stacey Zembrzycki, "Who's Afraid of Oral History: Fifty Years of Debates and Anxiety about Ethics," 338–66; and Daniel R. Kerr, "Allan Nevins Is Not My Grandfather: The Roots of Radical Oral History Practice in the United States," 367–91.

32. For more information, see Glenn Whitman, *Dialogue with the Past: Engaging Students and Meeting Standards through Oral History* (Lanham, MD: Rowman & Littlefield Publishers, 2004); and Barry A. Lanman and Laura M. Wendling, *Preparing the Next Generation of Oral Historians: An Anthology of Oral History Education* (Lanham, MD: Rowman & Littlefield Publishers, 2006).

33. For more information, see Cyns Nelson with contributions by Adam Speirs, *Oral History in Your Library: Create Shelf Space for Community Voice* (Santa Barbara, CA: Libraries Unlimited, 2018).

2

Planning Overview and Oral History Terms

Oral history methodology is a series of stages, each a part of what we call the oral history life cycle. The stages are a basic structure, the pieces of which oral history practitioners recognize as steps leading to creation of primary source documents (oral histories) created according to professional standards. The methodology is summarized in this chapter and discussed in detail in the following chapters. Although presented here in the context of an oral history project with multiple interviews, it applies equally to the recording of individual oral history interviews.

> Oral history methodology encompasses life cycle stages that support and focus the interview and make it available to users.

ORAL HISTORY LIFE CYCLE

As discussed in chapter 1, the oral history life cycle begins with an idea. The idea guides the development of a project and helps define the purpose for doing the interviews. It involves documenting first-person information, but the impetus for developing it can vary. For example, some ideas stem from an interest in building research collections, while others may have a specific end product such as a museum exhibit as a primary goal. Some take on what can be the challenges of social justice and trauma interviewing, bringing the voices of potentially vulnerable communities and individuals into an historical record. The motivations may vary, but the results are the same—a set of oral histories that stand the test of time.[1]

The oral history life cycle begins with discussing the idea. A helpful way to do this is to ask questions about what it is and how it can be developed. Answers can help focus the thinking about it, moving the steps into the more detailed planning process.

Steps in the planning stage identify strategies, set goals, outline tasks, identify a pool of possible narrators, and formulate a course of action. If a project is working on social justice issues or involves interviewing in times of crisis, planning can help with many challenging decisions, including those about documenting context and protecting narrators who may be in vulnerable positions. Generally, decisions include identification of funding or sources of support, review of legal and ethical issues, and determination of equipment to use. While it may be tempting to skip the planning stage and go straight to the interviews, coordinators and leaders will find that, by working through the steps in the planning stage, interviews often have a clearer focus and interviewers are more prepared and confident. The planning stage also lays the groundwork for documenting interview context and maintaining access to the interview information. The planning stage is covered in chapters 3, 4, and 5.

Budget information is a critical part of the planning process. It helps determine real costs, even if a project is relying on volunteers. Creating a budget also can serve as a guide to helping develop grant requests to various funding sources. Budget information and funding sources are included in chapter 3.

Decisions about legal and ethical issues are among the most important for oral history practitioners. They provide the basis for the trust relationship between narrator and interviewer that is basic to oral history. They also define the process for current and future accessibility of oral history interview information and guide the work of planners, interviewers, and other project personnel. Chapter 4 provides information about legal and ethical issues in oral history.

Equipment decisions also are an important part of the planning process and are some of the most discussed aspects of oral history project work. Making appropriate decisions about the equipment to use, especially in a time of rapid technological advances, results in more than ending up with a recording that has good sound or video at the time of the interview. These equipment decisions help determine the full range of potential uses of the recording as well as its future retrievability—basic considerations of oral history practitioners. Equipment decisions are covered in chapter 5.

Interview preparation is a critical part of the practice of oral history. With interview preparation, the development of the oral history moves into the interview stage of the oral history life cycle. In addition to developing and focusing interview content, preparation provides a structure for documenting the context of the interview information. Interviews are the products of an exchange between the narrator and interviewer; oral history methodology identifies both as co-creators of the interview. Careful documentation of decisions about what the interviewer and narrator will cover and why they will cover it helps provide a framework for use and an understanding of context, present and future, of the spoken memories in the oral history interview. Interview preparation is covered in chapter 6.

The interview is the central outreach, collecting stage in the oral history life cycle. During the interview, the interviewer and narrator collaborate to document the narrator's experiences and memories about the interview topics. While the interview is the best-known stage, it does not exist in a vacuum. The stages in the life cycle that precede it and that follow it are equally important. Conducting the interview is covered in chapter 7.

The preservation stage follows the interview in the oral history life cycle. With the steps in this stage, the oral history life cycle moves from creating oral histories to curating oral histories. The steps cover details to make sure the recordings and interview information are preserved according to the best standards of oral history methodology and that the circumstances surrounding the oral histories are carefully documented. The preservation stage, including preparing materials for ongoing curatorial care, is covered in chapter 8.[2]

Access and use are covered in the final stage in the oral history life cycle. Actions taken in this stage make oral histories available to the public, a critical part of identifying an interview as an oral history. Access covers the curatorial care that the repository gives the oral history and its support materials. Cataloging, storage in a climate-controlled physical facility or an online archive, and trained staff support all are part of the access stage. Use follows access and is based on the availability of the interview information. Access is covered in chapter 9 and use is discussed in chapter 10.[3]

Here is a summary checklist of the life cycle stages that will be covered in the remaining chapters of this book:

THE IDEA

- Identify the source and describe the idea
- Determine the reason for developing the idea into an oral history project, such as:

    Is my organization planning an event that includes oral histories? What types of information will be most helpful?

    Are members of my community interested in developing an oral history project, and where and why?

- Identify existing oral history projects that may cover the same or similar topics

    Ask: what will this idea add to the information in other oral histories about this idea? What is the contribution of this idea?

- Identify community engagement steps

    Ask: who in the community can help with a project about this idea?

    How much time will community members have for the project?

    What is an expected response to the idea and how will the response affect its development?

THE PLAN

- Identify project leaders and personnel
- Name the project
- Write a purpose or mission statement
- Identify and begin to work with a repository
- Select a project advisory board
- Establish a timeframe for completing the project
- Establish record-keeping procedures
- Develop a training session for interviewers
- Develop a publicity plan

BUDGET STEPS

- Develop a project budget, including the value of donations and volunteer help
- Find financial support and funding sources
- Plan to document volunteer help

LEGAL AND ETHICAL STEPS

- Identify legal issues
- Observe ethical standards

EQUIPMENT STEPS

- Decide on recording equipment and media
- Review impact of digital platforms
- Decide on microphones, cables, and other interview recording needs
- Decide on transcribing options

THE INTERVIEW

- Before the interview
- The interview
- Immediately after the interview

BEFORE THE INTERVIEW

- Draw on community resources to help identify information helpful for the project
- Begin background research and develop a bibliography
- Working with co-creators, make a list of the themes or topics to pursue in the interview
- With community partners, identify potential narrators and determine the topics or themes to be covered with each of them
- Conduct narrator-specific research
- Develop an interview outline or guide
- Train interviewers
- Schedule the interview

THE INTERVIEW

- Check the interview setting
- Determine microphone and recording equipment (audio and video) placement; do a sound check
- Review release forms with narrator
- Record the introduction
- Record the interview

IMMEDIATELY AFTER THE INTERVIEW

- Sign release forms
- Thank the narrator

PRESERVATION

- Process the materials, preparing digital and hard copies in preparation for ongoing preservation
- Make provisions to care for the oral histories per the project plan

- Catalog the oral histories and develop finding aids including keywords

ACCESS AND USE

- Include stewardship steps in the ongoing care of the oral histories
- Provide access to the oral histories
- Review models for use of oral histories

ORAL HISTORY TERMS

Oral historians use a variety of terms. While most of these are common, sometimes their meaning is specific to the work of oral historians. As we have seen in chapter 1, this extends to the term *oral history* itself, which can have a variety of meanings.

Listed in what follows are the most common oral history terms and their meanings. These are the terms and definitions used throughout the manual.[4]

Abstract: see recording abstract

Acid-free: There are no consistent standards for acid-free paper. Many consumer products, while labeled acid-free, will develop damaging acids as time goes on. For paper products, acid-free means lignin-free and alkaline, with a pH greater than seven. Lignin is an acidic element found in wood products. Alkaline is the opposite of acidic. For archival markers, acid-free refers to the use of acid-free pigment rather than dye as the coloring medium.

Analog: A recording process that imprints sound in a continuous pattern on magnetic tape.

Archive: A place, often part of a repository, that maintains historical records and documents.

Archivist: A person who cares for and manages collections of historical information, such as oral history, in an archive.

Artificial intelligence: "Technology that enables computers and digital devices to learn, read, write, talk, see, create, play, analyze, make recommendations, and do other things humans do."[5]

Audit check, also called audit edit: An interview processing step in which the recorded interview is carefully listened to while reading the transcript to correct transcribing errors.

Biographical information form: A part of the interview record-keeping system, this form contains background information about the narrator.

Community engagement: Building relationships through work with a community for the purpose of co-creating interviews.

Copyright: The exclusive legal right to print or otherwise reproduce, publish, or sell copies of original materials, such as oral history interviews, and to license their production and sale by others.

Curate: Manage the long-term care of historical documents for maximum preservation and access.

Digital: A recording process that stores sound as bits of data the way a computer stores information.

Donor form: see release form

Finding aid: The description of related archival materials. Finding aids often are hierarchical, beginning with a broad description of the materials and becoming more detailed within each section or series.

Informant: see narrator

Interviewee: see narrator

Interviewer: The person responsible for conducting the oral history interview. This person should have both general and interview-specific background, understand and be able to use open-ended questioning techniques, be able to build effective human relationships in the interview setting, and work to the standards of the Oral History Association.

Interview information form: The first action in processing the interview, it identifies the narrator and interviewer and helps document interview context including the date of the interview, its length, the type of recording equipment and media used, keywords, and an abstract or summary of the interview contents.

Legal release agreement: see release form

Life cycle: A model encompassing sequential stages that lead to a tangible result, in this case, the creation of an oral history interview.

Life interview: An oral history interview that focuses on one person, usually in a series of interviews. This process results in detailed documentation of the person's life experiences. See also project interview.

LOCKSS (lots of copies keeps stuff safe): A preservation principle referring to making multiple copies of an oral history to help preserve it and its contents.

Log: see recording abstract

Master file: A non-circulating file that contains all information about an interview and is permanently kept in the repository as part of the oral history collection.

Narrator (also sometimes called interviewee or informant): The person being interviewed. This is a person with firsthand knowledge about the subject of the interview and the ability to effectively communicate the information.

Oral history: Primary source material created in an interview setting with a witness to or a participant in an event or a way of life for the purpose of preserving the information and making it available to others. The term refers both to the process and the interview itself.

Oral History Association: The US-based professional organization for practitioners of oral history. It supports and encourages an understanding of the ethical principles and standards that guide oral historians in their work.

Oral history interview: The recorded question-and-answer session between an interviewer and narrator characterized by well-focused, clearly stated, open-ended, neutral questions aimed at gathering information not available from other sources.

Oral history project: A series of individual oral history interviews with a number of narrators focusing on one subject or event.

Preservation master: The interview recording, kept intact to preserve the interview. Preservation masters are kept in permanent and appropriate storage with the master files; user copies are made from them for preservation and access.

Primary source: Firsthand information with no interpretation between the document and the researcher. Examples are oral history recordings and transcripts, diaries, correspondence such as letters from family members, or government records. See also secondary source.

Processing: The steps taken to help make oral history interview information accessible to present and future users.

Processor: The person who works with oral history materials, including recordings, to help make the interview information accessible to users. Processors can include those who develop interview abstracts as well as transcribers.

Project interview: An oral history interview that focuses on a specific topic, place, or event. Interviews for the Library of Congress Veterans History Project, for example, focus on one subject or one part of a narrator's life. See also life interview.

Recording abstract: A list of interview subjects noted in the order in which they were discussed. See also transcript.

Recording equipment: The equipment, audio or video, used to record an interview.

Recording media: The physical materials on which recordings are made.

Release form (donor form): The document that transfers copyright of an oral history interview to the designated repository and may list restrictions on use of the interview information. It is signed by both the narrator and the interviewer, and any other person whose voice is heard on the recording, as soon as the interview session ends even if more interviews are planned with the narrator.

Repository: A facility where historical materials, including oral history materials, are deposited and permanently kept.

Secondary source: A publication or other document created using various types of historical information, including primary sources. See also primary source.

Transcribe: A verbatim (word-for-word) conversion of spoken information into written form.

Transcript: A verbatim written copy of interview information. See also recording abstract.

Website: A group of webpages on a single topic or on related topics accessed through a single network address

NOTES

1. Nancy MacKay, Mary Kay Quinlan, and Barbara W. Sommer, *Community Oral History Toolkit*, five volumes (New York, NY: Routledge, 2013); Oral History Association, *Guidelines for Social Justice Oral History Work*, https://oralhistory.org/guidelines-for-social-justice-oral-history-work/, accessed November 29, 2023.

2. For detailed information on curatorial care of oral history materials, see Nancy MacKay, *Oral Histories: From Interview to Archive*, second edition (New York, NY: Routledge, 2015).

3. The finding aids and catalogued oral history materials at the Brooklyn Historical Society (New York) offer an example of preservation and access from a physical repository (http://www.brooklynhistory.org/). Oral histories in the Densho Digital Archive offer an example of preservation and access through a virtual archive (https://densho.org/).

4. For additional information, see the Oral History Association, "Principles and Best Practices: Glossary," https://oralhistory.org/best-practices-glossary/, accessed December 6, 2023.

5. IBM, https://www.ibm.com/topics/artificial-intelligence, accessed February 21, 2024.

3

Planning and Budget

When thinking about oral history, it is easy to confuse the interview with the oral history. The interview is the vehicle through which oral history information is collected. Its success is based on the work that precedes it, the interviewer's skills, and the work that follows it.

This chapter covers oral history planning steps. Whether you choose to do one oral history, a multi-interview life history, or a topical oral history project, pay careful attention to planning and organization. Planning actually covers two major areas in the creation of oral histories:

- Process planning helps set up basic project organization—for example, which recording equipment will be used, the number of people who will be interviewed, the wording of forms covering the legal status of an interview, preservation plans for the completed oral histories, and length of time the project will last.
- Content planning focuses on the interview—it helps determine the topics to be covered, the questions to be asked, and the people who will be interviewed.

The first—basic process and budget steps—are covered in this chapter. Chapter 6 covers interview preparation and content planning.

THINKING LIKE AN ORAL HISTORIAN

Planning begins the work of thinking like an oral historian. We recognize that interviews are the central and most visible part of oral history, but oral historians understand how and why decisions made during the planning processes help identify the interviews as oral histories. This is thinking like an oral historian.

Begin by identifying and describing the idea for the project or set of interviews. Write it out, then discuss it; review questions about its proposed purpose. Why is the project being considered? What purpose would it fill? How would it fill this purpose? Is it duplicating existing information, and why would this be recommended? Is it generating new information? Where and how would this information fit into the historical record?

Think about the reality of successfully carrying it out, and make a decision on whether to carry it forward. If the decision is to carry it forward, move on to the following planning steps.

The first thing to think about in project planning is community engagement. This is true if project organizers are from a community, if a project originates outside a community, or if a project is focusing on a particular group within a community. Community engagement involves actions taken by oral historians to reach out to communities they want to work with. It is a broad concept, but its application can have subtle distinctions, depending on the project planners and involved communities. As has been defined by the Oral History Association, "It is a scholarly and interpretive act to both co-create an interview and give meaning and context to what is shared."[1] Its purpose is for a "mutually beneficial exchange of information and resources through partnership and reciprocity."[2]

Community engagement means working with a community as a collective, focusing on a collaboration between the community and oral historians. It is:

- community-situated—taking an idea and developing it into a research topic of practical relevance to the community and carried out in community settings;

- collaborative—community members and researchers share control of the research agenda through active and reciprocal involvement in the research design, implementation, and dissemination; and
- action-oriented—the process and results are useful to community members in making positive social change and to promote social equity.[3]

The goal of community engagement is community empowerment.

In oral history, community engagement can take another subtle turn. It begins with project planners reaching out to community members to help shape a project and continues after the oral history interviews are completed through sharing of information. Outreach based on the completed oral histories, through meetings and discussions, can, in some cases, support development of new, broader, and deeper senses of community as "a group of individuals bound together by a sense of shared identity."[4]

When thinking about the interviews, the concepts of shared authority and sharing authority weave through a discussion of community engagement. As Michael Frisch wrote in 2003, both concepts involve an understanding of the balance of authority when working with oral histories in a community and in an interview. Frisch described sharing authority as an approach to doing oral history "more collaboratively" and shared authority as "shared by definition . . . in the dialogic nature of the interview."[5] Both concepts help guide the making of connections to and within a community in the practice of oral history. They are critical considerations in oral history project planning.

Also keep in mind the tangible benefits that planning offers. It frames the process of recording new information and helps guide the work of filling in gaps in existing information. The planning process may raise new questions and open new and otherwise unrealized avenues of inquiry. This can help oral historians identify information that otherwise might have been missed and determine whether to include the information in an interview. It may even lead to the discovery that what seemed like a simple little project to interview a handful of people could become much broader and deeper in scope and content.

Planning helps in another way, too, by fully documenting information about the interview for its ongoing use. This begins with the planning process and incorporation of information that verifies interview context.

Participants and trainer at "Designing and planning your oral history project" one-day training course in London, United Kingdom, organized jointly by National Life Stories at the British Library and the Oral History Society, c.2019. Photo courtesy of The British Library, used with permission. *British Library.*

Oral-Visual History in Minnesota's Deaf, DeafBlind, and Hard of Hearing Community

In 2010 and 2011, the Minnesota Historical Society awarded the Minnesota Commission of the Deaf, DeafBlind, and Hard of Hearing, a state advocacy agency, a grant through its Arts and Cultural Heritage Fund. The funded project was a collaborative, public history/oral-visual history project of the commission and the community it serves. Through this grant, the community achieved a variety of accomplishments, including placing Charles Thompson Hall—the state's deaf cultural center—on the National Register of Historic Places, placing a trove of historic photos documenting the community in the Minnesota Digital Library, and making accessible four sets of oral-visual interviews, previously recorded interviews, and interviews recorded through the project. The seven video oral-visual histories recorded through the project were American Sign Language interviews with deaf narrators, translated to audio-recorded English by interpreters chosen by the narrators, transcribed and captioned; tactile sign language interviews with deafblind narrators followed by the same accessibility steps; and English interviews with the hard-of-hearing narrators, transcribed and captioned. Teika Pakalns, project director, said that the narrators "discussed the importance of recognizing the Minnesota deaf, deafblind, and hard of hearing community as a cultural community and provided information about the steps each (narrator) took to advocate for the needs of the community and its members." All project materials are held by the Minnesota Historical Society. To access information about the project and the oral-visual histories, go to the "Commission of Deaf, DeafBlind, and Hard of Hearing Minnesotans," Government Records, Minnesota Historical Society, http://www2.mnhs.org/library/findaids/gr00098.xml (scroll to find oral-visual histories).

For excellent information on recording interviews with deaf narrators, see "Filming Deaf Stories: Interviews in American Sign Language" by Jean Lindquist Bergey and Zilvinas Paludnevicius, *Journal of Folklore and Education*, 6 (2019): 21–33, https://jfepublications.org/article/filming-deaf-stories/, accessed February 22, 2024. Both authors are affiliated with Gallaudet University in Washington, DC. See also the Drs. John S. and Betty J. Schuchman Deaf Documentary Center, www.gallaudet.edu/drs-john-s-and-betty-j-schuchman-deaf-documentary-center at Gallaudet University; the Gallaudet University American Sign Language and Deaf Studies Department, Digital Journal, http://dsdj.gallaudet.edu; and "Case Study: Interviewing Deaf Narrators," https://www.nps.gov/articles/000/case-study-interviewing-deaf-narrators.htm, accessed February 22, 2024.

Note: Terminology for this sidebar is all-inclusive.

A number of factors can affect the telling of information in oral histories. The purpose of an interview, the topics it covers, and the questions that are asked are important; this information helps define the structure of an interview. The relationship between an interviewer and narrator is another factor; it can affect an interview through interactions between the individuals and the responses of a narrator to questions. Discussions about documenting information in the planning stage help define oral history content and support accurate interpretation and use of the interview information.

Oral histories are spoken, subjective, based on memory, grounded in an interaction and relationship between interviewer and narrator, and full of first-person information that often can be found nowhere else. Documenting context helps preserve this information for accurate ongoing use by future generations of researchers and others.

Working through each of the oral history planning and budget steps in this chapter helps solidify and clarify the support structure for the interviews. This increases the probability of recording strong, focused, and well-thought-out oral histories that remain accessible and stand the test of time. Coordinating with people from the community on the needs of project planning, the next steps help lay out the details.

PLANNING STEPS

The oral history planning stage helps define the structure for doing oral history interviews.

IDENTIFY KEY LEADERS AND PROJECT PERSONNEL

This is a critical step—begin by finding people to do the work. Oral history projects are labor intensive. They offer opportunities for many people to be involved in various capacities in addition to the people who will be doing the interviews. When beginning a project, think first about who will lead and guide it to completion. Look for planners or coordinators who can make the time commitment to see the process through to its end. An oral history project resulting in fifteen to twenty interviews can take several years to complete.

Whether your project is run by paid staff or volunteers, it helps to designate one or two people as coordinators or administrators. An effective project coordinator is dependable, forceful, tactful, dedicated, able to work collaboratively, and single-minded in managing a project. Project coordinators, working with community members and others in the project, help determine its purpose, focus, budget, interview themes, number of interviews, processing techniques, and the timeframe within which the interviews will be completed. While these tasks may be assigned to a leader as a guide for project development, they ideally are carried out by project coordinators with community members serving, for example, as a task force, advisory board, or leadership team.

In addition to the project coordinators, oral history projects have other personnel needs. These often include:

- Interviewers
- Support staff
- Indexers or transcribers

Interviewers are the people who do the oral history interviews. Project coordinators also may be interviewers, but do not confuse the work of the two. Interviewers should be able to give at least twenty to thirty hours per interview. This includes completing research and interview preparation, doing the interview, processing, and turning interview products over to the project director. The more complex the interview topics and themes, the more preparation time interviewers need.

Projects often have support staff. A secretary or data entry specialist can be helpful if the project has money to hire someone or can find a volunteer. A person who is familiar with the equipment and can handle training and maintenance also is an asset.

Despite increased availability of computer applications that convert audio to text, finding someone to index or transcribe the interviews often is a hurdle for oral history project coordinators. Although users of oral history materials often want ongoing access to the voices on the recording, indexes and verbatim transcripts can help guarantee access to the interview information. Full transcription ensures the information will remain accessible at least in written form for many generations. Transcribing can be done using transcribing apps, by volunteers or, if projects have funds, by paid transcribers.

Some oral history projects also include researchers to help with background research about project topics. They can aid project coordinators and interviewers with this important task.

With project personnel in place, it's time to move on to the next planning steps.

NAME THE PROJECT

Give the project a name. This is how it will be known. It helps give the project definition and a clear and consistent identity during the interviewing phase and for preservation and access purposes. If project letterhead or business cards are printed, use the name on these materials.

WRITE A MISSION STATEMENT

A mission or purpose statement defines why you are doing the oral histories. It helps bring all those involved in a project to an agreement by answering the question: "What are we trying to accomplish?" It may sound easy to write but often is one of the more difficult planning assignments.

The statement includes information on key areas of interest and importance. It defines project focus but is flexible enough in its language to allow for new directions that might evolve as a project progresses. It can become the yardstick to decide who will and will not be interviewed if the number of potential narrators outstrips resources. And it reaffirms the importance of conducting the work to the standards of the Oral History Association.

A mission statement for a narrowly focused, one-time project can be as simple as this one developed for the Pioneer Farms Oral History Project, the product of an interdisciplinary arts, agriculture, and oral history collaboration at the University of Nebraska-Lincoln:

> The mission of the Pioneer Farms Oral History Project is to collect, preserve, and make available to others oral history interviews with members of Nebraska farm families recognized as pioneer farmers, whose land has been in the same family for 100 years or more. The project is funded by the Nebraska Rural Futures Institute.[6]

Mission statements for ongoing oral history work conducted by major institutions may be more extensive, describing a broader scope of work. They also identify specific activities and frames of reference that guide the work of their oral historians. Here are several examples.

ASSOCIATION OF NATIONAL PARK RANGERS ORAL HISTORY PROJECT

In commemoration of the [National Park Service (NPS)] Centennial, the Association of National Park Rangers (ANPR) has launched an oral history project. ANPR's goal is to record, transcribe, archive, and share 50 interviews with Park Service personnel who have shaped the agency's history during its second half-century.

The first priority is to interview longtime employees who helped create the modern Park Service. They joined the agency in the 1950s, 60s, and 70s, and they occupied leadership positions during decades of great change. During their tenure, the NPS expanded significantly, the country adopted laws that challenged the Service's management policies, and the demographics of the agency's workforce and its visitors underwent a significant shift. The audio recordings and transcriptions of the oral histories will be archived at the Harpers Ferry Center in West Virginia and are already being shared via publications and websites.

ANPR's oral history project joins a long tradition in the NPS of using interviews to safeguard the collective memory and expertise of those who have shaped the Service over the years. These oral histories speak to issues such as relevance, stewardship, and workforce development—all of which will guide the Park Service in its second century. The information collected during these interviews can be used immediately as part of the workforce development and leadership succession. It is also vital to the long-term stewardship of the agency's history and the education of its early-career employees.[7]

Note the statement identifying the purpose of the project and the project organizers, and the clear definition of interviewing priorities in the ANPR statement. This is an excellent guide for project planners. The next example, from California State University, Fullerton, an ongoing project, defines the mission and goals of its work serving the campus and the community.

THE LAWRENCE DE GRAAF CENTER FOR ORAL AND PUBLIC HISTORY

The Lawrence de Graaf Center for Oral and Public History at California State Fullerton was established in 1968 as a teaching, training, research, publication, and public service archive located in the Pollak Library at California State University, Fullerton, California. It contains more than 6,000 oral histories covering topics from California and beyond.

Mission Statement:

The Lawrence de Graaf Center for Oral and Public History (COPH)—a component of the Department of History and the College of Humanities and Social Sciences at California State University, Fullerton—embraces a three-fold mission. First, COPH collects and preserves the stories of distinctive individuals and diverse communities whose historical experiences have shaped the collective memory of Southern California, defined national and transnational identities, and reflected life in an era of globalization. Second, COPH undertakes and provides support services for public history projects, particularly those designed to share oral histories with public audiences in South-

ern California and beyond. Third, COPH trains CSUF students in the research methods of collecting oral histories, interpreting these histories, and presenting important regional, national, and global stories to the public. Ultimately, COPH seeks to combine the strengths of oral history and public history in order to build better connections between Cal State Fullerton and the communities—local, national, and global—to which it is tied.

Description of Activities and Goals:

With over 6,000 recorded interviews and related transcripts, photographs, and other materials, COPH maintains the largest oral history archive in the state of California. The collection stands out nationally for its grassroots nature and the wide range of communities represented. The genesis of this archive came with the creation of a student-driven oral history program at Cal State Fullerton in 1968. Today, we continue to train students to create oral histories and generate new collections. We recognize that certain obligations accompany ownership of these collections, in particular the maintenance of a suitable storage environment and access for users, including students, scholars, educators, community members, journalists, filmmakers, and policy makers. We endeavor to employ the most appropriate, up-to-date technologies to achieve both of these ends.

The public history projects that COPH undertakes and supports include projects designed not only to tell the stories of Southern California but also to connect those stories to national and global contexts. COPH's public history projects, like its oral history projects, are student-driven. COPH trains students to curate museum exhibitions, engage in historic preservation initiatives, and complete other projects related to community history, public art and culture, oral history performance, heritage tourism, digital history, and archival management. Many of these projects are collaborative and serve as capstones for graduate students pursuing the M.A. in History.

COPH's highest goal is to provide service to students, researchers, and the public. An array of courses, projects, and internships prepare students to become engaged community members and global citizens, effective historians and educators, and successful public history professionals. Groundbreaking oral history projects, sponsorship of the Hansen Lectureship and Fellowship in Oral and Public History, and full array of support services for researchers make COPH a vibrant center of scholarly and creative activity. Oral history workshops, consultation services, and community-based projects allow COPH to serve the diverse communities whose members have shared their memories with us. [8]

The Samuel Proctor Oral History Program (SPOHP), another campus-based program, is designed to serve both the academics and the public community. Through use of its collections and its active interviewing project program, it reaches well beyond its campus location.

THE SAMUEL PROCTOR
ORAL HISTORY PROGRAM

This award-winning program is the oral history program of the University of Florida. Founded in 1967, its members have conducted over 8,000 interviews. More than 150,000 pages of transcribed material from these interviews may· be found in the SPOHP archives and Digital Collections at the University of Florida. Our mission statement is:

One Community, Many Voices.
Our mission is to gather, preserve, and promote living histories of individuals from all walks of life.

- SPOHP teaches the craft and intellectual traditions of oral history through university seminars as well as through community-based workshops.
- SPOHP teaches students, independent scholars, and community organizations how to bring history to life.
- SPOHP consults on an ongoing basis with local historians, civic leaders, and educators in Florida and beyond who are interested in initiating oral history projects in their towns and municipalities.
- SPOHP engages in the scholarly and educational life of the University of Florida, our state, and the world through public history programs, academic conferences, and scholarly collaborations.
- SPOHP emphasizes that oral history is an interdisciplinary methodology that draws on ethnography, literature, social theory, and memory studies—among other academic fields.
- SPOHP facilitates rigorous collaborative research, civic engagement, digital technology, and other techniques that make history accessible, democratic, and fun.
- SPOHP guides students, scholars, and communities throughout the world in gathering, preserving, and promoting living history through academic publications, public programs, electronic media, and other forums to document the human condition.[9]

PLAN FOR PRESERVATION

If your project already is operating under the sponsorship of a historical society, academic institution, library, or museum, planning for preservation may not be an issue. But if that is not the case, finding a permanent home for your project materials is an important decision. It will determine who will have ongoing curatorial

(preservation and access) responsibility for care of project products, including permanent storage of and access to media, interview information, indexes, transcripts, and all related materials. It is a responsibility not to be taken lightly. Suitable candidates will depend on the terms of a legal release agreement and, if a permanent repository, available storage, facilities, preservation and access options, and staff.

Project leaders should approach a place to care for the oral histories and discuss legal questions as early as possible in the planning process. Physical and digital repositories often have requirements for accepting collections. Leaders will want to make sure interview materials will be held by a place that has the ability to safeguard the collection and make it as widely available as appropriate for the project.

Even if narrators maintain ownership and control over their interviews, look for a place that will manage project materials in accordance with the prevailing archival and curatorial standards and the standards of the Oral History Association. Review written policies governing access to and care of the collections. Look for a rights and permissions statement clarifying use and copyright guidelines. Discuss the possibility of depositing copies of interview materials in other accessible locations. And remember that the internet is not a repository. Use it to disseminate project information, but never consider it a permanent repository.

Summarizing, what are the most important repository items needed for long-term care of oral histories? Here are some tips from archivists Michele Pollard and Mollie Spillman, drawing from their experience working with historical organizations in a large metropolitan area. Basic items include:

- Environmental controls that help provide protection for long-term care of interview recordings and transcripts
- Dedicated computers with enough space to support preservation and access of oral history recordings and funding to support their ongoing access
- Use of offsite facilities and/or the Cloud to provide collections backup and offsite computer space to maintain a full archival copy of the oral histories
- Use of a cataloging program that is flexible enough to accommodate the needs of oral history
- Use of shelving that meets archival standards
- Acid-free containers for all oral history materials, digital and hard copies[10]

If, for some reason, oral history project materials are not put in a standard repository, the chances of their being lost can increase. Oral history projects that end up permanently stashed under someone's bed or in a closet or attic are as inaccessible to the general public as items lost from the internet. As historian and oral historian Donald A. Ritchie has written: "An interview becomes an oral history only when it has been recorded, processed in some way, made available in an archive, library, or other repository, or reproduced in relatively verbatim form for publication. Availability for general research, reinterpretation, and verification defines oral history."[11]

See chapter 8 for a more detailed discussion of ongoing care and access guidelines for oral history materials. The Oral History Association's "Archiving Oral History: Manual of Best Practices" provides additional information about archiving that is helpful for oral history project planners. It also emphasizes why it is useful for project planners to proactively find an appropriate home for their oral history materials early in the planning process; this will make preservation and access steps run more smoothly.[12]

SELECT A PROJECT ADVISORY BOARD

A project advisory board is a group of people who can provide guidance and support for the project. This can be an area of interactive community engagement; advisory boards also can include project supporters from a variety of additional backgrounds. Its purpose is to represent the community, guide the development of the project, and provide help with questions. Selecting an advisory board or task force is a way of building a network of project support.

The people on a task force or advisory board should be committed to the project and its goals and thoroughly understand their roles in the work of community outreach, engagement, and support and why they were asked to serve. They may be community leaders who will help find funding sources or equipment when needed, experts on the general subject of the interviews, and those with a good grounding in history chosen to help guide the project on the most effective use of its time and resources. A liaison with a sponsoring institution also often serves on this board. Choose members for the support they can give to the project or their access to the types of expertise and community support that the project needs. Individual advisory board members, for example, may be asked to answer questions or to help with a phase of the work, depending on the particular knowledge or skills they bring to the project.

Community engagement can take as much time as needed to fully understand and be a part of a project. It may begin with a meeting at the beginning of the project, include regular meetings to incorporate suggestions and discuss directions and progress, and conclude with a celebration of the results.

ESTABLISH A PROJECT TIMEFRAME

A project timeframe establishes goals for project milestones—completing the research, preparing interview guides, and completing interviews. Allot time for:

- Identifying interviewers and providing interviewer training
- Selecting narrators
- Research, including narrator-specific work
- Scheduling and conducting interviews
- Processing interviews

Define blocks of time for various project tasks. The time it takes to adequately prepare for interviews, acquire equipment, do the interviews, and prepare them for post-interview preservation can take a toll on even the most enthusiastic project participants. Developing a timeframe helps you think through the project, identifying the necessary tasks and the time that can realistically be allotted to complete each one. Remember that oral history projects can change as new information is uncovered, so be prepared to remain flexible rather than just adhering to your timeframe. Laying out expectations, even if they change during the project, can help everyone better orient to a project and understand its needs.

CREATE A RECORD-KEEPING SYSTEM AND ESTABLISH PROCEDURES

After you reach agreement on post-interview care, begin to develop record-keeping systems that will serve post-interview needs. A relatively invisible part of project development, record-keeping documents context and provides continuity and support necessary for both interviewer and narrator. You don't want to get bogged down in paperwork, but developing standard forms at the outset can help keep a project on track. The forms also document critical information about interview content and context that aids in development of finding aids and in future use of the interview information. See sample forms in appendix A.

Some of the most commonly used forms are:

- Donor (legal release) form
- Project design statement (documents project planning)
- Biographical information form (narrator and interviewer)
- Interview summary form (documents interview context and content)
- Interview tracking form (tracks preservation and access steps)

- Photograph and memorabilia form (documents artifacts and other archival materials identified through an interview)

The donor or legal release form covers ongoing ownership and access to the interview materials. Common options are transfer of copyright, use of a Creative Commons license, and public domain. Each is designed to give future researchers and others access to the interview information. An agreement covering copyright is an essential part of the support materials for an interview and must be signed to help provide ongoing care. If using a legal release agreement, fill out and sign the form after each interview, even if another interview is planned with the same narrator. For further information and a more detailed discussion about the specific types of donor or legal release forms, see chapter 4.

The biographical information forms contain basic biographical data about a narrator and an interviewer. Depending on how the project is organized, an interviewer will fill out their form and then work with a narrator to complete that person's form. It may be filled out at the beginning of an interview or during a preliminary meeting or telephone conversation between the interviewer and narrator. If questions about possible vulnerability of documenting information about a narrator come up, try to get them answered as quickly as possible. Also document the decisions for interview context. The forms document who the interviewer and narrator are, both for project purposes and for the benefit of future users of the interview. For more information, see chapter 6.

Fill in the interview summary form as soon as possible after an interview. It lists the names of the narrator and interviewer, the project name, interview date and length, recorder or recorders used, and the number and type of media. It also confirms that legal issues have been covered and contains a one- to three-paragraph statement about interview contents. This form documents context and provides immediate access to the interview information as well as information for full processing (transcribing, indexing, access conditions, and development of finding aids). For further discussion, see chapter 8.

Some projects use additional forms. As an example, project research often will uncover names of people whose information could be important to the project. The potential narrator information form is a place to keep up-to-date information about prospective additional narrators. It also should include a brief summary about the person's background and information about their ties or links to the project.

A letter of agreement for volunteer interviewers and a letter of agreement for indexers or transcribers spell out the responsibilities of each position. Projects using paid interviewers will want to become familiar with the work-made-for-hire doctrine and the work-made-for-hire agreement. For more information, see *A Guide to Oral History and the Law*.[13]

FORMS TO HELP YOU GET STARTED WITH RECORD-KEEPING AND PROCEDURES

Oral historians have several forms that can help get an interview or a project started. They are the project design statement, the photograph and memorabilia form, and the interview tracking form. Each one helps document interview-related decisions in the oral history planning stage.

The project design statement covers the decisions that project leaders, whether planning one interview or a series of interviews, make in preparation to begin the interviewing stage. They include:

- Project name: this is the formal name that will identify the interview or set of interviews in the archival record; naming the project during the planning stage will help with its ongoing identification throughout the interviews and into the preservation and access stages.
- Basic details including mission, goals, and name of project director: oral history projects benefit from a project director committed to seeing a project through, though the form can be updated if the director changes. Development of project mission and goals help define the project and its purpose from the outset.
- Project content: decisions about project content details identified in this section of the form will guide the project to completion and further define interview context. All are necessary; making them during the planning stage and entering them on the form documents agreement on each point—a useful tool as work on the project moves forward.
- Project management: agreeing to and documenting details of project management from the outset also is helpful. Determining the number of narrators and the expected duration of the project provides everyone involved with helpful parameters that can both guide a project and offer an opportunity for setting and maintaining its pace.

Oral history interviews are generally done in a narrator's home or other community location where a narrator is comfortable, and interviewers can learn during the course of an interview about additional information, including photographs and memorabilia that narrators sometimes wish to give to the project repository. The photograph and memorabilia form helps project organizers know how to proceed if, or when, this happens. Its use can help planners train interviewers about what to do if this happens. Use of this form encourages a conversation with representatives from the project repository about what types of materials they are set up to accept, to identify other repositories that may be willing to accept other materials, and to discuss how to involve the repository when narrators offer such materials. The form helps keep track of these materials, identifying items, their owners, and the requested course of action.

The interview tracking form identifies all contacts with narrators. It shows the progress of each interview, its length and processing status, and provides a capsule summary of project progress at any point in time.

NON-CIRCULATING MASTER FILE

A non-circulating master file is a place to keep information about each narrator and interview. Its information contributes to documenting context; it usually contains:

- Background and contact information of the narrator
- Correspondence with the narrator
- Notes from conversations with the narrator, whether by telephone or in person
- Biographical information about a narrator and an interviewer
- Potential narrator information forms
- Completed interview information forms
- Original copy of a signed donor or other form dealing with legal issues
- Interview guide (topics and questions)
- Narrator-specific research materials
- Interview notes
- Lists of people and place names mentioned during the interview with the narrator's spelling corrections
- A photograph of the narrator, often taken in the interview setting
- A more formal photo given by the narrator, if desired
- A draft of the transcript containing the narrator's comments and corrections

This information can be adjusted if documenting a narrator's name or location would be a possible danger to the person.

EQUIPMENT DECISIONS

Recording equipment decisions often provoke lively discussions. This also is one of the larger oral history expenses. Equipment decisions include whether to use audio or video or both, how to combine the two if both are to be used, and what types of equipment will produce final products that fit a budget and serve a project's needs.

Planning decisions about equipment have far-reaching consequences. What type of equipment will work best for a particular project? Will the decision include using audio recordings, video recordings, or both, and why? What format and SD card will the recordings use and why? What types of recordings is a repository, or other places for preservation of the interviews, equipped to accession, preserve, care for, and make accessible? If a specific product, such as a museum exhibit, YouTube video, or podcast, is planned, what equipment and formats will best serve its needs and why? What recording formats are recommended for short-term and long-term preservation and access?

As digital guidelines continue to change, specifications for recording, preservation, and access of oral histories will change with them. In response to the need for ongoing, up-to-date information, several leading oral historians developed the *Oral History in the Digital Age* website. Through a series of essays, the *Oral History in the Digital Age* website connects oral historians to the "latest information on digital technologies pertaining to all phases of the oral history process."[14] For more information about oral history equipment options and the *Oral History in the Digital Age* website as a resource for oral historians, see chapter 5.

INTERVIEW CONTEXT IN PROJECT PLANNING

The practice of oral history is guided by certain standards, defined by the Oral History Association in its "Best Practices," updated regularly. The "Best Practices" are presented through each of the four key elements of oral history: preparation, interviewing, preservation, and access; they are applicable both to long-time standard oral history interviewing practices and to the more recent rapidly changing processes, such as use of Zoom and other distance recording techniques. "Best Practices" also cover interviews that can almost be said to blur the lines between oral history and journalism, documenting events in real time using oral history methodology.

Careful documentation of interview context is an important part of oral history "Best Practices." According to Oxford Languages, context is defined as "the circumstances that form the setting for an event, statement, or idea, and in terms of which it can be fully understood and assessed."[15] When working with an oral history interview or project, keep in mind the importance of documenting context as part of work on each stage of the oral history life cycle. Clearly state the purpose of the project; for example, is it designed to support development of a museum exhibit? Or to help a community document a part of its history? Perhaps it focuses on political or social justice purposes. Begin by documenting context in the planning stage and continue after the interview. Provide information that will help researchers accurately understand and interpret the oral histories.

Handle documenting context with care. Generally, it involves basic but thorough narrator identification including full name, community of residence, and relevance to the project. It also can include birth year or a range of years and place of birth, though all information has to be handled with care to protect a narrator from the possibility of identity theft or other harm.[16] Context also can include a discussion about the focus of an interview and reasons for choosing a particular focus, discussion about the choice of interview topics, description of an interview setting, biographical background as appropriate on the interviewer and narrator, discussions on why and how a narrator became part of a project, a narrator's response to being interviewed, a narrator's response to the interview focus and interview topics, discussions about various points of view and backgrounds and their impacts on the interview, and comments about expected preservation and access status. This is basic contextual information needed for accurate understanding and use of interview information.

This information is helpful but can be more difficult to document when working with narrators who are members of potentially vulnerable populations. In these cases, full identification of a narrator may not be possible or appropriate. It may be necessary to provide background information about a narrator and a narrator's response to interview questions in ways that would not violate narrator privacy or put them in a difficult situation. In these cases, an interviewer, working with a narrator, can make decisions that are helpful in understanding interview content while remaining protective of a narrator and, if necessary, an interviewer.

TRAIN INTERVIEWERS

The ideal situation is to find trained oral history interviewers who are familiar with a project's subject. Whether using experienced or novice interviewers, arrange for interviewer training and project orientation sessions as part of the planning and development process. This is essential to creating good oral history interviews. An orientation and training workshop should include discussion of your project's goals as well as general background about the oral history process. Would-be interviewers, no matter how much experience they have, need to learn about the unique characteristics of each project. Interviewers also should be trained in setting up interview locations, including controlling sounds of barking dogs and running appliances, as well as placement of recording equipment. As new interviewers join a project, follow-up training always should be offered.

Training interviewers is integral to a project's success. Haphazard or insufficient training is certain to be a project's downfall. Even the best-planned oral history projects can fizzle if interviewers lack the skills they need to get started or to improve their work once the interviewing phase is under way.

Training is available from a variety of sources. The Oral History Association's annual fall meetings include informative workshops for beginning and advanced oral history practitioners, and state or regional oral history organizations often schedule workshops as well. State historical societies, state or regional museum associations, local colleges and universities, and state humanities councils can be resources for oral history training. And experienced oral historians often are available to create workshops customized to meet a project's needs. For more information, see the Oral History Association "Find an Oral Historian" webpage.[17]

PREPARE FOR UNEXPECTED SITUATIONS

Oral historians can run into a number of unexpected situations when recording interviews. One example is learning about collections of photos and memorabilia held by the narrator during an interview. Sometimes, a narrator will unexpectedly bring out historic photographs (which may either be copied and returned or permanently accessioned into a repository's collections) and other archival materials and artifacts. Such collections can add an important dimension to an oral history interview, but they also can disrupt it or draw an interviewer into new and unanticipated areas of discussion. When this happens, ask for basic identifying questions of each photo or artifact as the narrator holds the item. Take careful notes and document as much information as possible.

An example of unexpected memorabilia occurred during an interview recorded with a former Civilian Conservation Corps (CCC) enrollee many years after the end of the New Deal program. Toward the end of the interview, the narrator asked for time to show the interviewer a CCC camp souvenir he had, fifty years earlier, as a young enrollee far from home, sent his mother. The interviewer waited as the narrator rummaged through upstairs closets and then came down with a CCC souvenir pillow embroidered "Mother." The interviewer contacted the project repository about accessioning it into the CCC collections, where it became a prized item. The narrator was pleased his gift of many years ago had a new home, and the interviewer was pleased to provide a home for this rare and cherished item. When situations like this occur, contact the repository and use the artifact and memorabilia form to document information about the item and the person who has it; turn the information over to the repository

CCC pillow. *Civilian Conservation Corps. Minnesota Discovery Center, Iron Range Research Center. Used with permission.*

for further action. If accessioned by the repository, these materials can become part of project collections.[18]

Emotions of narrators during an interview are another example of an unexpected occurrence. During an oral history project organized as a memorial for a recently deceased governor of a Midwestern state, the interviewer was surprised when one of the first narrators cried during the interview. The interviewer, thinking this was a mistake, carefully reviewed the situation. Though originally unplanned and unexpected, as the interviews went on, the interviewer realized emotions were part of each narrator's memories of the governor. Most narrators—state business and political leaders and top members of his administrations—cried during their interviews. One narrator, when asked to participate in the project, told the interviewer that he cried when talking about the governor and asked if this would make a difference in participating in it; the interviewer assured him it would not. The interviewer learned to bring a package of tissues to the interviews and to give the narrators space and tissues when they became emotional. The interviewer put the recorder on pause and gently gave the narrators time to compose themselves before continuing; they also purposefully designed the last questions to focus on happier memories, ending the interview on a positive note.[19]

Oral histories can bring up varieties of intense memories from the past. This is often the case in interviews with veterans. When interviewing someone who may be affected by post-traumatic stress disorder or similar issues, discuss the situation with the narrator and plan for ways to help the veteran, such as keeping a phone number handy to call for support if needed. Some narrators

prefer to have someone familiar with the situation nearby during their interviews; if so, include this in the project plan. Intensity of memories can be unexpected, but it also is a situation that advance planning can help cushion.

Oral historians also have stories about interview surprises, ranging from overly friendly pets who knock over a recorder (hopefully not in the middle of an interview) to difficulty in controlling background noises such as street traffic or ticking clocks to doing interviews in unexpected places such as the back of a pickup truck. SD card/media failures, though rare, are disconcerting to even the most experienced oral historians. It is a good idea to anticipate possible concerns and prepare for them as much as possible.

Here are a couple of tips:

- Assemble and carry a backup kit as part of equipment and other interview materials. As an example, a kit can include a package of tissues, extension cords, extra SD cards/media, batteries, and a microphone windscreen—materials to meet a variety of situations.
- Check with narrators about pets during an interview (this can go for small children too).
- And, especially if interviewing outdoors, be prepared for rain, clouds, changing weather, wind, and needs of a narrator for a comfortable place for an interview.

Think through your needs for the possibility of an unexpected situation.

DEVELOP A PROJECT BUDGET

Oral history is an exciting and invigorating process. But the reality of financial needs can stop a good project before it gets off the ground. It helps to create a budget early in the planning process and to include all possible project costs. With this, you can begin to determine realistically what you can and cannot accomplish. Even if your project will be staffed largely by volunteers, it will incur expenses; donations and volunteer time also can show added value. While some of those costs may be met through volunteer time or donated materials, it is still important at the outset to determine realistically what funds will be required and when. The costs of developing and carrying out an oral history project often are underestimated. Mapping out expected costs early in the project helps everyone understand its needs.

Developing a project budget helps determine the full cost of doing an interview. A budget is helpful even if a project is run by volunteers.

What are the financial needs of an oral history project? Oral historians ask this question almost as often as they ask what equipment to use. Oral history is not cheap. Committed volunteers can help underwrite project costs and provide considerable manpower. But unless everything—time, space, and materials—is donated, projects need cash to survive.

Oral history is labor-intensive work. If you think only in terms of interview costs, the project will be woefully underfunded. Although this is a project's most visible product, the interview may only take several hours; careful preparation beforehand and meticulous processing afterward are time-consuming. Adequate budgeting for that time plus the cost of equipment and other supplies is a critical part of successfully completing an oral history project. Identifying all project costs and sources of revenue can make the difference between a good idea and a successfully completed project.

The full costs of an oral history project are not immediately obvious, as many project organizers have found to their dismay. Include the following elements in a project budget.

ONE-TIME OR NON-RECURRING EXPENSES

- Recording equipment, including carrying case
- Microphones and accessories, including cables
- Duplicating equipment
- Interviewer training costs
- Transcriber or transcribing apps
- Backup kit
- Consultant fee, if needed

OVERHEAD COSTS

- Administration, including salaries for any paid project staff
- Advisory board meetings, per diems for advisory board members
- Honoraria and per diems for project guests
- Interviewer training
- Photocopying
- Postage
- Telephone, email, texts
- Printing costs, such as letterhead, business cards, project brochures
- Office space
- Office equipment, such as file cabinets
- Other costs, including equipment repair and unexpected items

INTERVIEW COSTS

- Interview research and preparation
- Media for each interview and for all copies that will need to be made

- Payment to interviewers
- Payment to narrators
- Payment to videographers
- Transcribing
- Printing transcripts (acid-free paper, acid-free folders)
- Travel (interview research/interview)

BUDGET DISCUSSION

Each of the budget elements is a project cost, whether donated, in-kind, or purchased. Among all project costs, equipment is one of the largest. Once purchased, it will be available for the duration of the project. The number of recorders and microphones needed will be based on available funds, the size of the project, and the number of project interviewers.

The amount and type of media will depend on the number of narrators. Digital recordings are made on one type of media and saved on another. Following the LOCKSS principle (lots of copies keeps stuff safe), plan to save an interview in at least two forms and to make at least three additional copies of each recording: a processing copy, a public user copy, and a courtesy copy for the narrator.

Photocopying, scanning, printing, and postage are standard project costs and will depend on the size and scope of the project. Travel costs should cover both research and interview needs.

Processing costs support making copies of the interviews as well as transcribing and transcripts. While transcribing software increasingly is available to speed the transcription process, time is still needed to carefully check the transcript against the audio recording to assure accuracy.

Personnel costs vary, depending on project participants. Is this a volunteer-run project, a project run by paid staff, or a combination of the two? An estimate of personnel costs can be determined by looking at salaries of equivalent staff at local museums and libraries. Interviewers sometimes are paid by the interview. Videographers are paid by the hour, studio hour, or interview. Some projects pay narrators, and in some circumstances, a gift also may be given.

Oral history projects often rely on volunteers. Doing oral history requires firm resolve and many hours of time on the part of project participants. Volunteers should make every effort to keep to the schedules and guidelines the coordinators establish. Projects in which this understanding has been well defined from the beginning have the best chance of success.

Whether using volunteer or paid staff, oral history training is an essential expense. A workshop for project participants, including planners, interviewers, and processors, can save everyone unnecessary mistakes and loss of time. Attending a one-day workshop to learn and practice appropriate interviewing techniques should be a minimum expectation for volunteers who want to be involved in a project. Don't forget to budget for workshop training costs.

Finally, to help determine the number of interviews a project can reasonably afford, develop a per-interview cost. Identify all costs associated with an interview, using an average interview length of one-and-one-half hours. Basic interview costs include:

- Interviewer payment
- Narrator payment
- Transportation
- Technology (recorders, recording media)
- Transcribing
- Making a copy of a recording and transcript for a narrator

Add the figures for these items together for a basic per-interview cost. Multiply per-interview costs by the number of planned project interviews for a ballpark project cost estimate. The Oral History Association "OHA Statement on Freelance, Contract, and Independent Labor" offers helpful guidelines in determining cost figures.[20]

NARRATOR COMPENSATION

The topic of narrator compensation has been a thread of conversation among oral historians for a number of years. Focusing originally on the ethics of paying a narrator because of concerns about coercion or credibility of interview information, payment often was made as a gift of a copy of an interview recording and transcript in lieu of cash. If a legal release agreement was written as a contract, it would often include a token payment of, for example, one dollar. Conversations are now increasingly turning to viewing narrator payment as a planning and budget item. In this scenario, an interview is seen as labor and a narrator as someone who should be paid for this labor.[21] Oral historians are looking more closely into ongoing narrator payment questions such as avoiding narrator coercion, sensitivity to issues that could worsen inequality or highlight vulnerability, and taking care that use of narrator compensation meets oral history ethical standards.[22] Community engagement advisors can be helpful in answering narrator payment questions including amounts and how to make the payments.

The concept of viewing an oral history interview as paid labor is encouraging oral historians to take a new, and deeper, look at this issue. With this in mind, they are developing project payment guidelines, identifying criteria to set payment types and amounts, and determining how to make payments that meet narrators' needs.[23] Funders also are beginning to include social justice goals as part of a "more general culture of payment."[24] All of these steps can help support narrator compensation as paid labor.

Projects involved in ongoing discussions about narrator payments have a variety of options open to them. Narrators may be paid in cash or through direct deposit into a bank account. Other often-used suggestions range from paying for interview meals and transportation costs to giving narrators copies of their interviews. Oral historians also can widen compensation opportunities by delivering meals and groceries; helping with, and advocating for, narrator educational and legal questions and needs; providing support for healthcare needs broadly defined as medical care, housing care, and food; and providing gifts such as prepaid cell phones.[25] All of these ideas recognize the importance of providing narrator compensation and can be designed to meet narrator needs.

Overall, as the topic of oral history narrator compensation continues to be discussed, oral historians are finding a variety of ways to provide support for the contributions of narrators—the people with the knowledge and information key to the work of oral historians—that can fit into project budgets and meet ethical guidelines. The thread running through the discussion of narrator compensation acknowledges narrator knowledge and offers support for recording it. See chapter 4 of this manual for a detailed discussion about changing thoughts on narrator compensation as an evolving ethical question.

FIND FINANCIAL SUPPORT AND FUNDING SOURCES

Finding funding can be an ongoing process. Oral history projects take time and can be expensive. Unless full funding already exists, start laying the groundwork for obtaining funding as soon as you have defined the project and developed a budget. Even volunteer projects have costs that donated time and materials cannot cover. Funding sources can include outright grants, loans of equipment and other materials, in-kind contributions, self-funding by institutions, grants from state or local historical societies or state humanities councils, and programs run through public libraries. Experienced oral historians know that while all are good options, the available amount of per-project funds from each of these sources often is relatively small and that many or all may be necessary to successfully complete a project.

Competition is keen for grants from national sources. The National Endowment for the Humanities, for example, has funded oral history work, although such projects have had to show evidence of national significance, pass rigorous reviews, and show strong evidence of planning and preparation. Many projects look for funds from other sources to support initial planning work before considering an application for federal funds.

Funding and Support Suggestions

An oral history project can be an expensive undertaking. If available, volunteers can help offset some expenses. Other sources of funding and support can include the following.

Civic organizations: A group may want to sponsor the project, providing printing, postage, photocopying, media—or funds.

Local businesses: Sometimes local businesses are willing to support a community effort through gifts of photocopying, postage, fax, and other administrative needs.

Radio and television stations: Both have to document community service as part of licensing requirements. They may be willing to help with equipment.

Schools (secondary and post-secondary): They may have equipment to loan to a project. Parents groups or service clubs may also be willing to sponsor a project.

Libraries, historical societies, and other non-profit organizations: They may have resources to give to a project, including grant options. They can also help identify possible grant sources and offer grant-writing expertise.

Newspapers: They may be willing to help provide publicity.

Some state historical organizations offer support for oral history projects. The Kentucky Oral History Commission, for example, manages its own active system of workshops and grants designed to encourage statewide participation in oral history. Grant categories include oral history projects, transcribing/indexing, and technical and preservation assistance. In addition, its oral history preservation and access commission offers archival accreditation support for archives in Kentucky that want to become permanent repositories for oral histories created through the oral history grants program.[26]

Educational institutions often develop and carry out oral history projects, as do libraries, archives, and museums. Many major colleges and universities have ongoing flagship programs with work done primarily by faculty, graduate students, and research assistants. The oral history program at Columbia University with its Oral History Master of Arts; the Center for Oral History Research at the University of California, Los Angeles; and the Oral History Center at the Bancroft Library at the University of California are some of the longest-established and best known of these programs. Now many colleges and universities have active programs that emphasize both teaching and building collections that can help document the history of their community.

Community-based oral history projects developed with volunteer support also are growing in number. Community members interested in documenting specific events or time periods may want to explore resources in their communities or through the local and state historical societies and the Oral History Association to develop their projects.

Local secondary school history or social studies teachers are another possible source of support. Although class schedules and days are full for students and teachers, the possibility of school-community collaboration may be of interest. Teachers across the country have successfully integrated oral history into the curriculum, offering students an exciting opportunity for hands-on learning while preserving community history that might otherwise be lost.[27]

Professional associations, businesses, and interest groups related to a project's theme are potential sources of financial support. Some may be willing to provide in-kind (non-cash, donated) support such as offering a place to meet or providing supplies. Local governments and corporations may be other sources.

City- and state-based foundations and local businesses can be sources of funds if project purposes meet their grant guidelines. Local libraries often have information on grants opportunities that can be a help. Many non-profit organizations and local foundations sponsor grant-writing workshops that can help in locating funding sources and writing grant proposals. Some coordinators find private sources, but if these sources are used, care should be taken to ensure donors do not control project results.

Chapter 5 provides detailed information about the types of equipment and media recommended for oral history projects. The standards are high because using good equipment maximizes the life of the recording. But don't be deterred by the price tag and think that you must abandon the project if you cannot immediately go out and purchase such equipment. This is another area where community sources of support may be able to help. Organizations that may not be able or willing to fund interviews might fund equipment purchases. Other agencies, including radio and television stations, school districts, or state historical societies, might be willing to loan equipment to the project or permit you to use specialized equipment. Borrowing equipment, in fact, is sometimes preferable to buying it.

Finding funding sources does not mean just looking for outright grants but, depending on circumstances, identifying any and all possible means of support. For some projects, local businesses might provide in-kind support for equipment, media, printing, postage, or photocopying. Community-based organizations for another project may be willing to help with travel expenses and transcribing interviews. Finding and monitoring community support can be time-consuming, but in some circumstances, it can help assure successful completion of a project.

Project coordinators should keep careful records of gifts and loans of materials and time because in-kind support can help show potential funders the value of commitment to a project. Start keeping track of all time and materials beginning with the first planning meetings and continue this practice throughout the life of the project. And, as a reminder, keep in mind the purpose of the project you want to develop, and, while gratefully accepting help and support, don't let the wishes of supporters influence project outcomes. This is not easy, but it is important to the final results.

This discussion of budgeting for an oral history project does not include the costs of creating products from oral history interviews, such as websites, museum exhibits, books, pamphlets, or podcasts. It focuses only on the development of the oral history interview as a primary source document. If you wish to develop additional products after the project has been completed, or to develop a project in phases, you will want to budget for this, too.

DEVELOP A PUBLICITY PLAN

Be sure to give some thought to creating a project publicity plan. This is an essential, but often overlooked, element of any successful oral history project. The oral history interviews, when completed, will represent an important addition of new information or new perspectives to the historical record. Publicizing the collection's existence should not be neglected. Project publicity includes everything from letting people know it is taking place to encouraging use of the completed interviews. Publicity will help all stages of the project by encouraging support—financial and material—and maintaining participant and community enthusiasm.

A publicity plan can include a brochure that describes the project and lists the names of coordinators and supporters. This can be useful both for the general public and as a handout for prospective narrators. Project coordinators also may want to print project stationery as a way of reinforcing its public identity.

Sometimes project coordinators think it will help generate good publicity if they issue a press release or turn to social media asking for would-be narrators to step forward. A public request for narrators implies a promise to interview anyone who comes forth, which may not be in the best interests of your project, unless the project has unlimited resources or is intended to be permanently ongoing. The choice of narrators, depending on the purpose of a project, often is guided by community engagement discussions, planning, and research.

Although some work on the publicity plan will take place at the beginning of the project, most will occur after the information has been collected and the project is complete. At that time, announce project results to the general public. Send brief press releases to all local news media and other organizations—local, state, national, or international—that might have an interest in the information you've collected. And use appropriate social media channels and other forms of outreach to spread the word.

SUMMARY

Support for oral history projects varies depending on the community, project coordinators, and available resources. As with all stages of project development,

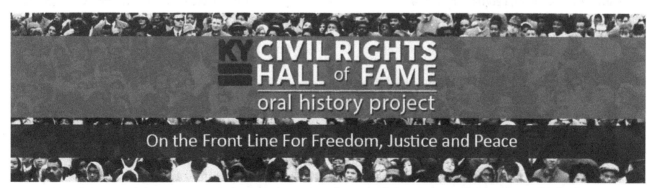

Kentucky Historical Society Civil Rights Hall of Fame Project. Participants: Kentucky Civil Rights Hall of Fame Oral History Project, Kentucky Oral History Commission, in partnership with the Louie B. Nunn Center for Oral History, University of Kentucky Libraries, the University Office of Community Engagement, and the Kentucky Commission on Human Rights.

however, good planning helps. Always let potential supporters know what you want to accomplish and why it is important. If you have multiple sponsors, coordinate among them. Show a clear plan of work and a realistic, clearly defined budget to everyone you are working with. Explain what the results of the project will be and how the oral history materials will be made available in the future.

Planning is time-consuming, but it pays dividends from the beginning of an oral history project or a series of interviews. It provides a stable foundation for recording oral histories that meet project goals and methodological standards.

NOTES

1. Oral History Association, "Guidelines for Evaluation of Professional or Academic Oral Historians for Promotion, Tenure, or Other Review," https://oralhistory.org/oha-guidelines-for-the-evaluation-of-oral-historians/, accessed October 15, 2023.
2. Carnegie Classification, "The Elective Classification for Community Engagement," https://carnegieclassifications.acenet.edu/elective-classifications/community-engagement, accessed October 15, 2023.
3. Winona Wheeler, Charles E. Trimble, Mary Kay Quinlan, and Barbara W. Sommer, *Indigenous Oral History Manual: Canada and the United States* (New York, NY: Routledge, 2024), 33.
4. Mary Kay Quinlan, Nancy MacKay, and Barbara W. Sommer, *Community Oral History Toolkit*, volume 1 (New York, NY: Routledge, 2013), 28.
5. Michael Frisch, "Commentary: Sharing Authority: Oral History and the Collaborative Process," *Oral History Review*, 30:1 (winter/spring 2003): 113.
6. Pioneer Farms Oral History Project Agreement, Nebraska State Historical Society, 2016.
7. Courtesy of Lu Ann Jones, National Park Service historian (retired), email to Mary Kay Quinlan and Barbara W. Sommer, February 15, 2024.
8. The Lawrence de Graaf Center for Oral and Public History, California State University, Fullerton, https://coph.fullerton.edu/, accessed September 7, 2023.
9. Samuel Proctor Oral History Program, University of Florida, https://oral.history.ufl.edu/welcome/mission/, accessed November 15, 2023.
10. Michele Pollard, archivist, Hennepin History Museum, Minneapolis, Minnesota, conversation with Barbara W. Sommer, June 14, 2023. Mollie Spillman, curator/archivist, Ramsey County Historical Society, St. Paul, Minnesota, conversation with Barbara W. Sommer, June 13, 2023.
11. Donald A. Ritchie, *Doing Oral History*, third edition (New York, NY: Oxford University Press, 2015), 8.
12. Oral History Association, "Archiving Oral History: Manual of Best Practices," https://oralhistory.org/archives-principles-and-best-practices-complete-manual/, accessed November 11, 2023.
13. John A. Neuenschwander, *A Guide to Oral History and the Law*, second edition (New York, NY: Oxford University Press, 2014), 3–19, 123–29. See also: Oral History Association, "OHA Statement on Freelance, Independent, and Contract Oral History Labor," https://oralhistory.org/oha-statement-on-freelance-independent-and-contract-oral-history-labor/, accessed November 29, 2023.
14. *Oral History in the Digital Age*, https://oralhistory.org/oral-history-in-the-digital-age/, accessed November 12, 2023. The project and site was developed under the intellectual leadership of Doug Boyd, director, the Louie B. Nunn Center for Oral History, University of Kentucky Libraries; Steve Cohen, research faculty, Michigan State University Digital Humanities Center, Matrix; Brad Rakerd, professor, Department of Communicative Sciences and Disorders; C. Kurt Dewhurst, professor, Director of Arts and Cultural Initiatives, and senior fellow for University Outreach & Engagement, Michigan State University; and Dean Rehberger, director, Matrix.
15. Oxford Languages, https://languages.oup.com/google-dictionary-en/, accessed September 5, 2023.
16. Oral History Association, "Principles and Best Practices: Glossary," https://oralhistory.org/best-practices-glossary/, accessed November 29, 2023.
17. For more information, see "Find an Oral Historian" on the Oral History Association website, https://oralhistory.org/directory/, accessed February 21, 2024.
18. Civilian Conservation Corps Documentation Project, Minnesota Discovery Center, Iron Range Research Center, Minnesota Civilian Conservation Corps documentation project finding aid–Oral History Collection–IRON RANGE RESEARCH CENTER Archival Collections, oclc.org, accessed February 23, 2024.
19. Governor Rudy Perpich Oral History Project, Minnesota Discovery Center, Iron Range Research Center, Friends of the Iron Range Interpretative Center records finding aid–Manuscripts Collection–IRON RANGE RESEARCH CENTER Archival Collections, oclc.org, accessed December 4, 2023.
20. For information on interviewer and narrator payments, see the Oral History Association, "OHA Statement on Freelance, Independent, and Contract Labor," https://oralhistory.org/oha-statement-on-freelance-inde

pendent-and-contract-oral-history-labor, accessed October 15, 2023. Project leaders in academic institutions can check with the institution on pay rates. And leaders of all projects should check on pay rates with people providing community engagement guidance.

21. Alissa Rae Funderburk, "Oral History Narrator Compensation Alternatives," *OHA Newsletter*, Spring 2023.

22. "Proposed Framework for Narrator Compensation in Oral History," Incite at Columbia University, https://docs.google.com/document/d/1Lwg6kE1mKujINSpgqf7Ic6VwBNwritt5Jw6gnljpgow/edit#heading=h.omk8peuyg0rt, accessed January 25, 2024.

23. Fanny Julissa Garcia and Nara Milanich, "Money Talks: Narrator Compensation in Oral History," *Oral History Review*, 50:2 (2023): 148–68.

24. Garcia and Milanich, 156, 163–65.

25. Funderburk.

26. Kentucky Oral History Commission, Kentucky Historical Society, "Oral History Grants," http://history.ky.gov/resources/kentucky-oral-history-commission/, accessed November 18, 2023.

27. For more information about oral history in the classroom, see Glenn Whitman, *Dialogue with the Past: Engaging Students & Meeting Standards through Oral History* (Lanham, MD: Rowman & Littlefield Publishers, Inc., 2004); and Oral History Association, "Oral History in Education," http://www.oralhistory.org/education/, accessed November 18, 2023.

4

Legal and Ethical Considerations

Oral history projects often are born of a desire to capture the memories of elderly community members or to increase knowledge about people, places, events, or times past. But enthusiastic planners often have no idea they're embarking on a project with important legal and ethical dimensions. And just as the digital revolution has changed the way we shop and the way we stay in touch with grandkids, so also has it changed some of the ways oral historians think about legal and ethical aspects of their work. This chapter will:

- introduce the basic legal and ethical considerations that underpin oral history practice;
- discuss how legal and ethical issues affect stages of an oral history project's life cycle, including project planning and administration, technology decisions, processing, and the end use of the oral history interview;
- discuss the legal and ethical dimensions of rapidly changing technology and financial issues that affect oral history practice;
- explore evolving concepts of social justice and ethical oral history practice; and
- examine ethical and legal considerations relating to oral histories involving potentially vulnerable narrators, particularly in the context of oral history in times of crisis.

But this chapter will not:

- offer a shortcut to law school;
- provide legal advice; or
- recommend archives management policies. Many legal and ethical considerations affect procedures for handling interview recordings and transcripts. This

chapter will describe the range of issues and options to consider, but it is no substitute for professional archival information, which can be obtained from qualified archivists. The Society of American Archivists and the American Association for State and Local History are good sources of information about archives management issues.

The primary legal framework for oral history work in the United States rests on the established legal premise that an oral history interview creates a copyrightable document as soon as the recorder is turned off at the end of an interview session. Decide during the planning stage of the oral history life cycle how to secure copyright (the exclusive legal right to reproduce, distribute, display, perform, or create derivative works) from the interview's creators and how to handle responsibly the materials your project creates. This chapter will help you accomplish that.[1]

Oral histories came to be treated as copyrightable documents in the earliest days of institutional oral history practice at Columbia University where the interviews or oral memoirs were deemed analogous to written autobiographies, which authors clearly could copyright. Over time, the practice evolved of asking narrators to give their copyright interest to institutions sponsoring oral history programs, thus alleviating the need for the narrators themselves to control access to the materials. Narrators or interviewers legally could insist on retaining their copyright interest and simply grant project sponsors permission to use their interviews in a specific way—with or without certain restrictions. Such arrangements, however, are cumbersome at best.

Instead, institutions that sponsor oral history programs or repositories that include oral histories in their collections typically hold the copyright for those materials and are responsible for making them accessible under whatever conditions they deem appropriate, subject to any restrictions noted on the donor forms. Transfer of copyright is consistent with the legal and ethical standards promulgated by the Oral History Association (OHA), the national professional organization of oral history practitioners. Moreover, most institutions or organizations that sponsor or maintain oral history collections are reluctant to accept interviews without clear legal rights to use them and make them accessible to others, which a copyright transfer ensures.

A host of legal and ethical issues arise at virtually every stage of the oral history life cycle. The OHA describes in its online publication "Principles and Practices" the ethical standards that guide oral historians.[2] These principles and best practices define oral history and outline an oral historian's responsibilities for pre-interview preparation, appropriate conduct of an interview, and the use and preservation of interviews.

The ethical framework that the OHA describes is based on these general principles:

- Narrators should be fully informed about the purpose of an oral history interview and freely give their consent.
- Narrators should be informed that they hold copyright to their interviews unless or until they transfer copyright to an institution, with or without restrictions on use. Narrators' stories, of course, still belong to them and may be retold and used however they wish, and legal release agreements often give narrators lifetime rights to the story as it was told in the interview.
- Oral historians are obligated to conduct interviews with integrity, asking historically significant questions based on thorough preparation and respecting narrators' responses.
- Oral history narrators should be identified by name, except in highly unusual circumstances.
- Oral historians should use the best recording equipment available within their financial means to facilitate preservation and access of interviews as historical documents.
- Interviewers should not make promises they cannot keep, including any guarantees about control over and use of the interview materials beyond terms of the release form or promises of an ongoing relationship between the narrator and interviewer.

If you're planning an oral history project, become thoroughly familiar with the OHA "Principles and Practices" before starting. You also should study *A Guide to Oral History and the Law*, second edition, by John

A. Neuenschwander,[3] a past OHA president, emeritus history professor, lawyer, and retired municipal judge. Originally published by the OHA as part of its pamphlet series, the book-length Oxford University Press edition of *A Guide to Oral History and the Law* is the single most complete source of information about this topic. It provides considerably more detail about legal issues potentially affecting oral historians than this manual can offer, and it should be a part of every oral historian's library. But even it is not a substitute for competent legal advice, which all projects should seek during the planning stages as a way to prevent legal problems down the road. Project coordinators should provide their institution's legal advisers with copies of the book, too.

The rest of this chapter will outline the legal and ethical issues to consider at each stage of an oral history project.

PLANNING A PROJECT

The first—and most important—legal issue project coordinators must address is who will hold and maintain the materials the project ultimately creates. While it may seem premature to think about what should be done with materials that don't yet exist, it is fundamental to the rest of the planning process because it determines who will hold the copyright to the oral history interviews, maintain the materials, and govern access to them.

> The donor or legal release form transfers copyright to the designated owner, the Creative Commons, or to the public domain. The narrator and interviewer should sign a donor form after each interview

Because an oral history interview is considered a copyrightable document from the moment the interview ends, both interviewer and narrator—and anyone else whose voice is on the recording—have a copyright interest in the material on the recording and may grant or withhold permission to use it. Thus, to make the oral history interviews readily available for researchers and others to use, both interviewer and narrator sign a donor or legal release form at the end of each interview session giving their copyright interest to the project. In recent years, some oral historians have turned to an option offered online by Creative Commons, a licensing system instituted by a non-profit organization of the same name that allows creators of all kinds of material to retain ownership of their copyright interest but allow widespread sharing as long as the information is attributed to its creators. By 2023, Creative Commons reported that more than 2.5 billion works worldwide were licensed under the Creative Commons regime, including data, research publications, photographs, videos, music, and more. Creative Commons licensing options allow creators to grant users varying levels of permission to use content users find online that is marked with a Creative Commons license. Users are expected to attribute the content to its creator and abide by any restrictions, such as not using it for commercial purposes.[4] Creative Commons appeals to some oral historians because it represents an easy way to facilitate widespread use of interview materials published online and also addresses the philosophical objection some oral historians have about asking narrators to relinquish ownership of their interviews by signing over their copyright interest.[5]

Some oral historians advocate yet another option. Instead of securing a transfer of copyright or registering a Creative Commons license, oral history projects might choose simply to relinquish ownership claims altogether and donate materials to the public domain, which is where material will end up anyway after its copyright expires. If oral histories are donated to the public domain, no restrictions could be imposed on their use. And interview participants simply would sign a release form renouncing their copyright interest in the interview.

Beyond the legal matter of copyright and ownership of materials an oral history project creates, project planning includes the important ethical dimension of documenting the context in which the project takes place. What was the frame of reference of those who crafted the mission statement? Who served as advisers? Why were they chosen? How and why were narrators chosen? Were some potential areas of inquiry purposely omitted? If so, why? Oral history project planners need not be defensive about their choices of whom to interview and what topics to cover, but they do need to be transparent about why they've chosen to proceed as they have. If, for example, community organizing is an overt purpose of a project, planners should say so, describing in project planning materials their specific aims. Similarly, a project intended to celebrate a company's anniversary might choose to focus only on the corporation's retirees, a pool of narrators whose views might differ markedly from those of current employees. But whatever a project's immediate purpose, as long as it is conveyed openly and in detail, future users of the oral histories will be able to understand the context in which they were created and take that into consideration as they evaluate previous projects.

Describing a project's context—including how the work might evolve while it is under way—is particularly important as oral historians, often during and in the immediate aftermath of crises, increasingly engage in real-time interviewing. Journalists would call it "breaking news" coverage. Such projects may not have the luxury of carefully researching potential narrators and selecting them for their particular background knowledge or experience with the subject at hand. Rather, selection of narrators, by necessity, may be based largely on their availability and willingness to participate.[6] Describing such a project's purpose and its narrator selection process provides important context for subsequent users of the oral history materials.

Oral history projects that anticipate involving potentially vulnerable narrators also need to consider at the outset of a project the extent to which such participants' identities can or should be protected and document those decisions in detail. Such decisions likely will be critically important to the repository where oral history materials will be deposited, and appropriate arrangements need to be part of an initial discussion with all project partners. The nature of a particular project and the specific life circumstances of narrators may lead them to ask that they not be identified by name in the project. If project planners agree to use a pseudonym, that should be the only name associated with the interview and related materials. But it would be very difficult for a project to guarantee absolute anonymity for a narrator. Oral histories by definition include details about a person's life, which others might be able to recognize, even if a fictitious name is used. Restricting access to interviews for a specified period of time is an option for repository managers to consider that might mitigate narrators' concerns about being identified. Again, these are matters to consider early in the project planning process.[7]

PROJECT ADMINISTRATION

Handling the paperwork an oral history project generates is an ongoing responsibility of project coordinators. One of the most critical documents associated with oral history projects is the donor form or legal release form, which gives the project repository (the place that holds and maintains the materials) the right to use and disseminate the oral history materials, or an appropriate Creative Commons license. Without such documentation public access to and use of the information would be possible only if the narrators and interviewers or their heirs granted permission to specific requests for access, a prospect repositories generally would deem impractical and unworkable. If you're working with a repository that already has an oral history collection, the repository itself likely will already have donor forms suitable for oral history projects, which might be customized for particular purposes. If, however, the oral history materials will be held by an institution unfamiliar with such release forms, you'll need to write one, with the advice of informed legal counsel. It is worth noting that oral history might be an unfamiliar concept to many lawyers, so be prepared to explain thoroughly what you are doing and provide relevant materials, such as Neuen-schwander's book. Above all, be prepared to insist that any documents narrators and interviewers are asked to sign be written in commonly understood language, not legalistic mumbo jumbo. Narrators cannot give informed consent if they cannot understand the document they're asked to sign. Simple one-page forms are the best. Planners should be prepared to provide forms written in languages used by project narrators and interviewers. If a project is likely to include narrators who cannot read, ethical planners will develop appropriate in-person, oral explanations of donor or release forms. Sample release forms can be found in appendix B. Other samples are included in *A Guide to Oral History and the Law*. These samples can be useful, but resist the temptation merely to copy these release forms or forms from another oral history project. Instead, be sure the donor agreement you use meets *your* project's needs.[8]

A donor form can be either a contract or a deed of gift. To be complete legally and thus enforceable, each of these documents must contain specific elements that are discussed briefly in the following. The key distinction between the two is that a contract must provide for what is known legally as "consideration," or payment. Some oral history projects use a contract form, stipulating, for example, a token one dollar payment or promising the narrator a bound copy of the interview transcript or a copy of the video or audio recording. The token or symbolic payment approach is related to an underlying concept that an oral history interview could be seen as providing a service or a gift to a community rather than a product or commodity for which they should be paid.

Some oral historians, particularly those whose work deals with marginalized or potentially vulnerable narrators, however, have raised important questions about narrator compensation. As with many ethical questions, there may be no easy answers. For example: What type of service is a narrator providing? What impact does being paid have on an interview, a narrator, and the information they provide in an interview? Does paying for an interview monetize oral history? Where and how do the concepts of shared authority and active community engagement fit into this discussion?

Practical questions come up, too. Oral histories often operate on lean budgets and volunteer time. What is the value of the service both in narrator time and in content, and how is this determined? Where would funds come from to pay project narrators? Will a project grantor allow narrator payment as a line item in a grant budget? Often, it is narrators who are most marginalized who would benefit most from a payment—how can they be reached for payment? Unless narrators will be paid directly in cash,

how can funds be transferred to reach narrators who, in some circumstances, may live in different countries and may not have bank accounts or comparable access to funds? If narrators are in another country, what is involved in making international payments? And, even if the payments are relatively small by many standards, are there tax or government reporting regulations that need to be met? What types of payments can be best used by narrators? Money, in-kind, gifts? Other? Cultural expectations also may need to be considered. In Indigenous communities, for example, symbolic gifts often are given in exchange for something of value. Is this a factor in an oral history project, and how should it be handled by projects within a community? By those who are working with the community but are outside the community and culture? What types of gifts or payments are considered culturally appropriate? All such questions about paying narrators should be answered through thorough discussions among all parties involved in an oral history project as part of the planning process.[9]

Generally less complex than contracts, and considerably more common, is the deed of gift form, a voluntary transfer of property without any payment. Indeed, some projects call their donor form a "gift of personal memoir." Avoid creating a hybrid donor form that includes elements of both a contract and a deed of gift. Such hybrids are more difficult to defend legally because they fall outside the boundaries of the conventional legal framework.

Whatever form you use, it should include:

* clear identification of the name of the narrator, unless some other arrangements have been made to anonymize potentially vulnerable narrators;
* clear identification of the project repository;
* a statement that the narrator and interviewer are transferring "legal title and all literary property rights to the interview, including copyright" to the repository;
* a place for the narrator to sign; and
* a place for the interviewer to sign.

US copyright law specifies that for a copyright transfer to be valid, it must be in writing and signed by the copyright owner. So be sure the donor form contains a specific reference to copyright, and not some generic, legal-sounding language about "all rights, title and interest" without specifically mentioning copyright.

Donor forms and Creative Commons licenses also may include restrictions on how interviews may or may not be used. Such restrictions might allow use of the material in various formats for non-profit use but prohibit use of the materials for commercial purposes without the narrator's written consent or that of their heirs. Try to resist the temptation to create overly specific lists of possible future uses of the material, which run the risk of creating an inflexible project that legally cannot be used in new creative formats. Any restrictions on access or use of oral history materials generally specify an end date rather than being open-ended. Archivists also may choose to restrict access to interviews deemed to contain sensitive information for a specified period of time.[10]

Of particular interest in recent years is the now commonplace publication of oral history materials online. The ethical arguments over the merits of internet dissemination of oral history materials will be discussed subsequently, but any project that contemplates doing so should include in its donor form a specific reference to electronic distribution as well as archival deposit and copyright. Holding the copyright to the oral history materials might clearly give a project the legal right to put materials online, but most oral historians would consider it a serious breach of ethics to do so unless narrators are fully informed about the intent to do so and agree to it in advance. Many oral history collections considering online dissemination of archived oral history materials face the daunting prospect of retroactively seeking permission from narrators (or their heirs) whose memories were recorded long before the digital age. So even if project coordinators don't currently plan electronic distribution of oral history materials, they should consider including a specific reference allowing it to alleviate future complications. Narrators always may stipulate that they do not wish online publication of an interview, which should be noted clearly in the signed legal agreement. When new forms of online access evolve, such as the proliferation of podcasts using oral history interview excerpts, creators might consider following up with narrators, if they're available, to determine if they want to opt out of podcast distribution, even if the "electronic distribution" phrase in a donor form would permit it. Decisions in potentially ethical gray areas often are made case by case.

Other situations occasionally occur that will affect the donor form. As you plan your project, consider possibilities such as those discussed in the following list and decide how to handle them should they arise.

- Narrators—or interviewers—who are reluctant to assign copyright to the project because they want to use the material for their own written memoirs or other work before the interviews are opened to the general public. You can handle this dilemma by including a sentence in your donor forms stipulating that the narrator or interviewer has the right to use the material during their lifetime. This amounts to the copyright holder—the project's sponsor or repository—granting a license for use of the material. Alternatively, language could be included stipulating that the gift of copyright doesn't preclude use of the

interview itself by the narrator or interviewer. These kinds of situations call for careful consultation with the project's legal adviser to arrive at language that meets everyone's needs.

- Narrators who want to close access to all or part of their interviews. This usually occurs when a narrator has something unflattering, highly controversial, or potentially defamatory to say about someone. Such information can be important to the interview because of the context it provides, and, in these circumstances, an oral history project may agree to close access to the interview materials for a specified number of years. Defamation issues will be discussed more fully in connection with processing and archiving oral history materials, but understand—and make sure narrators understand—that while materials can be closed to researchers, they are unlikely to be protected from subpoena. As Neuenschwander has repeatedly noted, US courts generally have not recognized an archival privilege or scholar's privilege analogous to the legal protections that apply to communications between spouses or between doctors and patients. Similarly, state and federal open records laws can affect the ability of a project sponsored by a government agency or publicly funded institutions to restrict access to oral history materials. Open records laws vary, so you'll need to determine what conditions prevail in your jurisdiction. Some oral history projects include specific language in donor forms that notes a restricted interview may still be subject to a subpoena or public records request. A sample of donor form language allowing a restriction may be found in appendix B.
- A highly prominent narrator who insists on having an intellectual property lawyer negotiate a unique donor form. The vast majority of oral history interviews do not fall into that category. Indeed, oral history work reflects a long tradition of documenting the lives and putting on the historical record the voices of people who have otherwise been overlooked or forgotten. But if prominent historical figures are part of an oral history project, customized forms might need to be negotiated. Note, however, that customized donor forms for each interview in a collection could be an archivist's nightmare, and management issues associated with such one-of-a-kind legal documents should be considered carefully in a project's planning stages.
- Volunteer or freelance interviewers who refuse to relinquish work in progress if the oral history project disintegrates. Actually, if that happens, it's likely too late to prevent messy entanglements. That's why it's best to have volunteer or freelance interviewers—or anyone working for the project as an independent

contractor—sign an agreement at the outset making clear who has rights to the ownership and possession of the oral history materials in case the project fizzles out before it's completed. Again, Neuenschwander offers a complete discussion of this issue.

ORAL HISTORY INTERVIEWING EQUIPMENT

While equipment selection is not a legal matter, myriad other considerations affect the choice of equipment for an oral history project. Chapter 5 provides complete details on the technical aspects of the many audio and video equipment choices available. But equipment choice and use also has an ethical dimension to keep in mind. Here are some examples:

- While all recording equipment has a presence in the interview setting, video equipment in particular can be more intrusive than the equipment needed for an audio-only interview. Even in a visual communications era in which many narrators may expect to be video recorded, oral historians need to be sensitive to any narrators' reluctance to appear on camera and respect their right to refuse to participate in a video interview. During the planning process, arrangements can be considered that will enable either audio or video recording formats.
- Oral history projects that choose to record interviews on video should make sure camera operators avoid unflattering camera angles and lighting that create harsh portrayals of narrators. While a video oral history interview is not a documentary or a polished, rehearsed performance, it should not portray people negatively.
- Legal release forms for oral history projects that video record interviews should include specific permission for displaying the interviewers' and narrators' names and images in online or other publications of visual productions.[11]
- Some oral historians argue that there is an ethical dimension to selecting recording equipment that fails to meet the test of time. As this manual makes clear, good oral history requires substantial planning and thorough research. To do that and then have the interview materials themselves deteriorate rapidly or otherwise become unusable is a disservice to everyone who participates in a project, but particularly to narrators whose time, energy, and memories made the project possible. Make every effort to maximize the quality of the equipment you choose, within the limits of your financial resources.
- Whatever the equipment choices, interviewers always should be thoroughly trained in its use. Failure to do so disrespects narrators by wasting their time

and resulting in a low-quality interview of limited usefulness.
- Video interviews have greater potential for attracting interest from video production companies and other commercial interests, and narrators should be told that in the interest of fully informing them about the nature of the project. Some repositories, however, do not allow commercial use of their materials.

PROJECT BUDGET

Well-done oral history projects don't come cheaply, but creative project coordinators become adept at finding resources. Projects sponsored by companies and large institutions often are self-funded, and those sponsored by local non-profit, volunteer-run organizations often rely on funds from a wide variety of sources.

No matter what your sources of funds may be, always strive to maintain the intellectual integrity of the project and guard against any attempt by financial backers to control the content of the project or dictate topics or themes that must be pursued as a condition of funding. Include information about sources of funds or project sponsors in publicity about the project, public exhibits, or other materials developed as a result of the project, as well as permanent records of the collection, including online descriptions and access.

INTERVIEW PREPARATION

The preparation required before an oral history interview is fundamental to its success, and, like the other steps in the oral history process, it has an ethical dimension.

Oral historians conduct background research to the highest standards of scholarly integrity, taking care to document fully the sources of information consulted in the project's research phase. Providing such documentation makes it possible for future users of an oral history collection to put the interviews in context and understand the background against which the interviews took place.

The interview preparation steps, discussed in detail in chapter 6, are the point at which potential narrators are identified, and here again, ethical issues arise. Narrators invited to participate in an oral history project should reflect the full range of perspectives about the topic or issue on which the oral history project focuses, in keeping with the project's mission statement, goals, and community needs. This sometimes can be difficult precisely because oral history projects aim to find and collect previously undocumented accounts of often controversial events. But oral historians with a strong sense of ethics will commit themselves to creating a full-fledged historical record within the scope of their project.

THE INTERVIEW SETTING

Practical considerations govern most of the decisions about where interviews take place. But just as equipment choices have an ethical dimension, so also do the choices about interview setting. While an oral history interview is not a relaxed social occasion, you can maximize the quality of an interview by assuring that it takes place where the narrator will be most comfortable. This is particularly important when narrators are elderly, have special physical needs, or may be potentially vulnerable.[12] Likewise, the interview location, if not in the narrator's home, office, or similar personal space, should be in a reasonably neutral location and should not exploit a narrator in any way. Narrators and interviewers can work together to determine interview locations, keeping in mind that settings where audio and video quality can be maximized are also part of the equation. Ethical oral historians never try to coax narrators to conduct their interviews in settings that would make them uncomfortable, no matter how visually interesting the settings might be for a video oral history project.

COVID-19 Sparks New Approaches to Oral History

On March 11, 2020, the World Health Organization declared COVID-19 a pandemic.[1] The city of Wuhan, China, was already under quarantine. COVID-19 was spreading on cruise ships. Scientists and public health experts were desperately analyzing available data. There were more questions than answers.

In the weeks that followed, quilt guilds frantically sewed cloth face masks; hand sanitizer demand skyrocketed; restaurants, bars, and churches closed; schools switched to remote learning, exposing inequalities in access to broadband in rural areas and big cities alike; no one visited grandmas in nursing homes; COVID-19 case counts exposed stark differences in health care in communities of color; and news reports showed refrigerated trailers serving as temporary morgues at New York City hospitals.

Oral historians recognized that the unfolding pandemic represented a critical opportunity to engage in real-time or crisis oral history work to document the beginnings of a story whose impact continues to be felt. Hundreds of COVID-19 projects emerged along with thoughtful, self-reflective questions about remote interviewing practices that evolved when in-person interviewing was off the table.

For example:

- Is it really necessary to do this interview right now?
- How do you establish rapport with a narrator who appears in a box on your computer screen?
- What are the ethical decisions associated with interviewing first responders, nursing home workers, and others coping with trauma? Is it therapeutic or retraumatizing?
- What about the mechanics of remote interviewing? Technology availability? Audio quality? Reliable internet connections? Confidentiality concerns?
- What does archival quality even mean in a Zoom setting? Does it matter?
- How will you make sure narrators will have access to their interviews?

By the end of August 2020, an Oral History Association Remote Interviewing Resources Task Force published a colorful, easy-to-follow decision tree and extensive guidelines addressing key planning, technical, and ethical issues, enabling oral historians to make informed decisions about whether and how to conduct remote interviews.[2] Although COVID-19 limitations on in-person encounters may be a thing of the past and in-person interviews remain the preferred standard for oral history interviews, situations could occur in which remote interviews would be appropriate. So the guidelines for remote oral history practice remain useful and represent a good first step for oral historians who envision incorporating remote interviewing in their work.

NOTES

1. Centers for Disease Control and Prevention, "CDC Museum COVID-19 Timeline," https://www.cdc.gov/museum/timeline/covid19.html, accessed November 27, 2023.
2. Oral History Association, "Remote Interviewing Resources," https://oralhistory.org/remote-interviewing-resources/, accessed November 27, 2023. See also *Oral History Review*, 47:2 (September 2020), for a special section "Oral History and COVID-19" for wide-ranging discussion of crisis interviewing during the pandemic.

THE INTERVIEW

Ethical conduct of the oral history interview is fundamental to the integrity of an oral history project. While chapter 7 describes the process in detail, any discussion of oral history legal and ethical issues must stress the importance of respect for narrators and their stories as the underpinning of ethical interviewing. It begins with assuring that narrators are fully informed about all aspects of the interview process and their involvement in it. Projects may ask interviewers to review with narrators all the steps of the process, from interview to transcript review to creation of end products, and ask narrators to confirm, either orally or in writing, that they consent to participating in the project. Narrators also need to be assured that they can withdraw their participation at any time without penalty.

Interviewers also show respect by:

- thorough preparation and training that enables them to engage appropriately with narrators, including the ability to listen carefully and ask probing follow-up questions in a professional manner;
- familiarity with the equipment so they can operate it with confidence, thus ensuring a high-quality recording and preventing the equipment from becoming the focus of the interview;
- being sensitive to diverse cultural and life experiences that inform their narrators' perspectives and shunning thoughtless stereotypes that cloud understanding of people and issues;
- refraining from making promises that can't be fulfilled, such as guaranteeing that the oral history interview will be used in a particular way; and
- assuring that the narrator and interviewer properly sign a donor form at the conclusion of each interview session. Some oral historians advocate summarizing the content of the form while the recorder is turned on—either at the beginning or end of the interview—and getting the narrator's verbal agreement with the terms of the document in addition to the concurrence in writing.

PROCESSING THE INTERVIEW

Processing and archival issues that relate to how the content of an oral history interview is to be made public raise a host of legal and ethical concerns.

If you plan for full transcriptions of the interviews, narrators customarily are asked to review drafts of the transcripts, in whatever language or languages were previously determined, to make corrections before the materials are made public. To streamline that process but still maintain the ethical duty to allow narrators to review their transcripts, some oral history projects include in their release form a clause saying that the narrator has the right to review the transcript before it is put in final form. The document transfers copyright to the project but commits the project to returning the transcript for narrator review before making it public. Such release forms also often specify that if the narrator fails to return the transcript within a specified period of time—at least thirty days—it will be assumed that the transcript is correct and thus can become part of the oral history collection. In situations involving narrators with special needs that make it difficult or impossible for them to review a printed transcript, oral history projects can arrange for helpers to review transcripts with them.

In addition to the copyright issue discussed earlier, another major legal issue comes into play in processing and archiving oral history materials. Make sure you have a procedure for reviewing the content of interviews to see if they contain potentially defamatory statements, which *Ballentine's Law Dictionary* defines as "anything which is injurious to the good name or reputation of another person, or which tends to bring him into disrepute." Defamatory statements can be spoken (slander) or written (libel).[13]

Neuenschwander's *A Guide to Oral History and the Law* makes clear that oral history collections that include narrators' potentially defamatory statements could be found equally guilty of defamation for disseminating such statements as the narrators who made the statements in the first place. While it's unclear just how frequently oral history narrators make slanderous remarks, be aware of the possibility and be sure that interviewers alert project coordinators whenever such statements occur in an interview. Generally, words held to be defamatory relate to accusations of criminal, unethical, or immoral behavior; professional incompetence; financial irresponsibility; or association with despicable people.[14]

> Oral history project planners need to be aware of the potential legal pitfalls of disseminating potentially defamatory statements narrators might make. In general, words held to be defamatory relate to accusations of criminal, unethical, or immoral behavior; professional incompetence; financial irresponsibility; or association with despicable people.

Established legal defenses against accusations of libel or slander fall into several categories. Among other points, they include the following:

- The person about whom the defamatory statement was made is dead; only the living can be libeled.

- The person about whom the defamatory statement was made is a public figure, not a private individual. While case law makes it much more difficult to libel a public official, the legal determination of just what constitutes a public or private figure often becomes the contentious part of a defamation claim.
- Truth is an absolute defense against charges of libel.

Rather than banking on the prospect of successfully defending a libel claim in court—likely an expensive prospect at best—many archives or repositories with oral history holdings rely on one of several options to protect themselves: editing out offending words in the transcript, masking the identity of the person about whom the libelous statement was made, or sealing offending portions of the interview. Again, sealing portions of an interview or closing it altogether for an extended period of time still would not protect a restricted interview from being opened by court-ordered subpoena or, in some cases, a public records request; a narrator should be told of this possibility.[15]

GROUND RULES FOR ORAL HISTORY ON CAMPUS

For the first time in decades, oral historians at colleges and universities, beginning in 2019, welcomed the prospect of planning and carrying out oral history projects without being subject to review by campus Institutional Review Boards (IRBs). A proposed change in federal rules governing policies aimed at protecting human research subjects made clear for the first time that oral history and journalism, among other activities, would no longer be subject to the federal research regulations. The rule change marked the culmination of two decades of concerted efforts by the OHA, the American Historical Association, and other scholarly organizations to untangle the confusing regulatory web that seemed to equate oral history interviewing with the kind of biomedical research that gave rise to the federal rules in the first place.

In the mid-1960s, the US Public Health Service began requiring recipients of its biomedical research grants to submit their plans in advance to committees that came to be known as IRBs, which would review them to assure that the rights of individual research subjects would be protected.[16] In the ensuing decades, expanded federal regulations and mission creep at many campus IRBs resulted in a tangled web of regulation, virtually defying generalization, that affected social science and humanities scholars as well as biomedical researchers. To many scholars, they also defied logic and represented a significant threat to academic freedom.[17]

Efforts by various scholarly organizations to track IRB activities found numerous instances of IRBs asking oral historians for detailed lists of all questions that would be asked, ordering the destruction of interview recordings, demanding assurances that oral history narrators remain anonymous, and prohibiting questions that might prove controversial—all of which directly contradict the best practices for research espoused by ethical oral historians. Moreover, oral historians do not regard their narrators as objects being studied, but rather as collaborators in a joint effort to shed light on people, places, and situations about which the narrators have firsthand knowledge. In an attempt to deal with the inconsistencies and confusion over campus IRB treatment of oral history work, oral history leaders and other scholars worked with federal officials for two decades to address those concerns.[18]

The scholars' persistence ultimately led to a new federal rule fully exempting oral history, journalism, and other similar forms of research from IRB review. The final regulation stipulates: "For purposes of this part, the following activities are deemed not to be research: (1) Scholarly and journalistic activities (e.g., oral history, journalism, biography, literary criticism, legal research, and historical scholarship), including the collection and use of information, that focus directly on the specific individuals about whom the information is collected."[19] With or without IRB review, however, oral historians on and off campus must commit themselves to ethical conduct in all their work. Standards promoted by the OHA describe best practices for the ethical conduct of oral history. Anyone contemplating an oral history project should affirm a commitment to those practices in the initial stage of developing a project and should continue to emphasize ethical conduct through all stages of the project's life cycle.[20]

ETHICS AND SOCIAL JUSTICE WORK IN ORAL HISTORY

While the formalized practice of oral history in the United States evolved primarily from major academic institutions, oral historians both in and out of academe increasingly have questioned some of those traditional practices that customarily privileged a hierarchical approach to oral history and instead have adopted a social justice frame of reference in structuring and carrying out oral history work. The OHA defines this social justice framework as: "An analysis of how power, privilege, and oppression impact our experience of our social and cultural identities. This analysis contributes to and becomes a main focus and topic of exploration for oral historians who collaborate primarily with vulnerable communities."[21] Publication of Michael Frisch's *A Shared Authority: Essays on the Craft and Meaning of Oral and Public History* in 1990 articulated the concept of an oral history interview as being the co-creation of narrator and interviewer.[22] OHA's "Guidelines for Social Justice Oral History Work" additionally emphasize that a social justice frame of reference aims at "empowering the narrator at every step" of the oral history process.[23] Rather than creating an oral history project based largely on the perspective that researchers or interviewers bring to oral history, social justice oral history work prioritizes a flexible approach that privileges narrators and their communities and is based on relationship building, co-creation, and power sharing among all parties throughout the oral history process. Indeed, some social justice oral history work, in addition to preserving historical information, may also become an important tool in a community's efforts to achieve social justice.

Proponents of a narrator-centered frame of reference advocate alternative ethical approaches to narrator consent, interview ownership, and archiving and access concerns.[24]

Particularly important from a legal standpoint is the concept of narrators remaining co-owners of their oral histories rather than relinquishing legal ownership through a donor form that privileges a repository, even if narrators retain the right to use their own stories. The OHA's "Independent Practitioners' Toolkit for Oral Historians" cites "post-custodial archives" concepts, "which view the archive, museum, library, institution or university as a place that *shares* and *stewards* cultural resources, but does not need to or explicitly should *not* own them" (italics in the original). It's an approach that recognizes a long history of anthropologists, folklorists, ethnomusicologists, oral historians, and others extracting information from Indigenous communities in particular without their involvement or consent. Similarly, oral historians dedicated to a social justice framework also advocate alternative forms of narrator consent. Known as rolling consent or iterative consent, the approach reflects the importance of interviewers and other project participants building ongoing relationships with narrators. All oral historians, of course, are expected to fully inform narrators about all aspects of a project before interviewing commences and to document narrators' consent to participate. Oral historians engaged in social justice projects suggest, however, that rather than giving one-time consent, narrators should be offered the opportunity to consent to participating in specific phases of a project, from interview, transcript editing, publication, or other end uses. Such an approach takes into account how a project might evolve and how narrators might decide to change their minds about participating or not participating in various aspects of it. A step-by-step approach to informed narrator consent, advocates suggest, is a more transparent way to pursue narrator-centered work and assures that narrators feel free to end their participation at any time or ask that portions of an interview be redacted or withdrawn altogether without penalty. The approach reflects a belief that social justice oral history work is an ongoing community collaboration.

Because social justice oral history generally involves potentially vulnerable communities and individuals, project planning necessarily includes careful consideration of potential risks to the safety of narrators and their families and associates and possible ways to offset those concerns through the use of pseudonyms or limits on outsider access to oral history materials through the use of digital firewalls or other means. Oral historians and archivists, however, also need to inform narrators that such protective efforts are not absolute and that project information would be subject to release in response to a subpoena or, in some cases, to public records requests. The OHA's "Guidelines for Social Justice Oral History Work" also suggest as a protective consideration "providing legal assistance/consultation for individual participants left open to political harassment" as a result of their participation in an oral history project.[25]

Other social justice oral history considerations that recognize potentially vulnerable narrators' agency will be discussed in chapters 6 and 7.

ETHICS AND CRISIS INTERVIEWS

Dictionaries say history is the study of past events.[26] But the past need not be long ago; it may be as recent as yesterday, a reality that oral historians recognized in a dramatic new way when terrorists flew airplanes into New York City's World Trade Center towers and the Pentagon on September 11, 2001. Within days, Columbia University's Center for Oral History had put in place its September 11, 2001, Oral History Narrative and Memory Project. Designed as a longitudinal study, the effort eventually involved five discrete projects and ultimately resulted in some nine hundred recorded interview hours with more than six hundred people.[27] And it called attention to the role oral historians can play in documenting manmade or natural disasters as they unfold, before public discourse settles on an accepted narrative of the event.

In the decades since, widespread media coverage of emerging crises on an ever-increasing number of platforms has contributed to oral historians' awareness that such crises are more complex than media coverage can capture, particularly because national and international crisis coverage often leads to a prevailing narrative that misses critical parts of complex times. Thus, oral historians increasingly are using the techniques of oral history—with its emphasis on asking open-ended questions, casting wide nets to find narrators, and planning for long-term preservation of and access to oral history materials—that go beyond the framework journalists bring to the task of covering breaking news. Notably, oral historians' involvement in real-time information gathering goes back to the early days of oral history, when the US Army assigned combat historians to accompany soldiers in battle and interview them soon thereafter.[28] When Army historian Forrest C. Pogue picked up a wire recorder on a hospital ship off Omaha Beach in June 1944 and began doing interviews with soldiers wounded in D-Day battles, he might not have been thinking of oral history. Although he was collecting first-person information, the term had yet to be formally applied to the methodology. But his work, done under the direction of chief army historian S. L. A. Marshall, helped lay the groundwork for the development of oral history as a research technique.[29] Throughout World War II and the Korean and Vietnam Wars, combat historians also evolved the practice of relying on group discussions in which soldiers could collectively verify details of specific engagements.[30]

As interest among oral historians to engage in documenting emerging crises grew after 9/11, one of the biggest challenges they discovered was slow turnaround in grant funding requests to support such work. So the OHA decided in 2005 to create an OHA Emerging Crises Oral History Research Award as at least one source of modest funding with a shorter lead time than some other sources. The first award was made the following year, just six months after Hurricane Katrina struck the US Gulf coast. The OHA award defines crises as situations that include "wars, natural disasters, political and economic/ethnic repression, or other current events of crisis proportions."[31] Grant recipients have included oral historians engaged in crisis fieldwork in China, Columbia, Nicaragua, Mexico, Egypt, Cameroon, Thailand, Malaysia, Puerto Rico, the Virgin Islands, Italy, and Azerbaijan, as well as the United States. And while internationally recognized events like 9/11, Hurricane Katrina, and the COVID-19 pandemic might exemplify a typical understanding of crises, they are not the only examples of events oral historians have documented as crises. A chemical spill that poisoned a river in Charleston, West Virginia, in 2014, for example, was certainly a crisis for the three hundred thousand people in nine counties whose public water supply was cut off, although at the time it attracted primarily local and regional news coverage. The OHA-funded grant to researcher Luke Eric Lassiter for crisis oral history interviews eventually led to the 2020 publication of *I'm Afraid of that Water: A Collaborative Ethnography of a West Virginia Water Crisis*.

Oral historian Stephen Sloan has summarized several elements that characterize professional, ethical approaches to crisis oral history, which empowers narrators to own their narrative and explore the meaning of a crisis on their own terms, avoiding opportunistic or voyeuristic approaches that can exploit vulnerable people in the midst of crisis. First, crisis oral history projects need to remain flexible. Despite best-laid plans, conditions on the ground may require a change in plans. And even the premise of a project from the point of view of an outsider oral historian may change as narrators describe different realities. Next, disaster or crisis oral histories ideally adopt a broad framework, pursuing life stories of their narrators, and not just characterizing them as traumatized victims of circumstances beyond their control. And third, crisis oral history projects always have a public purpose, thus requiring a plan for preserving the interviews and related materials and making them accessible so others can seek to understand the unique characteristics of a particular time, place, and event through the voices of those who lived it.[32]

ETHICS AND TRAUMA

Oral historians whose projects embody a social justice framework or seek to document unfolding crises of necessity share a concern with interviewing narrators who may be experiencing trauma or who may be asked to talk about prior traumatic events. In such situations, a host of ethical considerations comes into play.

To be sure, oral history interviews often can be emotionally intense for narrators and interviewers alike. In-depth questions on many topics can evoke laughter, anger, and tears. And ethically prepared oral historians try to anticipate such reactions. But recalling past events that may bring some narrators to tears—recalling the funeral of a loved one, for example—can be the same sort of events that other narrators take in stride. When oral historians think about trauma in interviews, however, they often are considering narrators whose experiences may include violent, terror-inducing events, like Holocaust or genocide survivors, refugees from war or famine or civil unrest, prison inmates, undocumented migrants, victims of all sorts of human rights violations, or those who experience the aftermath of all manner of natural and manmade disasters, from school shootings to deadly floods of biblical proportions.

In such cases, oral historians who want to make ethical choices have pondered whether engaging in such interviews helps narrators cope with a traumatic experience by talking about it or whether talking about it only serves to retraumatize them. Moreover, interviewers themselves can experience vicarious trauma from engaging with traumatized narrators. However narrators react, ethical oral historians remind themselves that they are not trained therapists (unless, of course, they actually *are* trained therapists). In *Listening on the Edge: Oral History in the Aftermath of Crisis*, psychologist and psychoanalyst Ghislaine Boulanger reminds oral historians that their primary interest is in the narrative, whereas mental health professionals' concern is the narrator.[33] "From the oral historian point of view, obtaining individual narratives is crucial to providing a more nuanced understanding of history."[34]

Boulanger suggests that the way in which oral historians introduce and explain a project to prospective narrators can go a long way toward eliciting participation by creating "a set of expectations that can help respondents override their fears of reviving memories that will not stay dead." She cites as an example Columbia University's September 11, 2001, Oral History Narrative and Memory Project, in which interviewees told prospective narrators that their unique perspectives would help historians in generations to come to understand the scope of the tragedy. "This is an important message to potential respondents who feel they have been cast aside by history and for whom there has been no public acknowledgment," Boulanger says.[35] Indeed, Mary Marshall Clark recalls one 9/11 project participant who described in detail a man jumping from one of the towers. "Telling my interviewer the story of what I saw kept the image of it from burning into my brain and destroying my mind," she told Clark. "It saved my life."[36]

There is no way to know, of course, whether that narrator's experience is unusual or commonplace. But whenever oral history projects contemplate interviewing people who have experienced traumatic events, ethical preparation is critical. Planners can find an array of useful advice from organizations like the Shoah Foundation, which has archived tens of thousands of interviews with Holocaust survivors and others; Voice of Witness, a non-profit organization that uses oral history to advance human rights; individual scholars, like award-winning author Sarah C. Bishop, whose research focuses on the dysfunctional US asylum system; and the OHA journal *Oral History Review*, which regularly publishes information to advance the practice of ethical oral history.[37]

The following are some key recommendations for ethical conduct of interviewing survivors of traumatic experiences:

- Never press a potential narrator to participate in an interview, no matter how important that person's experience might seem to be in furthering a project's goals.
- Narrators are always more than survivors of trauma. Be willing to find out about their lives before and after the traumatic experience in question. Focusing on traumatic experiences alone paints them as one-dimensional characters.
- Let narrators know in advance the kinds of questions you plan to ask so they are not caught off guard. The Shoah Foundation advises interviewers to ask narrators ahead of time if there are topics they don't want to discuss. In any case, don't push narrators to answer something they don't want to share but leave

room for narrators to tell their story however they wish. It is, after all, *their* story.
- Make sure potential interviewers understand the challenges associated with interviewing narrators who have suffered from traumatic experiences and make available post-interview support for interviewers who experience vicarious trauma.

Because social justice oral history work, emerging crisis oral histories, and concern about related interviews with narrators who have suffered trauma are continually evolving, oral historians who engage in these areas are encouraged to seek more detailed information than this manual can provide.

ETHICS AND ACCESS

In the contemporary oral history world, only Luddites resist the idea of having an online presence for their oral history projects. Indeed, oral history projects sometimes begin with a goal of creating a comprehensive online presence for their work. Oral history is a fundamentally egalitarian pursuit, and the near ubiquitous access to digital communications gives oral historians access to a publication platform with a potential reach exponentially greater than earlier generations of oral historians could have imagined. Widespread computer literacy coupled with user-friendly online tools and increasingly accurate automatic speech recognition make it possible for oral history projects to easily share online transcripts of interviews as well as full audio and video recordings of interviews, and to employ tools that enable users to search interview content quickly to their heart's content. An important option for streamlining access to oral history interviews emerged in 2008 when the Louie B. Nunn Center for Oral History at the University of Kentucky Libraries developed a free easy-to-use tool for indexing digital oral history interviews, particularly those that have not been transcribed. Known as the Oral History Metadata Synchronizer, the web-based system allows for keyword searching of digital audio material in the same way that one could keyword search a text file. Users can enter search terms, and the system locates specific segments of audio or video interviews that match the terms, greatly simplifying and streamlining the otherwise laborious process of listening to an entire interview—or reading a transcript—to locate particular information of interest to a user. Doug Boyd, who directs the Nunn Center, has noted that the Oral History Metadata Synchronizer makes it possible for institutions with oral history collections "to provide an effective, user-centered discovery interface for oral history on a large scale for a fraction of the usual cost."[38]

Oral historians also can easily add greater context to interviews by incorporating photographs, maps, music, and various other forms of documentation in online exhibits based on their interviews, with links to related material and opportunities to engage with visitors to their sites. In short, online publication of oral history materials has become the norm, and funding for oral history projects can sometimes hinge on innovative plans for digital dissemination of interview materials.[39]

But it wasn't always thus. Oral historian Mary Larson, then at the University of Alaska Fairbanks, was among the early wave of oral historians who adopted digital tools for publishing oral history beginning around the mid-1990s when oral historians had to learn HTML coding themselves or hire information technology specialists to accomplish online publication. Because the process was arduous and expensive in both time and money, oral historians gave careful consideration to every step of the process, including ethical considerations, according to Larson. Project planners contemplating online dissemination asked themselves: "What were the implications of placing material online—for the interviewees, their communities, the oral historians, and the archives?"[40] But as online publication has become considerably more manageable with widely available tools, putting oral history materials online has virtually become a given, with oral historians sometimes failing to give adequate consideration to critical ethical aspects of doing so. As Larson has pointed out: "Ultimately, the impact has probably been more far-reaching than any of us might have imagined."[41]

Widespread access to oral history materials is a two-sided coin. Vastly greater numbers of people can read, hear, see, learn from, and share interview information than ever would have visited a library or museum's special collections archive housing oral history recordings and transcripts. At the same time, vastly greater numbers of people can read, hear, see, learn from, and share interview information that, unless restricted in some way, might be used—or misused, some would say—in ways that diminish the important trust relationship an oral history interviewer and narrator must establish.

Some oral historians worry that the narrator's knowledge that an interview is to be accessible to virtually anyone in the world who has access to a computer will affect the content of the interview itself. Will such widespread access lead narrators to engage in self-censorship to the point of blandness, where potentially valuable but controversial insights will be lost or never revealed? Or will the reverse happen, wherein narrators envisioning a cameo role on a global stage get carried away with their accounts?

Such concerns about the impact of online dissemination are not merely theoretical. The proliferation of internet searching capabilities and heightened concerns in some quarters about national security have raised questions about online publication of oral histories that go beyond concerns about copyright violations or unauthorized profiteering from such material. One oral history collection administrator has reported that a man, originally from India but who had lived in the United States for thirty years, was called twice by Federal Bureau of Investigation agents who questioned him about his connection to atomic bomb testing in India in the 1990s. He had nothing to do with atomic bomb testing, but, like other Indian Americans interviewed for the oral history project, he was asked about it in the oral history interview. The use of "atomic bomb testing" as a subject keyword in the online finding aid, in connection with his name, apparently drew the Federal Bureau of Investigation's attention. The administrator removed "atomic bomb testing" as a subject heading in the finding aid, replacing it with the term "current events," which is much less useful to researchers seeking details about the content of the oral history interviews, but which attempts to address concerns that oral history narrators might find themselves being targeted for something they said in interviews published online.[42]

Sherna Berger Gluck, emerita faculty member in women's studies at California State University, Long Beach, and director emerita of its Oral History Program, has expressed concern about online publication of oral histories, particularly those of political activists, because of just such surveillance activities. "While the [Federal Bureau of Investigation] and other agencies have tapped the phones of activists for almost a century and/or paid informants have been used to spy on organizations, the earlier extant technology made these somewhat more limited in scope. Now, however, anything posted on the Web, including oral history accounts of and by activists, can become grist for the mill and be used without permission or court orders."[43] Gluck noted that in at least one case, an oral history interview with the chair of the National Committee against Repressive Legislation, who was a victim of the McCarthy-era witch hunts, was conducted by his lawyer so as to establish an attorney-client privilege for the oral history interview.[44]

To address ethical concerns about online publication, oral historians have adopted several different approaches to creating an online presence for their interviews, depending on the nature of their material and the nature of the release forms narrators sign. These include:

• Full verbatim transcripts, full audio, and, sometimes, full video, although publishing video online tends to be much more resource intensive. Indices or other finding aids allow users readily to find interview segments of their own choice.

- Full verbatim transcripts, which may or may not include search features.
- Audio only, with interview abstracts or finding aids to help users navigate the content. Increasingly, assistive technologies are available that enable people with visual or hearing impairments to access online content, whether in text or audio only. Such technologies may help offset earlier concerns that full written transcripts and full audio of interviews were essential to facilitating access for such online users.
- Catalogs or directories of interviews in a collection, sometimes including summaries or selected excerpts, with information about how to request access to complete transcripts or recordings of interviews.
- "Click-wrap" access, in which users first must read and click on an agreement stipulating any conditions attached to using the online oral history materials.[45]

The online approach an oral history project chooses will depend on ethical considerations related to the interview content and narrators' interests. In all cases, oral history projects should pay particular attention to reviewing interviews for potentially defamatory content and include appropriate copyright or Creative Commons notices on digitally published material to discourage unauthorized use. Policing copyright, however, is widely considered to be problematic in an environment that seems to have abandoned the concept of intellectual property rights, instead subscribing to the myth: "If I can find it online, it must be free."

In any case, oral historians' first ethical obligation related to internet publication is to make sure narrators fully understand the scope of access to their interviews. Many narrators might welcome the prospect; others might not. Narrators' wishes regarding online publication should be honored. Indeed, Gluck argued a decade ago that ethical decision-making associated with online publication of oral histories should be considered a fluid process subject to renegotiation, an approach now widely advocated by those engaged in social justice oral history work. Narrators' circumstances can change, as can the degree of sensitivity associated with topics covered in an interview, which might justify reconsideration of online access.[46] Such an approach, however, likely would require reconsideration of how repositories administer oral history collections.

Canadian oral historians Anna Sheftel and Stacey Zembrzycki are among the thoughtful critics who have called for a closer examination of the ethical and practical implications of online dissemination of oral history materials, particularly noting the practice of detailed indexing to facilitate access. If access and user-friendliness have become the ultimate goals for oral history, they have stipulated, oral historians need to consider the consequences. "Indexing implies that we are listening principally for information rather than for the more subjective elements of an interview and, beyond that, the meaning they contain. How does one index a silence?"[47] Much like the child in Hans Christian Andersen's tale who dared point out that the emperor was naked, Sheftel and Zembrzycki also have pointed out that internet access does not necessarily mean anyone out there is paying attention. Web analytics that tally the number of hits a website gets and the average length of a visit or number of pages visited are of limited value in the absence of comparative data about oral history sites in general. "Online, even if a collection is receiving many hits, we have no way of knowing if someone is switching between a dozen tabs in a browser while playing a life story, if it is a single person or a room full of people doing the listening, or if the interview is playing in the background as listener(s) simultaneously engage in another distracting activity."[48] By contrast, oral history interviews in an archive might be accessed by fewer people, but that access is purposeful and generally uninterrupted, they note. "While it is certainly not the job or intention of the oral historian to completely control how others listen to interviews, if we want more thoughtful listening to occur, is there a way to disseminate them online that would privilege the act of stopping and watching and listening, rather than clicking for thirty seconds and then scrolling on to the next piece of media?"[49]

Other oral historians, such as Juliana Nykolaiszyn, have written thoughtfully about ways to use social media to create multiple points of access by which audiences can connect with online oral history collections.[50] Cultivating a community of social media followers could contribute to meaningful, ongoing engagement with oral history materials quite unlike that which a traditional archival collection might experience.

But even that can be a double-edged sword, Sheftel and Zembrzyki suggest. "When we put our lives, or our oral histories, online, we willingly commodify them, whether it is through data mining, targeted advertising, or the selling of our photographs or personal information to advertisers or security agencies." Social media companies are not altruistic enterprises. "They exist because they make people a lot of money," which suggests a possible ethical conflict with oral history's fundamentally democratic, egalitarian underpinnings. "Transforming lives into products is one of the troubling consequences of the digital age that has yet to be fully understood."[51]

Few oral historians would argue that the possible disadvantages of online publication of oral histories outweigh the value of greater digital access, but as oral historians continue to adopt and adapt to ever-changing realities of the digital age, new ethical and legal questions are sure to emerge. And the collaborative, communal nature of oral history is sure to foster lively discussion in the search for answers. The legal and ethical framework in which oral historians work has evolved over more than half a century, and it has successfully guided the conduct of untold numbers of oral history interviews. The digital age and the emergence of powerful artificial intelligence tools have introduced new dimensions to the philosophical and ethical debates, but nothing has changed the fundamental ethical requirement that an oral history project be guided by intellectual integrity and an overarching respect for the narrators who share their stories.

NOTES

1. Oral historians outside the United States who consult this manual should make local inquiry about copyright treatment and related issues. Such legal matters vary widely.
2. Oral History Association, "Principles and Practices," https://oralhistory.org/principles-and-best-prac tices-revised-2018, accessed November 22, 2023.
3. John A. Neuenschwander. *A Guide to Oral History and the Law*, second edition (New York, NY: Oxford University Press, 2014).
4. Detailed information about Creative Commons and how it works is available at https://creativecom mons.org/share-your-work/, accessed November 19, 2023.
5. For detailed discussions of Creative Commons in an oral history context, see Neuenschwander, *A Guide to Oral History and the Law*, second edition. Creative Commons also is discussed in Nancy MacKay, *Curating Oral Histories: From Interview to Archive*, second edition (Walnut Creek, CA: Left Coast Press, 2016); Barbara W. Sommer, *Practicing Oral History in Historical Organizations* (Walnut Creek, CA: Left Coast Press, 2015); and Jack Daugherty and Candace Simpson, "Who Owns Oral History? A Creative Commons Solution," *Oral History in the Digital Age*, http://ohda.matrix.msu.edu/2012/06/a-creative -commons-solution/, accessed November 19, 2023.
6. Oral historian Mark Cave documented how important it is for oral historians involved with crisis interviewing to pursue narrators who might not be immediately available as the crisis unfolds. In the wake of Hurricane Katrina, which devastated New Orleans in 2005, law enforcement and other first responders were widely criticized for what many observers considered incompetence. Many first responders were prohibited by their agencies from talking to the media. But in a 2009 project in connection with the Louisiana Department of Corrections after-action study of its hurricane response, Cave interviewed guards and other corrections personnel who offered new first-person details about the controversial evacuation of inmates stranded in a New Orleans prison, information unlikely to have been available to oral historians in the immediate aftermath of the storm. See Mark Cave, "Unlocked: Perspective and the New Orleans Prison Evacuation Crisis," in *Listening on the Edge: Oral History in the Aftermath of Crisis*, edited by Mark Cave and Stephen M. Sloan (New York: Oxford University Press, 2014).
7. Oral History Association, "Principles and Best Practices Glossary," https://oralhistory.org/best-prac tices-glossary/, accessed November 22, 2023.
8. The American Association for State and Local History and the Smithsonian Institution are additional sources of information about legal release forms.
9. For a more detailed discussion of narrator compensation, see Alissa Rae Funderburk, "Oral History Narrator Compensation Alternatives," *OHA Newsletter* (spring 2023); and Fanny Julissa Garcia and Nara Milanich, "Money Talks: Narrator Compensation in Oral History," *Oral History Review*, 50:2 (2023): 148-68.
10. See, for example, a case in which narrators who agreed to be named were "un-named" in transcripts out of concern for possible consequences of their participation in the research. Mia Martin Hobbs, "(Un)Naming: Ethics, Agency, and Anonymity in Oral Histories with Veteran-Narrators," *Oral History Review*, 48:1 (April 2021): 59-82.
11. John Neuenschwander, "Major Legal Challenges Facing Oral History in the Digital Age," *Oral History in the Digital Age*, http://ohda.matrix.msu .edu/2012/06/major-legal-challenges/, accessed November 19, 2023.
12. Oral historian Karin Mak interviewed some of her narrators, whose lives were endangered by cadmium poisoning from their work at a Chinese multinational battery factory, in a hotel room near the factory. It was air-conditioned, comfortable, and offered a safe space to talk. See Karin Mak, "Until Our Last Breath: Voices of Poisoned Workers in China," in *Listening on the Edge: Oral History in the Aftermath of Crisis*, edited by Mark Cave and Stephen M. Sloan (New York: Oxford University Press, 2014).
13. William S. Anderson, ed., *Ballentine's Law Dictionary*, third edition (Rochester: The Lawyers Co-operative Publishing Company, 1969), 321.
14. Neuenschwander discusses defamation issues in considerable detail in *A Guide to Oral History and the Law*, second edition, 35-50.
15. The prospect of successful subpoenas of oral history materials became starkly apparent to oral historians who watched with some dismay the untangling of overlapping legal fights—including one based on

an international treaty—connected with the Belfast Project. An oral history project housed at Boston College, the Belfast Project involved interviews in Northern Ireland between 2001 and 2006 with former members of the Irish Republican Army who were promised that their interviews would remain confidential until their deaths. That promise began to unravel in 2011 when the project director wrote a book based on the interview with a deceased Irish Republican Army member who referred to an unsolved murder, prompting Northern Ireland law enforcement authorities to subpoena interviews from the project. A complex and overlapping series of legal proceedings ensued involving Boston College, the United Kingdom, and the Belfast Project's director and chief interviewer. Ultimately, eleven interviews—far fewer than the eighty-five sought—were released to law enforcement authorities. And Boston College later announced it would return interviews to any of the narrators who asked for them. The Belfast Project sparked lively discussion among oral historians about poor planning and sloppy project administration that complicated the case. But a clear takeaway was that scholars cannot legally claim a "researcher's privilege" to protect their work from subpoena. For a detailed discussion of the Boston College case and other examples involving compelled release of oral history materials, see Neuenschwander, *A Guide to Oral History and the Law*, second edition, 20-34.

16. Zachary M. Schrag, "How Talking Became Human Subjects Research: The Federal Regulation of the Social Sciences, 1965-1991," *Journal of Policy History*, http://ssrn.com/abstract=1124284, accessed November 25, 2023. In his detailed historical analysis, Schrag notes that many IRB supporters mistakenly believe that application of IRB rules to social science research was a direct result of unethical research and experimentation on human beings beginning in the 1970s. But Schrag asserts that federal regulation of the social sciences actually can be traced to a New Jersey congressman's 1965 concerns about invasion of privacy related to psychological tests on federal employees and applicants for federal jobs. Clearly, however, medical research scandals in the 1970s, particularly a decades-long Public Health Service study of the effects of syphilis on African American men, sparked renewed congressional attention to medical research ethics, and the present system of elaborate IRB review of federally funded research began to evolve. A detailed discussion of how the policy grew over the years is beyond the scope of this manual, but readers interested in the details will find Schrag's exhaustive account highly informative.

17. The OHA, the American Historical Association, and the American Association of University Professors are among the academic organizations that took a leading role in focusing public discussion of the misapplication of rules meant to protect subjects of biomedical research to the work of historians and other humanities and social science scholars. Readers interested in more detailed background than this section provides will find extensive information about IRBs available from these professional associations.

18. In 1997, three OHA leaders met with federal officials to express oral historians' concerns, and past OHA president Richard Candida Smith reported that the officials indicated they had never talked to oral historians before and hadn't thought about what historians do. "Revised Rules Could Affect Oral Historians," *OHA Newsletter*, 32:1 (winter 1998): 6.

19. National Archives, "Code of Federal Regulations," https://www.ecfr.gov/current/title-45/subtitle-A/subchapter-A/part-46/subpart-A/section-46.102, accessed November 25, 2023. See also Zachary M. Schrag, "United States of America Frees Oral History!" *Institutional Review Blog*, January 18, 2017, http://www.institutionalreviewblog.com/2017/01/united-states-of-america-frees-oral.html#more, accessed November 20, 2023.

20. Oral History Association, "Principles and Best Practices," http://www.oralhistory.org/about/principles-and-practices/, accessed November 25, 2023.

21. Oral History Association, "Principles and Best Practices Glossary," https://oralhistory.org/best-practices-glossary/, accessed November 25, 2023.

22. Michael Frisch, *A Shared Authority: Essays on the Craft and Meaning of Oral and Public History* (State University of New York Press: Albany, 1990).

23. Oral History Association, "Guidelines for Social Justice Oral History Work," https://oralhistory.org/guidelines-for-social-justice-oral-history-work/, accessed November 25, 2023.

24. The OHA's "Guidelines for Social Justice Oral History Work," "Independent Practitioners' Toolkit for Oral Historians," and "Archiving Oral History: Manual of Best Practices" along with the Voice of Witness "Ethical Storytelling Principles," and the Texas-based Institute for Diversity and Civic Life's Oral History for Social Change certificate program are among various useful resources that offer detailed suggestions related to ethical conduct of oral history from a social justice framework. They comprise key sources in this discussion.

25. Oral History Association, "Guidelines for Social Justice Oral History Work," https://oralhistory.org/guidelines-for-social-justice-oral-history-work/, accessed November 26, 2023.

26. See, for example, Merriam-Webster Dictionary and Oxford Languages.

27. Columbia Center for Oral History Research, "9/11 Oral History Project," https://www.ccohr.incite.columbia.edu/911-oral-history-project, accessed December 4, 2023; Columbia University Libraries, "September 11, 2001 Oral History Projects," https://library.columbia.edu/libraries/ccoh/digital/9-11.html, accessed December 4, 2023.

28. Mark Cave, "What Remains: Reflections on Crisis Oral History," in *Listening on the Edge: Oral History in the Aftermath of Crisis*, edited by Mark Cave and Stephen M. Sloan (New York: Oxford University Press, 2014), 6.

29. Donald A. Ritchie, "Remembering Forrest Pogue," *Oral History Association Newsletter* (winter 1997): 7.

30. Cave, *Listening on the Edge*, 7.

31. Oral History Association, "Emerging Crises Oral History Research Fund," https://oralhistory.org/award/emerging-crisis-research-fund/, accessed December 4, 2023.

32. Stephen M. Sloan, "Conclusion: The Fabric of Crisis," in *Listening on the Edge: Oral History in the Aftermath of Crisis*, edited by Mark Cave and Stephen M. Sloan (New York: Oxford University Press, 2014), 269–73. See also Voice of Witness, "Ethical Storytelling Principles," https://voiceofwitness.org/, accessed December 4, 2023.

33. Ghislaine Boulanger, "The Continuing and Unfinished Present: Oral History in the Aftermath of Terror," in *Listening on the Edge: Oral History in the Aftermath of Crisis*, edited by Mark Cave and Stephen M. Sloan (New York: Oxford University Press, 2014), 112.

34. Ibid, 118.

35. Ibid, 119.

36. Quoted in Mary Marshall Clark, "A Long Song: Oral History in the Time of Emergency and After," in *Listening on the Edge: Oral History in the Aftermath of Crisis*, edited by Mark Cave and Stephen M. Sloan (New York: Oxford University Press, 2014), 255.

37. Sources consulted in this discussion include Mark Cave and Stephen M. Sloan, eds., *Listening on the Edge: Oral History in the Aftermath of Crisis* (New York: Oxford University Press, 2014); USC Shoah Foundation, "Interviewer Guidelines," University of Southern California, 2021; Sarah C. Bishop, *A Story to Save Your Life: Communication and Culture in Migrants' Search for Asylum* (New York: Columbia University Press, 2022); Anna Sheftel, "Talking and Not Talking About Violence: Challenges in Interviewing Survivors of Atrocity as Whole People," *Oral History Review*, 45:2 (summer/fall 2018): 288–303; Emma L. Vickers, "Unexpected Trauma in Oral History Interviewing," *Oral History Review*, 46:1 (winter/spring 2019): 134–41; Lindsay French, "Refugee Narratives; Oral History and Ethnography: Stories and Silence," *Oral History Review*, 46:2 (summer/fall 2019): 267–76; and Henry Greenspan, "The Humanities of Contingency: Interviewing and Teaching Beyond 'Testimony' with Holocaust Survivors," *Oral History Review*, 46:2 (summer/fall 2019): 360–79.

38. Doug Boyd, "OHMS: Enhancing Access to Oral History for Free," *Oral History Review*, 40 (winter/spring 2013): 106. For a more detailed description of how the Oral History Metadata Synchronizer indexing works, see also Doug Boyd, Danielle Gabbard, Sara Price, and Alana Boltz, "Indexing Interviews in OHMS: An Overview," in *Oral History in the Digital Age*, edited by Doug Boyd, Steve Cohen, Brad Rakerd, and Dean Rehberger (Washington, DC: Institute of Museum and Library Services, 2014), http://ohda.matrix.msu.edu/2014/11/indexing-interviews-in-ohms/, accessed December 9, 2017.

39. Canadian oral historians Anna Sheftel and Stacey Zembrzycki raise this and other important issues in "Slowing Down to Listen in the Digital Age: How New Technology is Changing Oral History Practice," *Oral History Review*, 44 (winter/spring 2017): 94–112.

40. Mary Larson, "Steering Clear of the Rocks: A Look at the Current State of Oral History Ethics in the Digital Age," *Oral History Review*, 40 (winter/spring 2013): 42.

41. Ibid, 43.

42. Barbara Truesdell, "FBI Use of Oral History Finding Aid," H-Oralhist, http:/2017/h-net.msu.edu/cgi-bin/logbrowse, September 28, 2007, accessed June 20, 2008.

43. Sherna Berger Gluck, "Reflecting on the Quantum Leap: Promises and Perils of Oral History on the Web," *Oral History Review*, 41 (summer/fall 2014): 247.

44. Ibid, 253.

45. Neuenschwander, *A Guide to Oral History and the Law*, second edition, 96–97.

46. Gluck, "Reflecting on the Quantum Leap: Promises and Perils of Oral History on the Web," 250.

47. Sheftel and Zembrzycki, 103.

48. Ibid.

49. Ibid, 105.

50. Juliana Nykolaiszyn, "Oral History and Social Networks: From Promotion to Relationship Building," in *Oral History in the Digital Age*, edited by Doug Boyd, Steve Cohen, Brad Rakerd, and Dean Rehberger (Washington, DC: Institute of Museum and Library Services, 2012), http://ohda.matrix.msu.edu/2012/06/oral-history-and-social-networks/, accessed November 26, 2023.

51. Sheftel and Zembrzycki, 109–10.

5

Recording Technology

What equipment should you use? Oral historians have faced this question since the first use of mechanical recorders. Equipment decisions are critical parts of an oral history plan. Misinformation or confusion about equipment basics can stall a project or result in loss of information. The purpose of this chapter is not to recommend one type of equipment or to recommend specific brands or models, nor is it meant to recommend or show a bias toward (or against) audio or video recording. It is, rather, designed to give you the background and tools to make the most beneficial choices for your project.

Given the relatively recent luxury of not only being able to read primary sources but to listen to or view them as well, equipment decisions continue to open up new options for users of oral history materials. Audio-visual archivists, the Oral History Association website, the *Oral History in the Digital Age* website, and other sources included in the notes for this chapter are excellent sources for updates about recording equipment and media.[1]

A BRIEF HISTORY OF RECORDING EQUIPMENT

Oral historians write about the digital revolution and technological advances. The transition from analog to digital—the digital revolution—had an impact on oral history projects and collections. It has not changed oral history but has changed "everything about" oral history.[2]

What do we mean by *analog* and *digital*? Both analog and digital recorders transform sound and images into electric current. Analog machines save signals on magnetized media in a continuous pattern as we see or hear them. The recorded signal is a direct analog to sound and image. Digital machines save analog signals as discrete averages of sound and images. Using various software programs and hardware, they take samples, mathemat-

ically balance them, and store them as bits of data. The recorded signal is a digitized average of the analog signal.

The necessity of adapting to changes in recording technology is not new. In the 1890s, ethnographers began using wax cylinders or discs (hard wax surfaces into which sound grooves were cut). Today, these fragile media are in museum collections, and efforts to save the information they contain are ongoing.[3]

Recording technologies that would give rise to oral history began with the invention of the magnetic recorder.[4] The wire recorder, an analog recorder that used steel tape or wire as the magnetized recording medium, was developed in the late nineteenth and early twentieth centuries. Prior to World War II, these machines were somewhat rare; during the war, most were used by branches of the service. In June 1944, Master Sergeant Forrest Pogue of the Army's Historical Division used one to record firsthand accounts of the D-Day invasion.[5] After World War II, wire recorders became more widely available. Allan Nevins of Columbia University, pursuing a prewar interest, began using them to collect oral histories. In 1948, he founded the Columbia University Oral History Research Office—the first organized program of its kind.[6]

The work of Pogue and Nevins helped establish oral history and its use of recorders to collect interview information inside and outside the archives. Others quickly saw the potential, including historians at the Bancroft Library at the University of California, Berkeley. Questions about the type of equipment to use, however, surfaced almost immediately. Post-war wire recorders, an improvement over equipment used before World War II, still were bulky and prone to breakdowns.

An early tape recorder, the Magnetophon, was developed in Germany between World War I and World War II. Tape coating experiments at Minnesota Mining and Manufacturing Company (now 3M) began in 1944. Discovery of several Magnetophones in Frankfurt, Germany, near the end of World War II furthered the work. Portable, self-contained reel-to-reel recorders appeared in 1951. Audiocassettes—audiotapes housed in plastic cases containing both the supply and take-up reels—went on the market in 1963. Analog recorders were universal, meaning any reel-to-reel or cassette recording could be played on any reel-to-reel or cassette equipment.

Digital technology—the use of discrete numerical values to represent data or information read by a computer—appeared in the early 1980s. Recording media for digital technology have included the Digital Audio Tape, compact discs (CDs), flash drives, and memory cards, among many options.[7]

Developments in video recording technology moved as fast as the audio recording field. Ampex began work on videotape and a videotape recorder in 1951. The first home videotape recorder was marketed in 1963. The first videocassette, the three-quarter-inch U-Matic, was introduced in 1969 and became the world standard for videocassettes. The first consumer video camcorder (its name is a contraction of *camera* and *recorder*) was introduced by Sony in 1980. The introduction of digital video brought additional variety to the market. The major medium was the digital versatile disc (DVD; also known as digital video disc), for which commercial standards were agreed to in 1995. Blu-ray discs, which use blue-violet laser to write and read data, and high-definition, which hit the market in 1998 with increased quality and resolution, were the next generation of digital video media. Oral historians now use SD (Secure Digital) cards and web-based systems.

The Digital Age, beginning in the 1970s when computers and computer technology came into common use, has had a major impact on recording, preservation, and access to oral histories. Digital technology allows oral historians to record and duplicate interviews without loss of quality, to bring oral histories off the shelf, and, through the internet, to give them widespread distribution. Artificial intelligence (AI) also plays a role. For example, AI audio transcription programs, using "natural language processing, machine learning algorithms, and vast databases of linguistic data," use this information to recognize and transcribe human speech.[8]

What is AI? If you ask Google (itself an AI tool) for a definition, you won't get just one.[9] But here's one that captures the gist of most of them in everyday terms. AI is a "technology that enables computers and digital devices to learn, read, write, talk, see, create, play, analyze, make recommendations, and do other things humans do."[10] The concept has been around since the 1950s, but dramatic increases in computing power, largely because of technology required for video gaming, spurred AI development. The release by OpenAI of its ChatGPT-3 program in late 2022, which enables users to readily create new text, propelled practitioners in virtually all technology-driven fields, including oral historians, to consider—or reconsider—the impact of such forms of AI. In general, ChatGPT and similar programs are enabled by software, known as bots, that trawl through websites collecting information in multiple forms, which then can be used to train AI programs to develop human-like responses to queries. That data-scraping process led to push-back from news organizations and content creators of all sorts who claimed copyright infringement for unauthorized use of intellectual property the bots collected. Major class action lawsuits for copyright infringement have been brought against OpenAI, Microsoft, and others, but whether or how those cases may result in new definitions of fair use, as permitted under copyright law, are likely to take years for courts to decide. By late 2023, hundreds of news organizations had installed blocking technology to prevent unauthorized access to their digital content. Alternatively, some publishers and other content creators have sought deals with tech firms to develop payment mechanisms for use of their digital content. After the emergence of ChatGPT, other companies introduced additional chat-based language models as well as image generators and sound creators that can generate new music and clone an individual's voice, making the person appear to speak any text you give it, raising additional concerns for oral historians, among many others.[11]

The rapid and ongoing AI evolution makes it advisable for oral historians planning projects to stay abreast of developments by consulting sources like the Oral History Association, *Oral History in the Digital Age*, and similar resources in the field. Rapid developments in AI also reinforce the importance of oral historians connecting early with a repository to assure that its digital practices align with the project's intent. For example, if the oral history materials will be published online, do project planners want the materials to be available to bots that accumulate data to drive AI training, or does the website host have the ability to block such access?

EQUIPMENT CHOICES AS PART OF THE ORAL HISTORY PLANNING PROCESS

As you can see from this brief overview of the evolution of recording formats, the one constant in recording equipment history is change. Formats are created and abandoned, and at any one time a number of different formats are available. Understanding the range of equipment types will help you make the best decision for a project.

This doesn't mean oral historians must be experts in recording technology. A working knowledge of the basics outlined in this chapter will help guide project decisions. Depending on your level of interest or expertise, you also may want to enlist help from a person with a strong background in computers and recording technology. But if you do, remember that ideally anyone you look to for advice should understand, or be willing to learn about, the specific recording needs of oral history, especially the need for continuing access to the full interview maximizing longevity and retrievability of the original recording.

Sources of information about recording equipment are mentioned throughout the chapter. Archivists and librarians, the Oral History Association and its H-Oralhist Listserv, and websites such as *Oral History in the Digital Age* all are excellent resources and good places to turn for the most up-to-date oral history equipment information. See "Ask Doug: Choosing a Digital Audio Recorder" on the *Oral History in the Digital Age* website for detailed information about various brands of recorders.[12]

BASIC RECOMMENDATIONS

Where to start? Think first about several basic recommendations:

- Use the best quality recording equipment to which you have access.
- Use high-quality external microphones.
- Use high-quality connecting cables.
- Use headphones.

Recordings that maintain long-term sound quality and accessibility are the goal of oral historians. The use of production-quality recorders is recommended whenever possible. High-quality external microphones, another item on the list, circumvent built-in recorder microphones and maximize recording quality for both analog and digital recorders. They provide the clearest and cleanest sound. High-quality connecting cables also help maximize recording or sound quality. Headphones allow the interviewer to monitor the sound as the interview is being recorded, helping avoid loss of the interview information.

PRODUCTION AND ARCHIVAL QUALITY

Oral historians work with production quality and archival quality standards. Production quality, also described as broadcast quality, is a recording equipment standard. The specifications refer to the most recent commercial recording guidelines.

Archival quality refers to the following:

- The approximate length of time the production-quality recording technology is expected to last
- The natural lifespan of the recording media
- The length of time playback equipment will be available[13]

Let's review each of the archival standards. The first, the approximate length of time the high-quality or production-quality recording technology is expected to last, is, at least ideally, an indication of stability and long-term access. If the recording equipment is not universal—meaning any recording can be played on any equipment—the recording and playback technology should at least be as widely available as possible. And equipment using proprietary technology—in which recording and playback options are restricted by software or hardware requirements and are linked to specific manufacturers—should be well documented.

The natural lifespan of the recording media is another standard. This refers to the amount of time the recording is retrievable. Reel-to-reel tapes were the recording and archival standard for four decades. With proper care and access to a recorder, they can be played for decades after an interview session. Digital interviews are recorded and stored in a variety of ways. The archival standard is to store several copies of the recordings on both physical media and a dedicated server. The general lifespan of digital formats has yet to be determined, although migration (transfer of information to the latest format) can extend accessibility.[14]

Rapid technological change makes it important to be aware of the length of time playback equipment is available. Obsolete playback technology can make oral history recordings inaccessible.

BASIC USE FACTORS

The next step is to consider basic use factors. They are:

- cost;
- project goals;
- audio and video; and
- project repositories.

COST

Recording equipment costs vary considerably. Although it may be tempting to save money on less expensive options, look carefully at equipment specifications before making a decision. Does the recorder have a removable memory card? This will allow for flexibility in long-term use. Does it have the option to record in unreduced sound, also referred to as uncompressed sound, a basic standard for digital oral history recordings? Are there proprietary factors in the software that can inhibit access to the recordings, either in the short term or the long term?

What about the cost of the recording media? Recording media, such as removable memory cards, are an extra expense to be factored into equipment costs. The physical media or server space needed to store the interview is another cost factor. While not a direct recording equipment cost, equipment and media needed for ongoing preservation and access are part of the cost of the digital age practice of oral history.

PROJECT GOALS

The second consideration involves project goals. What are the purposes of the project, and how and where will the recordings be used? Project directors will want to think about not only short-term access and use but access and use over decades. Will recordings be in formats that can continue to be accessible as the digital revolution races along? In what ways can your choice of equipment help maximize this possibility? What about options for "editing, indexing, incorporation into a database, dissemination, curation, presentation, and manipulation for research purposes, public consumption, and greater interactivity"? All lead to possible access questions that digital age oral history practitioners will want to consider.[15]

Ease of use in the interview setting is another factor. How easy is the equipment to use? How sturdy is it? Will it hold up through multiple users in a variety of interview settings and conditions?

AUDIO AND VIDEO

Here, your decision will be based on the project budget, project goals, type and availability of equipment, and narrator preferences. Each of these factors is important. Video cameras record in high definition, but used in uncontrolled environments, the recordings will be only as good as the lighting and environment in which they are made. Because video combines audio recording with visual images, it is a more complex medium and its use can require more planning. Carefully check options, including controlled environment needs such as equipment, lights, deflectors, and trained personnel.

Video equipment should be used by someone trained to handle the added technical elements that are part of a successful oral history video recording. Depending on the situation and the type of video equipment used, this can mean added expense. Oral historians generally record video from stationary camera positions, focusing on fully capturing the visual communications of a narrator. If projects use a professional camera operator, care should be given to emphasize that oral history videos do not use changing video positions and close-ups of narrators. As an overview, basic points to remember for video equipment users include the following:

- Document the type of equipment and recording format for preservation and access purposes.
- Confirm the interview setting puts the focus on the narrator.
- Confirm lighting is soft and focused on the narrator.
- Frame the photo (head and shoulders is usually recommended) and maintain a stationary camera position.
- Meet the most up-to-date archival video recording standards.

Using a digital video camera often allows one person to record in video; if this is the case, training sessions can provide an interviewer with needed information.

Recorders are oral historians' tools. When thinking about using video equipment, consider the following:

- What is the purpose of video? Is access to the context that video provides integral to understanding a narrator's story?
- What is the context the video will provide? Will it add visual information to the interview? If so, what type? How does the visual information strengthen the narrator's story? How does it contribute to the project purposes? Is the visual element needed to document the narrator's expressions and body language? How important is this to understanding the interview information and why?
- What is the setting? Is there an option to record in a location that is inviting visually or that adds to the information being discussed?
- Does the visual information document background footage that can be shot as a second interview after the initial audio recording?
- What are the short-term and long-term uses of the video information? Is it produced for immediate programming needs? Oral history guidelines stipulate that original recordings, audio and video, be kept intact and programming be done with copies. How does this affect the decision to use video?
- Will the project use production-quality video recording equipment? As with audio equipment, some video equipment may produce a recording that sounds and looks good in the short term but may not be sustainable in the long term.
- What types of media will be used, and how accessible and retrievable will the interview information be, short term and long term? Are there media types that can maximize accessibility and retrievability? If so, how available are they to the project?
- What are the video preservation needs? What are the unreduced (uncompressed) storage needs for

video data files? What are the video recording archival standards? What are plans for ongoing access to the video information?

Careful consideration of the impact on narrator and interviewer-narrator interaction is another part of the planning process. Just because video is available does not mean it must be used or even that it should be used. Audio-only interviews were the recording standard for decades, and they continue to have value. Here, community engagement can play a role in thinking through the considerations. Questions to ask about the impact of video on the interview participants include the following:

- Who will be in charge of the video interview? Is it the interviewer? Is it the videographer? What impact will this have on interview participants?
- What is the impact of using video on the interview and on the narrator? Video cameras and use of video are increasingly common, but interviews can be intense. Would the presence of video recording equipment be unsettling? What impact could video have on the interview information?
- How will the interviewer and narrator be perceived on camera? If the narrator is nervous, will this affect the credibility of the information presented? How important a consideration is this for the project?
- Will the video materials stereotype the narrator or other interview participants or create biases in any way? What are the narrator's wishes for the interview? What impact will this have on the project?
- What are the needs of the project, short term and long term? Sometimes video is necessary. Interviews done in sign language are a good example. Video interviews also document other non-verbal communications, such as gestures, facial expressions, and body language, and complex expressions that are difficult to translate into words. They collect information that cannot be communicated in an audio interview.

Video has other advantages. Although most oral history interviews are conducted one on one, video is useful if an interview involves more than one narrator since it makes it easier to see who is saying what. It also is useful if the narrator has items such as photographs or artifacts that visually enhance the interview. And video can provide material for possible exhibit or online uses, although development of useful footage also involves careful planning.

There are options for combining audio and video. First recording an audio interview and then working with the narrator to record visual images that supplement or complement it can be very effective. This allows projects to include video recording techniques while not relying exclusively on them. For example, thirty-two narrators were audio recorded through the Minnesota Historical Society's Minnesota Environmental Issues Oral History Project. After completing these interviews, project director James E. Fogerty followed up with video interviews with four narrators, each at a location that illustrated information given during the narrator's audio interview. Through careful planning for the video in a follow-up interview, Fogerty was able to gather additional information in a setting that maximized the use of visual images.[16]

We are an increasingly visual culture. Often the decision by oral history project leaders is to automatically assume that interviews will be video recorded. Many oral historians believe that what it brings to a project far outweighs anything else. As with all steps in the planning stage, care and caution are watchwords. Do not let technology drive the equipment planning process. Audio and video recording options are tools for oral historians. Use the tools that will best serve the purposes of your project.[17]

PROJECT REPOSITORIES

Many oral histories are held in repositories, permanent physical or digital facilities designed to care for historical documents. In this situation, the oral histories are given to the repository for ongoing preservation and care. If project planners choose not to use a repository for materials because of concern about protecting the interviews or other reasons, they will want to discuss how to handle ongoing care of the materials and document their decisions and the reasons for making them.

When using a repository, before making equipment decisions, talk with the manager where your collection ultimately will reside. Most repositories, small and volunteer-run or large multifaceted organizations, have format requirements and space limitations. Repositories generally will not accept formats they cannot support over the long term or that don't meet oral history archival standards. Repositories also look closely at the amount of storage space needed for storage of oral histories, with more emphasis on the large demands of video recordings. Don't forget to ask what kinds of recording equipment and media a repository will accept and can

Check with your repository for format requirements or guidelines when selecting equipment.

Ȟaȟá Wakpádaŋ/Bassett Creek Oral History Project

Ȟaȟá Wakpádaŋ (Falls Creek) is the Dakota name for a creek that flows through nine different suburban and urban municipalities before emptying into the Mississippi River in Minneapolis, Hennepin County, Minnesota (Mnísota Makhóčhe). Called Bassett Creek in English, the creek is a tributary to the Mississippi River, called Ȟaȟá Wakpá (Falls River) in Dakota. The Ȟaȟá Wakpádaŋ/Bassett Creek Oral History Project originated with Valley Community Presbyterian Church in Golden Valley, Minnesota, one of the suburbs, as a way for the church to go beyond its land acknowledgment statement in partnership with Indigenous communities.

Through the Ȟaȟá Wakpádaŋ/Bassett Creek Oral History Project, fourteen interviews were recorded with Indigenous people (Dakota, Anishinaabe, Ho-Chunk, and eight other tribes) connected to this suburban watershed. Indigenous scholar and oral historian Kasey Keeler (Tuolumne Me-Wuk and Citizen Potawatomi), whose work includes exploring the Indigenous relationship to suburbanization, co-led the project with oral historian Crystal Boyd and served as interviewer. Keeler described the project as amplifying Indigenous voices and sharing how Indigenous people experience the watershed as part of their historic and contemporary cultures. After the interviews were completed, the church hosted a thank-you brunch where Indigenous narrators identified their priorities for next steps. The interviews and all project materials are held in the collections of Hennepin History Museum in Minneapolis, Minnesota.

After writing the land acknowledgment statement, Boyd, with church members and Hennepin History Museum Director John Crippen, worked with Indigenous narrators and cultural advisers to develop a series of public programs around the interviews. Designed to raise awareness of the creek's Dakota name, the programs included nine community partner meetings and three discussion sessions, all of which were co-presented with Keeler or a narrator. Project leaders further expanded outreach by developing a podcast featuring the interviews, which was shared on a number of platforms including Spotify and YouTube. Also, an Indigenous filmmaker, Tiana LaPointe (Sicaŋgu Lakota), produced a video demonstrating how to pronounce Ȟaȟá Wakpádaŋ.

Through this post-interview community engagement, the Ȟaȟá Wakpádaŋ/Bassett Creek community has grown to more than seventy partners ranging from community leaders to ecologists to Indigenous scholars. In addition, hundreds of people have listened to the podcasts. Beginning with the oral histories, the project continues to build community engagement and support awareness of Indigenous cultures and histories in this suburban watershed. Future steps include developing education and arts materials and networking with government officials and non-governmental organizations whose work affects the creek.

For more information on the Ȟaȟá Wakpádaŋ/Bassett Creek Oral History Project, project partners, project sponsors, and the podcasts developed with the guidance of Carson Tomony, contact Hennepin History Museum or visit its website.

For more information about the land acknowledgment statement, a pronunciation video, project sponsors, and related information, see the website of Valley Community Presbyterian Church, Golden Valley, Minnesota.

For information about the Ȟaȟá Wakpádaŋ water ceremony organized for Minnesota's Indigenous People's Day 2023, see Maya Rao, "We Ask You to Bless This Water," *Minneapolis Star Tribune*, October 10, 2023, B1, B4.

---

continue to support. Ask also about any limitations on server space that may have an impact on project planning. When planning an oral history project, working with an archivist or other repository personnel to learn about their recommendations can save time and money.

RECORDERS, MEDIA, AND ACCESSORIES

When you have examined your options based on these guidelines, look at various types of recording equipment. The basic equipment questions you will want to ask when planning an oral history project involve use of:

- recorders;
- microphones, headphones, and cables; and
- media.

RECORDERS

Oral historians have a variety of types of audio recording devices from which to choose. The most commonly used audio recorders are solid state portable recorders with reusable flash memory, a memory card slot, headphone and microphone connections, and an AC adapter. They record in non-proprietary, cross-platform formats to removable, commonly available media. Memory cards are the preferred media. The most commonly used video recorders are portable cameras that record in high definition; have an option for internal memory and a memory card slot; record to memory cards in widely available, supported formats; and have a sensor, microphone and headphone connections, and an AC adapter. Let's review the basic features of each.

Regardless of the choice of recorder, digital audio recording equipment should have the following basic features: two external microphone jacks; a display window that shows recorder functions; manual volume control; a headphone jack; the option to record in unreduced (uncompressed) sound in a non-proprietary, cross-platform format; a removable memory card slot; a USB interface; an on/off switch; and an AC adapter.[18] Video recorders should have the following features at a minimum: high-definition recording option in a widely available and supported format, professional-quality microphone with XLR connections, headphone jack, manual volume control, removable memory card, tripod mountable, USB interface, and on/off switch.[19] Additional options for video equipment can include sound mixer, light stands and lamps, monitor (to review the video as it is recording), edit controller, and recorders with manual focus and white balance.[20] If the video recorder has just one microphone jack, a Y-cable or splitter will allow you to plug two microphones into one jack.

The most important audio equipment issue for oral historians to consider is sound quality of the recording. Production-quality equipment is the ideal, but it may not always be available. Oral historians can help determine whether recording equipment will fill a project's needs by examining sound and sound reduction specifications. The quality of digital sound is measured in sample rate and bit depth. Sample rate is the number of sound samples taken per second. The more samples (kHz), the better quality the sound. Bit depth is the number of bits of sound used to encode a sound file. The more bits of sound, the more accurate the sound.[21] The higher the bit depth and sample rate is, the larger a file is. For example, WAV, an uncompressed audio format used as the oral history audio recording standard, may be recorded in different bit rates and frequencies: 16-bit, 44.1 kHz generating 50 MB of sound; 24-bit, 48 kHz generating 82 MB of sound; and 24-bit, 96 kHz generating 164 MB of sound.[22] Each MB level generates a different file size; the decision for oral historians is to determine which, while meeting recording standards, is the most useful, has the best sound quality for a project's needs, will meet a repository's guidelines, and will best stand the test of time.

When choosing recording equipment, check current standards and equipment specifications. Oral historians work in unreduced sound and formats, also known as uncompressed sound and formats, with specified sampling rates and bit depths.

Most audio digital recorders have the option to reduce the data—that is, put it into a more compact form by discarding anything the recorder identifies as redundant. Let's look first at unreduced data. Unreduced data is represented in file format as WAVE and Broadcast Wave Format (waveform sound files, identified by the .wav or .bwf file extension) for PC computers and AIFF (.aif or .aiff file extension) for Macintosh users. Portable audio recorders often use a pulse-code modulation to digitally convert the recorded signal, saving it as the .wav or .aif file.[23] Check the recorder's user handbook for the sampling rate, bit depth, and file extension as a guide to sound quality.

When looking for video equipment, check sound and visual recording formats. Many archivists recommend MOV as an oral history audio/video recording standard. It produces a high-quality recording but generates large files. Questions to ask include: What formats are available? What are their video recording specifications? When looking for a recording format, check the aspect ratio—the ratio of width to height, often shown in a formula such as 4:3 or 16:9—and illustrated by the number of pixels that create the image.[24] Follow audio guidelines for sound quality wherever possible.

When sound and visual files are reduced, access to compacted materials comes through perceptual coding (a codec or algorithm that processes digital files) that works with the computer operating system. This reduces the data representing the sequence of recorded signals, encoding (translating recorded signals into digital format) differences between frames and discarding similarities. Codecs vary, depending on what they are used for, and are identified by the file extension. Lossy codecs, which process greatly reduced audio and video digital signals, are common because they can produce smaller files while retaining the data basics; users know the human mind can fill in any minor blanks.[25] Two of the more widely known are JPEG and MPEG (file extensions are .jpeg and .mpeg). Others include M4A, a compressed audio format, and MP4, a compressed audio and video format. When used to reduce sound, lossy codecs do not allow restoration of the data to its original acoustic condition. Repositories may ask for files in

WAV and MOV for archival preservation purposes and the smaller reduced files in M4A and MP4 formats for daily access purposes.

Lossless codecs also are an option for audio digital recordings. Lossless codecs reduce data but, unlike lossy codecs, do not discard data in the process. With lossless codecs, sound can be restored evenly across the range from high to low.[26]

Default settings on recorders usually are in lossy codecs. The recorder's handbook should include a process for reformatting into an unreduced format. An example of production and archival quality digital equipment audio recording standards is .wav or .bwf (unreduced) format. Video recording standards vary and include MOV, among others. For the most recent information on audio and video recording standards, check with archives, historical organizations, the Society of American Archivists, the Oral History Association, and the *Oral History in the Digital Age* website.[27]

RECORDING OPTIONS ON EQUIPMENT DESIGNED FOR OTHER USES

As advances in digital technology continue, options for types of recording equipment available to oral historians will continue to expand. Examples are direct-to-computer recording and use of smartphones as recording devices. Both, as with all options, benefit from careful research and testing to assure the creation of archival quality recordings. If using computers as recorders, review and apply recording standards and use connections and cables that maximize sound quality.

> Use oral history standards as a guide if recording interviews with equipment not manufactured to create archival-quality recordings as a primary function.

How can we apply oral history standards to the use of devices manufactured for other purposes but used as recorders? Let's use smartphones as an example. Here are some tips:

Before the Interview

- Confirm the selected recording apps work with the smartphone system and hardware requirements; check costs of the apps.
- Confirm the recording app has the capability to transfer recorded files to another device and how this is accomplished.

- Check the recording format on the phone. Whenever possible, record in WAV for audio and MOV for video. Be aware that these formats, recommended for archival recording quality, are proprietary and create large files. If asked, use the lossless setting.
- If using a repository, confirm it is prepared to preserve and care for large files.
- Check the smartphone for obsolescence and the amount of storage available; confirm there is enough to hold a recorded interview.
- Research available file storage options—Cloud storage, external hard drive/flash drive, stored on computer—and how each works with the smartphone.
- Practice recording with the smartphone; do a test recording to make sure it is recording as expected.

The Interview

- Confirm that all notifications on the phone, including incoming calls and texts, are turned off during the interview; turning on airplane mode during an in-person interview can help.
- Check the interview setting and the lighting. Generally, narrators are photographed in head-and-shoulders shots, front lit with soft or natural light; use landscape (horizontal) orientation.
- For in-person interviews, use an external microphone plugged into the smartphone. This can be either lavalier microphones for interviewer and narrator or a single omnidirectional mic attached to the phone.
- Check sound level balance between narrator and interviewer ensuring the narrator is clearly heard and the interviewer's voice doesn't overpower or overbalance the narrator.
- Use a tripod with a smartphone holder to maintain audio and visual quality and stability.
- Do a sound and visual test to confirm audio and video quality in the interview setting.
- Keep an eye on the smartphone to make sure it is not overheating; if it does, end the interview.

After the Interview

- When finished, copy the recording onto a dedicated computer or external hard drive.

Check the Oral History Association, the Library of Congress and its American Folklife Center Veterans History Project, the Oral History Society in Great Britain, and other national oral history organizations for the latest updates and guidelines on the use of smartphones as recorders.[28]

Remote interviewing options and use for oral historians grew considerably during the pandemic. Project development continued, but interviewing pivoted from in-person to distance work. Organizations such as the Baylor Institute for Oral History held worldwide training sessions looking at a number of options, and oral historians began to familiarize themselves with platforms like Zoom. Although many oral historians prefer in-person interviews whenever possible, the use of remote interviewing continues and probably, for convenience and flexibility, is here to stay. Here are a couple of distance interviewing tips:

- When considering use of remote interviewing, think carefully about all alternatives for the needs of the project, the needs of the narrator including situations involving health issues and access to physical recording sites, and recording standards. Choose the option that works well for the narrator and project.
- What is a narrator's experience with using a remote platform? What is the narrator's wish?
  - Many oral historians are finding that narrators are experienced in using remote platforms because distance conversations have become a common way of keeping in touch with family, including grandchildren.
- What formats do a distance learning app record in, and do these formats meet the needs of a project? How do they affect the quality of the interview recording?
- Are the platforms easy to use for a setting, like an oral history, that may be a little more formal than a family discussion? What directions are needed?
- What about privacy needs? Does the remote interviewing platform meet these needs for a narrator? For a project?
- Is there another way to reach a narrator? Remote interviews often are used for narrators at a distance or for those who find it difficult to come to an interview location. Narrator and interviewer travel needs and narrator mobility both can play a role in answering this question.
- What about interview recordings? The platforms have options from sending it to a local email address to Cloud file capture. What is the most workable option for your project?

Information in the "Remote Interviewing Resources" of the Oral History Association covers discussions about these and additional points. The Decision Tree, "Considerations for Remote Oral History Interviewing," adds an excellent visual component to the decision-making process.[29]

MICROPHONES, HEADPHONES, AND CABLES

A high-quality external microphone allows future listeners to clearly hear the interviewer and the narrator (that is, the full structure of the interview). Make sure the microphone is insulated to prevent picking up extra noise when touched. The options are lavaliers—small microphones clipped to the clothing—or microphones that use a stand or a pad.

Microphones come in two types: condenser or dynamic. A condenser translates acoustical signals into electrical ones using a variable capacitor (a voltage-storing component) that requires an external power source. A dynamic translates acoustical signals into electrical ones using a coil moving in a magnetic field. It generates its own electric current and does not need an external power source.

Microphones have several sound pick-up patterns. Omnidirectional patterns pick up all sound in a field around the microphone. Cardioid microphones pick up sound predominantly from the direction in which the microphone is pointed in a heart-shaped pattern. Unidirectional microphones pick up sound from one direction only.

Oral historians use either dynamic directional lavalier microphones—one for each participant in an interview—or one dynamic or condenser omnidirectional microphone placed to pick up everyone's voices. Each of these options will clearly pick up all voices in an interview.

> Use an omnidirectional microphone or directional lavalier microphones to pick up the narrator's and interviewer's voices. If more than one narrator or interviewer is involved, use microphones that pick up the voices of all interview participants.

When choosing a microphone, make sure it is compatible with the recorder. If using a microphone that needs a stand, it is essential to use a sturdy, stable microphone stand that allows the interviewer to position the microphone for optimum sound recording. These vary from free-standing models to those that clamp on to a flat surface to soft foam pads made especially to hold a microphone. As with all equipment decisions, if you have questions, contact an expert familiar with audio recording for advice.[30]

Equipment accessories also are important. Headphones permit the interviewer to monitor sound and resolve any audio problems that develop during the interview. Good cables help make good-quality sound. Make sure cables and connectors between the microphone and recording equipment are shielded (the conductors are wrapped) to reduce interference. Use coaxial cables (with inner and outer conductors) for video recording. Cables should allow for maximum flexibility in positioning the recorder and microphone.

MEDIA

Media are another equipment factor to consider. As with types of recording equipment, each has specific characteristics. Many digital recorders capture the sound or video on a memory card. The two most common are SD (secure digital) cards and CF (compact flash) cards. SD cards are the industry standard. Both card types come in different sizes, and SD cards come in different speeds—a factor when choosing a card for video recording. The number of megabytes (MB) and gigabytes (GB) of storage space each has will help determine its usefulness in recording an oral history interview in an unreduced format. Faster cards generally work better for video use.[31]

STORAGE

Unlike analog, digital recordings are not stored on the media on which they are recorded. Equipment decisions should include a plan for electronic storage of interview data files as part of your equipment decision list. This covers transferring interview files to a server, a hard drive, or a flash drive (also sometimes called a thumb drive). A disc (CD or DVD) can hold a user or back-up copy. When preserving and storing electronic files, the best approaches are to keep the original recording on the original flash card to preserve information about it, but do not use the flash card to provide archival-level storage for the interview. Follow the LOCKSS principle: lots of copies keeps stuff safe. As oral historian Douglas A. Boyd advises, "Make multiple copies in multiple formats and keep them in multiple places."[32]

"A memory card is temporary storage until a recording can be downloaded onto a server for preservation and future access. Card storage is never appropriate for access or preservation."
—Shawn Rounds, State Archivist and Head of Digital Collections Services, Division of Collections & Research Services, Minnesota Historical Society, St. Paul, Minnesota

A server environment that provides regular back-ups and automatic checks for monitoring and maintaining data file integrity (checking for data file corruption) is an optimum storage option. An external hard drive can be a back-up for a server environment, or it can be used as primary storage if a server environment is not available. Look for an external hard drive that provides options for automatically monitoring data files to make future conversions and migrations as easy as possible.[33]

CDs and DVDs are manufactured for short-term playback rather than long-term storage. They can provide limited access to interview data files and sometimes provide a secondary back-up, although volatility and threat of file loss are factors in this decision and many places have moved toward use of dedicated servers or the Cloud (servers that host software and infrastructure and are accessed over the internet).[34]

Video storage is more complex—an added factor when considering when and how to record in video. Video files involve as much as thirteen to thirty GB/hour of server space. Because of file size and technical needs, archival storage of video data files can be very expensive, as can the playback equipment needed to access the files. Look for server space that provides regular back-ups and automatic checks for monitoring and maintaining data file integrity. If an external hard drive can be incorporated into a storage plan, use one that will automatically monitor data files and make future conversions and migrations as easy as possible.

PRESERVING THE DATA

Metadata—data about data—is another area to consider when planning for oral history storage. Metadata standards such as Dublin Core help create a digital "library card catalog" to document technical, administrative, preservation, and descriptive information for archivists and librarians. The Oral History Association Metadata Task Force helps determine how to most effectively adapt and use metadata standards for oral histories. Check sources listed in this chapter for updated information about metadata and its application to oral history.[35]

INDEXING

Oral historians are now using indexing in ways that utilize digital age advances in technology. For example, indexes can be developed to access specific spots on recordings, allowing researchers to hear the voices on recordings. When considering steps that will be useful for preservation and access of oral histories, check on advances in indexing and determine which could be useful for a project.[36]

TRANSCRIBING EQUIPMENT

Transcribing guidelines are covered in chapter 8. Transcribing, however, also involves equipment. In-person transcribing equipment includes a headset, a foot pedal, a USB connection, and computer software.[37]

The use of transcribing apps is another ongoing development in the field of oral history. Although many are developed to provide quick documentation of meetings and other events, they also can be used to meet oral history needs. While projects also continue to use in-person transcribing, rapid developments in automatic speech recognition applications have tilted in favor of automated transcription. Some programs enable real-time transcription, while others require uploading digital files to be transcribed. In either case, automating transcription can be a significant cost saving for oral history projects. By late 2023, oral historians running trials of various automatic speech recognition programs found accuracy levels approaching and—in some cases—exceeding that of human transcribers. Again, as with other technology developments, oral historians can stay abreast of rapid changes by consulting sources like the Oral History Association and the Society of American Archivists. When reviewing transcribing apps, here are some steps to help evaluate them:

- Check the amount of time an app needs to transcribe a document and include it in project planning.
- Look into the features included with the transcript and determine if they are helpful for a project; some apps can include automatically generated lists of keywords and identification of main topics, which are often helpful to researchers.
- If translations among several languages are needed, look into the languages an app can translate and run a short sample to check for quality control.
- Look into the cost and what it includes; some apps are free, others are free within certain limits. Overall, prices are generally listed by the minute and vary with sound quality of the recording and specific transcribing needs.

Choose an app that has the features needed for the project. And despite increasing accuracy of automatic speech recognition programs, always plan for plenty of time to audit-edit the resulting transcript.

Plans for use of transcribing apps also require specific consideration. It is helpful to be reminded of the impacts of their use on standard recording guidelines; some of the most common are:

- Existence of background noise—check on the effects of ambient noise in producing a transcript

- Variations in speech—dialects, accents, and less than clear enunciation may make it difficult to accurately recognize spoken language
- Multiple speakers in an interview—when more than one person's voice is on a recording, check accuracy of voice recognition when audit-checking the transcript
- Context—depending on context of what is said, it may be difficult to understand spoken language
- Privacy—the use of appropriate controls over preservation and access are important

If project plans include use of transcribing apps, include plenty of time to audit-check and confirm the accuracy of the transcripts.[38] All transcripts must be checked for accuracy; this is especially true of transcripts generated by apps. No matter how accurate an app is, and they vary greatly even in transcribing the basics, even the best apps often cannot identify slurred words, words spoken softly, or words or phrases spoken by a narrator in a second language. An app also cannot know the spelling of names, especially names that sound alike but are spelled differently (Anna/Anne/Ann, Erik/Eric/Erich, or Karen/Karin to name just a few). And it cannot always identify homonyms (to, two, too, and the like). Audio checking a transcript generated by an app can take at least several hours, depending on its length and accuracy.

RECORDING EQUIPMENT AND MEDIA NOT RECOMMENDED FOR ORAL HISTORY USE

What about equipment not recommended for use by oral historians? This section is not meant as a heavy-handed set of rules, but as a guide to maximize full preservation and long-term access to oral history information.

Oral history projects generally do not need equipment made for high-end music recording, but you can maximize the life and use of the interviews with the best voice and/or visual production-quality recorders you can find. Over-the-counter audio recorders manufactured for home use, while perhaps sounding good at the time of the initial recording, do not always meet oral history standards. Neither do video recorders manufactured for home use. Digital age advances have led to greater recording quality, but they do not always result in production-quality recordings, and the long-term viability and retrievability of the recorded information is unproven. Check the Oral History Association, American Folklife Center, and *Oral History in the Digital Age* websites and with your local historical organization for the most up-to-date information.

Avoid mini-forms of media, whether it be the older mini-cassettes or micro-SD cards. Generally, avoid memory cards other than SD or CF recommended for use by oral historians. And avoid voice-activated recorders. They shut down when people are not talking, omitting pauses in the interview that can be important to understanding its context.

The rapid equipment and media evolution of the digital age has led to the relatively rapid appearance and disappearance of some types of equipment and media. Ideally, try to use equipment and media that meet the archival standards described at the beginning of this chapter.

The information in this chapter is designed to help you think through some basic equipment and media decisions. Always check for the most up-to-date information available. Consult archivists, the oral history listserv, the Oral History Association, the Society of American Archivists, the *Oral History in the Digital Age* website, and the sources listed throughout this chapter. Equipment issues and recommendations are a moving target. Your project and your interviews will benefit from the most recent information you can find.

WHAT OTHER QUESTIONS CAN HELP GUIDE EQUIPMENT DECISIONS FOR YOUR PROJECT?

Does the equipment conform to national and international standards regarding basic specifications, interchangeability, and compatibility among brands? Digital age equipment standards emphasize the broadest applicability and use of recording equipment and formats as possible. Cross-platform, non-proprietary formats are the preferred types.

Who will be doing the interviewing, and who will train interviewers to use the equipment? Thorough interviewer training on recording equipment is essential. Nothing is worse than sending someone out on an interview only to find that inexperience with the equipment results in either a poor-quality product or complete loss of the information. Inexperienced or untrained interviewers also pay more attention to the equipment than to the narrator, which can lower the quality of the interview. Choose equipment that project interviewers can learn to use with confidence.

Who is available for help and equipment/media support? Interviewer training does not completely solve the equipment use issue. Whether using volunteers, graduate assistants, or interviewers with many years' experience, there are times when it is helpful to have someone to turn to with questions about use of the equipment. Knowing your community and the kinds of support and expertise available for various types of recorders can help you choose equipment best suited to your needs.

What are the interviewing conditions? Conditions at the interview setting can affect your equipment decisions. What are the conditions in which the interviewers will be operating, and what type of equipment is best suited to these situations? Given that interviewers may not always have access to electricity, how well does the equipment operate on batteries? How rugged is it, and how well does it perform in a variety of situations?

What factors can cause loss of recorded signal, and how often does this occur? One of the greatest fears of oral historians is to find out, too late, that the great interview just completed didn't record because of equipment problems. It is always helpful to ask how to identify factors leading to possible equipment or media recording malfunctions. You will also want to ask, should the worst happen, how much information was lost due to malfunctioning equipment or media and how you can expect to retrieve it with the equipment you want to use. Also ask how this is done, what the cost of doing it is, and who is available to do it.

Including video in an oral history project is another critical equipment decision. Here are some questions to help guide you. Answers to these equipment planning questions can help you make your decision.

What is your project budget, and how will video enhance the final result? Video can be expensive. As with audio, the use of production-quality equipment—the camera, the external microphones, and media—is the oral history standard. How can you best maximize project resources? If limited resources exist, where and how will video fit best? What is most useful for your project and why? Does every interview need to be recorded in video? Why or why not? Could an interview benefit from combining audio and selected video recordings, using video to complement or supplement the audio where it is most useful?

Who and what will be on video? Will video provide talking heads, or will it be used to provide a visual element that complements or provides additional background to the information being collected? If video provides talking heads, how will this further the goals of your project? How will your project benefit from the use of video, and how is this reconciled with overall needs and budget resources?

Are camera operators or videographers available if needed to make video recordings, and how accessible are they to your project? What is their experience with oral history? What is the cost of using them?

Who will conduct the video interviews, and what experience does this person have with video oral history? Just as audio interviews should be researched and organized, video interviews must be carefully planned. Video interviews can involve one or more equipment operators or the interviewer working alone. Regardless, the interviewer is in charge of the interview and, working with the camera operator, makes final decisions on set, lighting, and camera angles.

What are the possible needs at the recording site, such as special lenses, lighting, microphones, cables and accessories, and necessary power sources? If these are not readily available, how can you provide for each? Are there resources through community engagement that can help meet these needs?

How will a video recording session affect the narrator and interviewer? It is helpful to think about the presence of video equipment and whether it will distract the narrator, preventing successful interaction between interviewer and narrator during the interview. It is also helpful to be aware of possible effects of video recording equipment on the interviewer and to try to incorporate video interviewing techniques into interviewer training sessions whenever video will be used.

What are the recording conditions for use of video? If the interview is to be recorded outdoors, do you know how this will affect the recording? How does this contrast with the use of a studio, the narrator's home or place of business, or other indoor settings? It is helpful to find out how to maintain production-quality audio and video standards in each setting. What will result in a video that furthers project goals?

What are the wishes of narrators? Do the narrators understand they will be recorded on video? Do they understand how the project plans to use the video? Do they understand there can be additional—but unknown—uses of the video in the future? Do they agree to be on video under these circumstances?

Will video be useful for future projects, and is this a determining factor for your project? You may want to think about the possible future uses of video interviews and then decide if meeting undefined future needs is part of your project goal or purpose.

WHAT ABOUT PLANNED PRESERVATION AND ACCESS TO INTERVIEW MATERIALS?

Preservation and access questions are major factors to consider when developing a project and choosing equipment. This becomes especially obvious when requests to use interview materials for projects, such as museum exhibits or websites, begin to come in. Although the fundamental purpose of oral history is to collect primary source material documenting firsthand information, project coordinators increasingly consider its use in audio or video products as an important project outcome.

Key access questions relate to potential uses of the materials, preservation and access choices, and interview processing techniques. Oral history projects typically record interviews for both immediate and long-term use, although immediate use, such as a publication, documentary, or museum exhibit, can drive project development. With this in mind, the type of project and the need

to quickly and easily gain access to oral history materials become factors in choosing equipment. These questions can help guide the planning process.

Who will be responsible for the oral history collection? When at a repository, what experience do the personnel have handling oral history materials and in handling your formats? Oral history collections need specialized care. Does the repository have the resources to care for the kinds of formats you want to use? Does the repository recommend specific formats? If not at a repository, what are the decisions for ongoing care, preservation, and access of the oral histories?

How many interviews will be recorded, and what are the equipment, media, and estimated server space needs for preserving the recorded information? What about the use of external hard drives? Digitally recorded interviews are stored on server storage space, on external hard drives, and/or in the Cloud. It may take several external hard drives to hold copies of interviews. When using external hard drives to store or back up multiple copies of interviews, keep the hard drives in separate locations that provide adequate storage conditions. Keep track of unreduced file sizes to determine the amount of server space needed for interview data file storage.

What is the plan for technological change? What about back-up strategies? Oral history projects will want to determine a repository's practices for retaining access to the interview materials.

What equipment should you keep on hand to play tapes or discs when needed? What software and hardware systems does the digital equipment use? What are the repository's policies for maintaining equipment and software and hardware systems that continue to provide access to the recordings?

Who is available to provide equipment maintenance needed for accessibility to the interview information? It is helpful to know about the types of maintenance the equipment needs, how it should be done, what is most likely to need repairing, and what the possible repair costs can be. Librarians and school audio-visual staff can be helpful sources of information on equipment maintenance and repair track records.

What are the plans for making copies of the interviews and for keeping the originals as the preservation masters? What equipment is available for copying? What medium will interviews be copied onto and why? What are the resources for making user copies of the material?

Who will be processing the information in the interview, and what equipment is available for this purpose? What type of processing (developing a transcript, a recording abstract) will be done, and what types of processing equipment are needed? What medium should materials be in for processing? What will it take to put the recorded interview material into a format for processing? If full transcripts are to be made (important for both audio and video interviews), access to the contents of the interview probably will be ongoing. But if you decide to rely only on a recording abstract, how will continued access to the spoken information be maintained?

How do you plan to use information from the interviews? While collecting oral history will add primary source material to repositories, oral history interviews often are used to provide material for museum exhibits, radio and television programs, podcasts, websites, and written materials, among many other uses. What are some possible uses of the interviews beyond primary source documents? What formats would make them more useful, and what kinds of personnel, equipment, and budget would be needed to put the interviews into these formats?

Do you have plans to put project materials online? You may be interested in streaming. Keeping in mind the internet does not replace the need for a permanent repository for project materials, what formats are needed for website development? What are your reasons for putting project information online, and how do they further overall project development? What is needed to put project materials into a format for use online? How do web-related needs affect other access issues?

WHAT ABOUT RECORDING TECHNOLOGY AND LONG-TERM ACCESS TO RECORDINGS?

Although it is sometimes difficult to think about the needs of researchers and others well into the future, the purpose of oral history is to collect and preserve information that could otherwise be lost. Once collected, this primary source material is as important and unique as a diary or as letters dating back hundreds of years. Just as people today still read first-person accounts about life on the Overland Trail in the diaries and letters written by nineteenth-century migrants, people in the future will turn to oral histories to learn from the information they contain. Oral history materials also are being sought more often for audio or video uses beyond those designed into the project. Although the lifespan of the recordings is finite, adherence to production and archival standards whenever possible will help you maximize accessibility to the recorded interviews.

This set of decisions in equipment planning is one of the most important, but it can also be one of the most difficult and confusing. Bruce Bruemmer, former archivist at the Cargill Corporation, pointed out in a 1991 *American Archivist* article that "oral historians are [often] producers, not curators."[39] This dilemma is reflected in what may be referred to as the contradictory needs of historic records maintenance. Paul Eisloeffel, former curator of audiovisual collections at History Nebraska, notes that archivists

are responsible for the long-term care of records and media created for a more immediate or very different purpose. The challenge is long-term care and maintenance of materials created in a variety of formats using a variety of media, each of which has its own preservation needs. This is even more of an issue today when oral historians have a variety of equipment types, software and hardware systems, and media from which to choose.

As software, hardware, and media change and are updated, archivists and others owning oral history materials will be faced with maintaining access to the information in the most up-to-date formats. Many institutions also regularly transfer materials to newer formats. The transfer processes are called digitizing (transferring analog to digital), refreshing (recreating files on new software-hardware systems), reformatting (moving files to software-hardware systems with different specifications), and migrating (moving data between media). Archivists recommend that digitized items be transferred to the latest formats every five years to keep up with changes in technology.

As you look at various types of recording equipment and media, consider the following long-term access issues for oral history materials.

Will analog recordings be digitized? Digitization should be done according to the most up-to-date technological standards available. If the original recording is in analog format, that is the archival master. After digitizing, it should be retained in the collections. Digitization is a process that puts the recording into a different format; never use it as a reason for discarding the archival master.[40]

What are the equipment, media, and estimated server space needs for preserving the recorded information? What is the plan for technological change? What about back-up strategies? Ask repository personnel these questions to help determine options for ongoing retrievability. As noted earlier, some oral history projects use multiple external hard drives as back-ups.

What about equipment obsolescence? What happens when the equipment needed to play the recordings is no longer available or the parts needed to maintain existing out-of-date equipment are no longer available? What plans does the repository have to hold on to and maintain out-of-date equipment to provide access to recordings for the lifespan of the media? This is as true for continued access to analog in reel-to-reel or cassette formats as it is for CDs, sound cards, and interviews stored on servers.

What about format obsolescence? Is the software and hardware you are using proprietary (unavailable for use without permission from the manufacturer), or is it open and standard? What happens when the software and hardware systems you are using are no longer available? How will this affect access? What are the plans for regularly upgrading software and hardware access systems?

Are the equipment and media backwards compatible and, if so, for how many generations? Backwards compatibility, also called downward compatibility, refers to the ability to use data and files created with earlier technologies on new equipment and media. For instance, will new technology accept and allow access to materials created with earlier versions of software? Backwards compatibility reduces the need to start over when technology is upgraded.

Are the equipment and media forward compatible? Forward compatibility, also called upward compatibility, refers to planning for access to data and files created with earlier technologies on future upgrades.

Is a lossy or lossless codec needed to read digitally recorded information? What do you know about its ability to provide ongoing access to the materials?

How is the interview information stored? Data reduction is a factor for oral historians because unreduced files are large, a consideration when storing large numbers of interviews. What about the availability of server space for long-term storage of the interviews? What about additional storage options? What is available, and what is the lifespan for maintaining access to the interviews?

What are the project's policies for long-term access to oral history materials (digital and analog, audio and video) in its collections? As software and hardware technology changes, how will the ongoing access be handled? Realizing analog is less complex than digital but that both have specific archival needs, what are the policies for long-term access to the sound archives?

If a repository has collections in several digital formats, what are its policies for maintaining access to each? Does it have collections in various formats? What are staff and budget priorities for maintaining access? What are its policies and priorities for standardizing formats?

What are staff and budget priorities for care of analog and digital materials, including ongoing access to refreshment technology, commitment to refreshing collections, and number of copies made? It is difficult to determine future budget commitments and needs, but a thorough discussion of these issues can be helpful.

What about sound quality throughout the migration process? Although the data reduction process normally runs smoothly, with too much reduction or an incorrect ratio, artifacts (sounds or images that shouldn't be there) can appear, and, if they do, they can permanently affect the quality of the digitized materials. You will also want to ask about the effects of data reduction on multiple copies made over time.

What are the most recent archival staff recommendations regarding long-term stability of your chosen format? This information may be obtained through local historical organizations, the media archivist at your state historical society, and the Oral History Association and the Society of American Archivists.

FINAL RECOMMENDATIONS

Deciding what equipment to use can be a thorny issue for oral historians. While the discussion in this chapter can help you make an informed decision about your interview needs as well as accessibility and retrievability of the recordings, keep in mind that this discussion highlights ideal choices. Projects rarely have the funding to acquire the full assortment of equipment and media covered here. When funding needs are an issue, the first priority for many projects is acquiring the best recording equipment they can afford along with a high-quality microphone and high-quality cables.

The final suggestion is: Always do your homework. The resources listed in this chapter are good places to start. You may find that the newest technology does not fit your needs or it may not be supported by your repository. If your budget is tight, you may find that equipment can be donated or loaned. Schools, two- and four-year colleges, and universities often have media centers with good recording equipment that can be sources of help or support. And always remember that although recording technology changes rapidly, informed and thoughtful equipment decisions during the oral history planning process enhance the immediate and long-term accessibility, uses, and retrievability of your oral history recordings.

> Always do your homework when deciding on equipment for your oral history project.

NOTES

1. Because of rapidly changing technology, equipment specifications can change quickly. For up-to-date oral history technology information, see the Oral History Association, "Resources," https://oralhistory.org/resources/, accessed October 21, 2023; H-Oralhist Listserv, https://oralhistory.org/h-oralhist-listserv/, accessed October 21, 2023; *Oral History in the Digital Age*, https://oralhistory.org/oral-history-in-the-digital-age/, accessed October 23, 2023; and the Vermont Folklife Center Field and Research Guides at the Vermont Folklife Center, https://www.vtfolklife.org/fieldwork-guides, accessed October 21, 2023.

2. Douglas A. Boyd, "Oral History and Technology," presentation at "The Start of Something New," University of Wisconsin-Madison Oral History Day Program, April 14, 2008.

3. Oral History Association at www.oralhistory.org; *Oral History in the Digital Age*, https://oralhistory.org/oral-history-in-the-digital-age/, accessed October 21, 2023.

4. Definitions for various technical terms in this chapter are from Brad Hansen, *The Dictionary of Computing and Digital Media: Terms & Acronyms* (Wilsonville, OR: ABF Content, 1999).

5. Donald A. Ritchie, "Remembering Forrest Pogue," *Oral History Association Newsletter* (winter 1997): 7.

6. For more information, see Rebecca Sharpless, "The History of Oral History," in *Handbook of Oral History*, edited by Thomas L. Charlton, Lois E. Myers, and Rebecca Sharpless (Lanham, MD: AltaMira Press, 2006), 19–42.

7. *Disc* is sometimes spelled *disk*. The authors have chosen the first spelling as the more common.

8. ClickUp, https://clickup.com/blog/ai-transcription-tools/, accessed February 24, 2024.

9. A curious, non-tech-oriented oral historian asked just that question of a highly tech-oriented colleague at an Oral History Association conference in 2023 and was told, with a grin: "Well, it all depends."

10. IBM, "What Is Artificial Intelligence?" https://www.ibm.com/topics/artificial-intelligence, accessed February 21, 2024.

11. Information in this discussion comes from personal interview by co-author Quinlan with Matt Waite, professor of practice, University of Nebraska-Lincoln College of Journalism and Mass Communication, November 2, 2023, and from Nick Robertson, November 1, 2023. Also see: Will Douglas Heaven, "6 Big Questions for Generative AI," *MIT Technology Review*, 127:1 (January-February 2024): 31–37; Nick Robertson, "The Guardian Says It's Blocking OpenAI from Building Off Its Content," *The Hill*, September 1, 2023, https://thehill.com/policy/technology/4183282-the-guardian-will-block-open-ai-chatgpt-from-content/; Nitasha Tiku, "Newspapers Want Payment for Articles Used to Power ChatGPT," *Washington Post*, October 20, 2023, https://www.washingtonpost.com/technology/2023/10/20/artificial-intelligence-battle-online-data/.

12. Doug Boyd, "Ask Doug: Choosing a Digital Audio Recorder," *Oral History in the Digital Age*, https://digitalomnium.com/askdoug, accessed February 21, 2024.

13. Robyn Russell, "Archival Considerations for Librarians and Oral Historians," *Oral History Association Newsletter* (spring 2004): 4–5.

14. Nancy MacKay, *Curating Oral Histories: From Interview to Archive*, second edition (New York, NY: Routledge, 2016), 139–44.

15. Anna Sheftel and Stacy Zembrzyciski, "Slowing Down to Listen in the Digital Age: How New Technology is Changing Oral History Practice," *The Oral History Review*, 44:1 (winter/spring 2017): 95; Mary Larson, "Steering Clear of the Rocks: A Look at Oral History Ethics in the Digital Age," *Oral History Review*, 40:1 (winter/spring 2013): 36–49.

16. Minnesota Historical Society, *Voices of Minnesota*, Minnesota Environmental Issues Oral History Project, St. Paul, Minnesota.

17. For more information, see Douglas A. Boyd, "Audio or Video for Recording Oral History: Questions, Decisions," in *Oral History in the Digital Age*, edited by Douglas A. Boyd, Steve Cohen, Brad Rakerd, and Dean Rehberger (Washington, DC: Institute of Museum and Library Services, 2012), http://ohda.matrix.msu.edu/2012/06/audio-or-video-for-recording-oral-history/, accessed November 21, 2023; Joanna Hay, "Case Study: Using Video in Oral History—Learning From One Woman's Experiences," in *Oral History in the Digital Age*, edited by Douglas A. Boyd, Steve Cohen, Brad Rakerd, and Dean Rehberger (Washington, DC: Institute of Museum and Library Services, 2012), http://ohda.matrix.msu.edu/2012/06/using-video-in-oral-history/, accessed November 21, 2023.

18. For more information, see Baylor University Institute for Oral History Workshop on the Web, "Introduction to Oral History," http://www.baylor.edu/content/services/document.php/43912.pdf, accessed November 21, 2023.

19. For more information, see Donald A. Ritchie, "Video Oral History," in *Doing Oral History: A Practical Guide*, third edition (New York, NY: Oxford University Press, 2015), 137–60; Scott Pennington, "Video Equipment: Guide to Selecting and Use," in *Oral History in the Digital Age*, edited by Doug Boyd, Steve Cohen, Brad Rakerd, and Dean Rehberger (Washington, DC: Institute of Museum and Library Services, 2012), http://ohda.matrix.msu.edu/2012/06/video-equipment/, accessed November 21, 2023.

20. Stacy Ericson, revised by Troy Reeves, *A Field Notebook for Oral History*, fourth edition (Boise, ID: Idaho Oral History Center, Idaho State Historical Society, 2001), 29; Douglas A. Boyd, correspondence to Barbara W. Sommer, September 22, 2008; Scott Pennington, "Video Equipment: Guide to Selecting and Use," in *Oral History in the Digital Age*, edited by Doug Boyd, Steve Cohen, Brad Rakerd, and Dean Rehberger (Washington, DC: Institute of Museum and Library Services, 2012), http://ohda.matrix.msu.edu/2012/06/video-equipment/, accessed November 21, 2023.

21. Doug Boyd, Steve Cohen, Brad Rakerd, and Dean Rehberger, eds., "24-bit,96 kHz," in *Oral History in the Digital Age* (Washington, DC: Institute of Museum and Library Services, 2012), http://ohda.matrix.msu.edu/gettingstarted/glossary/audioglossary/24-bit96-khz/, accessed November 21, 2023.

22. W. A. Production, "How to Understand Audio Quality Formats," https://blog.waproduction.com/how-to-understand-audio-quality-formats, accessed February 21, 2024; Douglas A. Boyd, "Digital Audio Recording: The Basics," in *Oral History in the Digital Age*, edited by Doug Boyd, Steve Cohen, Brad Rakerd, and Dean Rehberger (Washington, DC: Institute of Museum and Library Services, 2012), http://ohda.matrix.msu.edu/2012/06/digital-audio-recording/, accessed November 21, 2023.

23. Douglas A. Boyd, "Pulse Code Modulation," in *Oral History in the Digital Age*, edited by Doug Boyd, Steve Cohen, Brad Rakerd, and Dean Rehberger (Washington, DC: Institute of Museum and Library Services, 2012), http://ohda.matrix.msu.edu/gettingstarted/glossary/audioglossary/pulse-code-modulation/, accessed November 21, 2023.

24. Scott Pennington, "Video Equipment: Guide to Selecting and Use," in *Oral History in the Digital Age*, edited by Doug Boyd, Steve Cohen, Brad Rakerd, and Dean Rehberger (Washington, DC: Institute of Museum and Library Services, 2012), http://ohda.matrix.msu.edu/2012/06/video-equipment/, accessed November 21, 2023.

25. Lossy codec reduction rates generally are at least 10:1 for audio and 300:1 for video, resulting in files that are greatly reduced in size. Lossy codecs are the standard for recording devices. For more information, see Douglas A. Boyd, "Codec," in *Oral History in the Digital Age*, edited by Doug Boyd, Steve Cohen, Brad Rakerd, and Dean Rehberger (Washington, DC: Institute of Museum and Library Services, 2012), http://ohda.matrix.msu.edu/gettingstarted/glossary/videoglossary/codec/, accessed November 21, 2023.

26. FLAC (Free Lossless Audio Codec) is an example of a non-proprietary, cross-platform, lossless audio codec. As a cross-platform codec, it works with both Windows and Macintosh software packages. Its file extension is .flac. For more information, see "Sustainability of Digital Formats: Planning for Library of Congress Collections," https://www.loc.gov/preservation/digital/formats/fdd/fdd000198.shtml, accessed November 21, 2023.

27. For more information, see National Archives, "Federal Records Management," https://www.archives.gov/records-mgmt/initiatives/dav-faq.html, accessed November 21, 2023; Smithsonian Institution Archives, "Recommended Preservation Formats for Electronic Records," https://siarchives.si.edu/what-we-do/digital-curation/recommended-preservation-formats-electronic-records, accessed November 21, 2023.

28. Winona Wheeler, Charles E. Trimble, Mary Kay Quinlan, and Barbara W. Sommer, *Indigenous Oral History Manual: Canada and the United States* (New York, NY: Routledge, 2024), 50–51; Oral History Association, "Mobile Phone Recording," https://www.oralhistory.org/wp-content/uploads/2020/09/3b.-Mobile-Phone-Recording-Platform-Document.pdf; Library of Congress, "Veterans History Project Instruction Booklet," https://www.loc.gov/static/programs/veterans-history-project/documents/vhp-field-kit-complete.pdf, accessed August 4, 2023; Veterans History Project, "Frequently Asked Questions (FAQ)," https://ask.loc.gov/veterans-history/faq/369298, accessed August 4, 2023; Oral History Society, "What About Smartphones?" https://www.ohs.org.uk/for-beginners/equipment, accessed February 22, 2024.

29. Oral History Association, "Remote Interviewing Resources," https://oralhistory.org/remote-interviewing-resources/#decisiontree, accessed December 5, 2023.

30. Douglas A. Boyd and Charles Hardy, "Understanding Microphones," in *Oral History in the Digital Age*, edited by Doug Boyd, Steve Cohen, Brad Rakerd, and Dean Rehberger (Washington, DC: Institute of Museum and Library Services, 2012), http://ohda.matrix.msu.edu/2012/06/understanding-microphones/, accessed November 21, 2023.

31. Scott Pennington and Dean Rehberger, "Video Equipment: Guide to Selecting and Use," in *Oral History in the Digital Age*, edited by Doug Boyd, Steve Cohen, Brad Rakerd, and Dean Rehberger (Washington, DC: Institute of Museum and Library Services, 2012), http://ohda.matrix.msu.edu/2012/06/video-equipment/, accessed November 21, 2023.

32. Douglas A. Boyd, telephone conversation with Barbara W. Sommer, September 25, 2008.

33. Douglas A. Boyd, "Digital Audio Recording: The Basics," in *Oral History in the Digital Age*, edited by Doug Boyd, Steve Cohen, Brad Rakerd, and Dean Rehberger (Washington, DC: Institute of Museum and Library Services, 2012), http://ohda.matrix.msu.edu/2012/06/digital-audio-recording/, accessed November 21, 2023.

34. Nancy MacKay, *Curating Oral Histories: From Interview to Archive*, second edition, 91.

35. Oral History Association, "The OHA Metadata Task Force," https://oralhistory.org/the-oha-metadata-task-force-mtf/, accessed November 30, 2023; Nancy MacKay, *Curating Oral Histories; From Interview to Archive*, second edition, 139; Cyns Nelson and Lauren Kata, "The OHA Metadata Task Force," in *Oral History in the Digital Age*, edited by

Doug Boyd, Steve Cohen, Brad Rakerd, and Dean Rehberger (Washington, DC: Institute of Museum and Library Services, 2012), http://ohda.matrix .msu.edu/2015/10/the-oha-metadata-task-force -the-force-behind-our-task/, accessed November 21, 2023; Elinor A. Mazé, "Metadata: Best Practices for Oral History Access and Preservation," in *Oral History in the Digital Age*, edited by Doug Boyd, Steve Cohen, Brad Rakerd, and Dean Rehberger (Washington, DC: Institute of Museum and Library Services, 2012), http://ohda.matrix.msu.edu/2012/06 /metadata/, accessed November 23, 2023.

36. Douglas Lambert, "Oral History Indexing," *The Oral History Review*, 50:2 (2023): 169–92.

37. For more information, see local or state archivists and the Oral History listserv. See also Baylor University Institute for Oral History Workshop on the Web, "Introduction to Oral History," http://www.baylor .edu/content/services/document.php/43912.pdf, accessed November 21, 2023.

38. Scaler Topics, https://www.scaler.com/topics /speech-recognition-in-ai/, accessed July 23, 2023.

39. Bruce A. Bruemmer, "Access to Oral History: A National Agenda," *American Archivist*, 54 (1991): 494–501.

40. Digitization is a process that puts analog recordings into a different format; it should never be used as a reason to discard archival masters. For up-to-date information on digitization procedures and standards, see Scott Pennington and Dean Rehberger, "The Preservation of Analog Video through Digitization," in *Oral History in the Digital Age*, edited by Doug Boyd, Steve Cohen, Brad Rakerd, and Dean Rehberger (Washington, DC: Institute of Museum and Library Services, 2012), http://ohda.matrix.msu.edu/2012/06 /preservation-of-analog-video-through-digitization/, accessed November 21, 2023.

6

Interview Preparation

Now that you have established a solid plan, determined a budget, considered legal and ethical issues, and selected equipment appropriate for your project, the oral history process moves into the next phase of its life cycle: the interview itself. Although the interview is the most-recognized part of the oral history process, a good interview requires thorough behind-the-scenes preparation to the extent possible. Interview preparation lays the foundation on which to build the oral history.

Interview preparation generally involves two distinct types of research: general project research and narrator-specific research. Often, people are attracted to an oral history project because they know about its subject and want to talk with people about it. Project coordinators need to direct this enthusiasm to the interview preparation process so that the interviews themselves will live up to everyone's expectations.

> Interview preparation involves general project research and individual narrator research.

Everyone involved in the project should participate in general project research regardless of how familiar some participants may be with the people, places, events, or themes to be explored. When projects make an effort to engage the community, the research phase can help collect important background information that provides context for the project. On the other hand, if a project is focused on an emerging crisis, it may have limited time to engage in anything but the most basic background research. Nonetheless, initial joint research serves several purposes:

- It brings people together so they are all working from a common set of background materials toward a common goal.
- It makes participants aware of existing information and lays the groundwork for determining good oral history questions to fill in gaps in the historical record or to seek a deeper, more nuanced understanding of the matters at hand.
- It familiarizes interviewers with enough information about the subject to be able to keep the interview on track and spot the need for follow-up questions.
- It provides interviewers with details, such as names, dates, and places, which can facilitate a good interview.

BEGIN BACKGROUND RESEARCH

Research is essential for taking a project from the level of merely recording reminiscences to collecting the depth of information characteristic of good oral history. It is an important step even for those who are experts. Research helps define the project, provides background on topics to help explore them further, helps project leaders determine which topics are most important, suggests additional topics, and provides background information to inform interviewers so they will be as prepared as possible for the interview.

Planners can help with this stage of project development by pulling together a basic information packet for all participants. This packet—in hard copy, digital format, or a combination of both—can include copies of written histories, newspaper articles, maps, photographs, drawings, excerpts from letters, diaries, and other primary source materials. It can include as much information about the

Archival aide Michaela Peine working on archival and oral history materials for the Cathedral of St. Paul archives, St. Paul, Minnesota. *Used with permission.*

defined subject of the oral history project as planners deem necessary, but it should not be overwhelming. If a project, for example, involves documenting the experiences of Korean War veterans, it is not necessary to amass every book ever written about Korea or the Korean War. But summaries or published highlights of the war during the years project veterans were involved would help interviewers gain sufficient background to prepare an informed interview outline.

Internet access and powerful electronic tools for searching online databases are invaluable methods for quickly locating important and useful background information about nearly any topic imaginable. However, be aware of several potential electronic traps. First, unless the focus of your oral history project is fairly obscure or highly localized, searching the internet for material related to your project can lead to informational quicksand that will mire you in an overwhelming mass of related material that no one could hope to sort through, much less understand. So cull through the pages of links and pull out only the material that pertains specifically to

your project. Second, despite the appearance of providing a thorough search, internet inquiries will provide access only to information that someone has decided to put online. Valuable private collections of primary source materials—photographs, letters, personal papers, high school yearbooks, local community histories, and the like—may never be accessible electronically, but they could be like pay dirt when seeking background information for an oral history project. How do you locate such treasures? Mainly by asking around—local libraries, community museums, area history buffs—and getting lucky. One student, through a circuitous series of word-of-mouth recommendations, found a local resident with three-ring binders full of clippings, notes, photos, and other information about an aspect of the county's history that otherwise had all but vanished from public knowledge. Likewise, if a quick Google search of your oral history topic leaves you empty-handed, don't assume no background information is available. County courthouses, corporate archives, schools, community civic clubs, and endless other types of organizations keep records—many of which never will be electronically accessible but which may be available to oral historians who ask politely to see them as part of the process of collecting background research. Note, however, that marginalized communities often are poorly represented in some kinds of formalized documentary evidence. But communities themselves can often help fill information gaps in the background research process.

With the packet of information as a base, project participants may wish to do additional research. This can include visits to the public library, historical society, newspaper archives, local institutions, and other specific places that have materials relevant to the project. Depending on the topics, this may involve research in local, state, or national facilities or more online research. Project advisory board members may help by finding collections to review and in identifying possible topics. The goal of all background research is to give project participants, especially the interviewers, a good base of knowledge to use in the interviews. If interviewers are thoroughly prepared, they will be better able to engage with narrators, who, after all, are the experts in their own story. But because so much information can be available about some topics, planners will need to caution participants not to get bogged down at this stage by continually looking at yet one more source. Oral history interviewers need not become the world's living experts on topic X. Rather, they need to know enough about the topic to focus intelligently on the aspects of it that matter to their particular project.

Researchers may choose to make notes with pencil and paper, notecards, computers, or other electronic devices. In any case, it is always important to write down or enter any information that relates to the purpose of the oral history project. This includes names (with proper spellings), dates, facts, figures, and information (correct or incorrect) already on the record.[1] Interviewers will want to add to their basic packets any new information they find. All of this can help not only in defining interview topics but in later development of specific questions.

It is always important to document clearly the source of the information. Keeping unclear notes often results in having to go back to clarify things—a waste of time. Researchers often use smartphones to take pictures of pages of research, which archivists often encourage rather than photocopying. Such documents, when properly identified and cited, are often a helpful addition to a project's collections. Material also can be saved to shared electronic files if project participants will find that approach easy to use.

It is usually helpful to begin the research by looking into the areas of interest identified in the project's mission statement. Which information is already well documented? Is the documentation complete? Are there discrepancies or mysterious unanswered questions among various sources of information? What is already on the record? What information is missing or inaccurate and should be covered in an oral history interview? What is not documented well at all? How important is it to document that? What questions should be asked about a topic? What information comes to light that helps define each topic further?

Research will probably bring up new topics as well. As new topics come to light, they can be added to the list and the same questions applied to them. Reviewing the research that is collected will help project leaders determine what should be covered in the interviews and why this information should be collected.

Such a thorough approach to research may seem exhausting—and unnecessary—to community-engaged projects in which planners and likely interviewers and narrators already have firsthand knowledge of the subject at hand. But it is no less important than the research necessary for a project in which some of the participants are outsiders to the subject. Even for projects that grow out of community engagement, in which all the players may share certain experiences and interests, some basic research is still important. It enables everyone associated with the project to operate from the same basic set of facts. And equally important, including the research base in the project master files will lay a foundation for future users of the material to understand a project's origins. Such research also might uncover information in the published record that participants are unaware of or know to be false or incomplete and that can add new dimensions to the scope of the project.

COMPILE A BIBLIOGRAPHY

Project participants should keep a list of all information sources they use. This will be compiled as the project bibliography. It becomes an end product of the oral history project, and it serves as a reference tool for newcomers to the project and as a source for future researchers and others who want to know what background information created the foundation for the interviews.

DEVELOP AN OUTLINE RELATING TO THE INTERVIEW TOPIC

Using the background research, one person or a small group should develop an outline identifying milestones important to the topic. It may take the form of a simple timeline of dates, key events, and relevant players. It also might include a glossary of jargon and appropriate definitions of terms particular to the subject. Summarizing such basic information in a readily accessible form will help everyone to focus on the material. It also will result in a useful resource document. It can help guide continuing research because gaps in available information can become readily apparent, and it can help participants become familiar with vocabulary narrators are likely to use. When you're ready to begin the interviews, it also serves as a good interviewing tool.

USE THE RESEARCH TO BUILD AN INTERVIEW GUIDE

In addition to giving project participants information about the subject, general background research helps planners identify topics or areas where information is sketchy or ambiguous or reveals mysterious unanswered questions. These are all topics to cover in the oral history interviews. Oral history is used to document information—including opinions, interpretations, emotions, and points of view—that otherwise is unavailable and subject to loss. By familiarizing themselves with existing information, interviewers can identify gaps in what is already available and determine how to fill them through oral history.

> Developing a list of themes or topics is a first step in focusing an interview.

Background researchers should keep a list of topics either omitted or inadequately covered in the written materials and any other topic ideas to include in an interview. Coordinators should regularly look over these lists, analyzing how each topic relates to the mission statement, which sets parameters for the project to keep it in focus. All ideas that meet the criteria should be included on a master interview topic list that will form the basis for planning the oral history interviews.

The research process inevitably will uncover intriguing information about which project planners might have been unaware, and because a generic curiosity is a typical trait of oral history practitioners, it can be challenging not to keep adding themes to a project. But finite resources—financial, human, and time constraints—are a reality for most projects. So keeping the topics discovered during the research reined in so they relate to the mission statement is key to keeping a project focused. Limiting project themes to those envisioned in the mission statement does not mean new information that emerges through the research process should be ignored. The research, for example, might unearth new perspectives about the subject at hand that leads to a revised mission statement. Alternatively, information that might take the project in an entirely new direction could become the basis of a subsequent project that builds on the initial work.

This pre-interview research process might seem heavily focused on fact-finding: who did what to whom when. But fact-finding alone is seldom the focus of oral history interviews themselves. Rather, when interviewers and narrators sit down to co-create an oral history interview, a key focus likely will be on documenting why and how things happened and how narrators understand their experiences. But it is the background research that lays a foundation for the opinions, interpretation, and points of view the interview will document. New topics, of course, will emerge during the interviews, and familiarity with background research will help interviewers pursue that new information.

IDENTIFY POTENTIAL NARRATORS AND DETERMINE THEMES OR TOPICS TO COVER WITH EACH OF THEM

General project research is an essential way to identify potential narrators. Although you might know from the outset some of the people you'll want to interview, general background research often leads to others whose knowledge is essential to project success. Background research will also help identify additional, perhaps previously unknown, types of information needed to fill gaps in knowledge and understanding, leading project coordinators to seek out potential narrators who can fill those gaps. The background research also can help you decide which people might have enough information for several interview sessions, while others might require only a shorter, single interview session.

As a rule of thumb, be conservative in planning the number of interviews you can complete. If your initial goal is to interview everyone whose name surfaces, the task will be so daunting that everyone involved will be frustrated and defeated from the start. Instead, begin with no more than three to five interviews—up to ten hours of recordings. Set a goal of ensuring these are well researched, well structured, and fully processed. When this is done, look realistically at what it took to meet this goal and determine what is manageable for your group to complete additional interviews. A handful of well-done interviews can inspire confidence in the project and energize participants to keep going. Having something concrete to show for your efforts also can generate more financial support for future work.

Oral history focuses on collecting firsthand knowledge. As such, narrators should be selected because of their knowledge about the interview themes and topics. They also should represent a variety of perspectives and backgrounds. In fact, an oral history project often specifically intends to seek out perspectives that are not already on the record. This will enhance the results of your oral history project, broadening the base of information you collect.

Community-engaged oral history projects in particular may choose to focus on a specific perspective about the issue at hand precisely *because* a particular point of view has been ignored or otherwise omitted from public discourse. In such cases, it might be more challenging to identify a range of narrators whose identities are not already in the public record, but often they will be people who are widely known within the community.

A project Edward Nelson and Robert "Skip" Drake and others developed in the 1980s in Minnesota to collect information about the Civilian Conservation Corps, for example, easily could have used all of its available resources interviewing the hundreds of men who enrolled in the Depression-era camps. The network was still strong, relatively little documentation was on the written record about enrollees' time in the Civilian Conservation Corps camps, and narrators could be found quickly because many were willing to tell their stories. But they could only tell one part of the story. So the oral history project included others, such as US Army personnel who ran the work camps in which the enrollees lived; representatives from the agencies that developed the projects on which enrollees worked, including former forest service personnel and US Army personnel, and others involved with various projects or agencies; adult work leaders and crew leaders assigned to supervise enrollees at work; and members of racial or ethnic groups who were or were not always welcomed into the camps. Making an effort to include many perspectives from people involved in all sides of the issues enhances a project and gives it the depth that characterizes good oral history.

Lists of possible narrators are sometimes easily compiled. At other times, it can take considerable legwork to find people who have firsthand knowledge about the project's themes or topics and who are good prospective narrators. In addition to relying on project research to identify possible narrators, community engagement—whether formal or informal—can add to the list. Depending on the subject, informal networks can generate a long list of possible narrators that will have to be winnowed down to a manageable size.

Good narrators for an oral history interview are people who:

- have firsthand, previously undocumented information or perspectives about project topics or themes;
- have strong powers of observation;
- can articulate their thoughts and memories effectively;
- are willing to participate, including signing a donor form; and

- are reasonably comfortable with interview equipment in either audio or video settings.

Narrators inevitably bring their own biases to project topics or themes. Their memories also reflect their perspectives on what happened and why, the ways in which they have organized their understanding of the past, and their frames of reference on what is or is not important. They are also often influenced by thoughts and ideas that have occurred since the event or time period. Narrators are chosen for a project because their views about it are important. Each narrator brings a unique perspective to the project's topics or themes; collectively, those perspectives enrich the historical record.

It often helps to think about choosing possible narrators in terms of the information each can bring to your project. Narrators may be chosen for knowledge about a certain time period or because they represent a certain perspective about an event related to the themes or topics. They may be chosen because they have a long-term perspective, although it is never necessary to interview the oldest people around just because they are old. They may be chosen because of their knowledge about the themes or topics. It is also not always necessary to interview the most visible local historian or the most prominent person associated with an event. Often, in fact, such local notables have either told or written their stories many times and those accounts are already part of the existing record. Sometimes they have repeated the stories so often, almost as a rehearsed performance, that it's impossible for them to explore the event more deeply, which ideally is what you want in a good oral history interview. Project coordinators should instead look for people who have firsthand knowledge and are willing to communicate this information clearly and effectively, answering the interviewer's questions to the best of their ability. Often, they may be people who have information about just one theme or one aspect of the project but whose perspective is nonetheless central to fully exploring the topic.

Oral history projects seeking to cast a wide net to identify potential narrators could consider crowdsourcing names by reaching out through social media or other means to seek participants with a particular connection to the subject at hand. Other projects might consider a narrower approach to finding narrators by issuing press releases or targeted public announcements designed to reach particular audiences. Such approaches could yield large lists of potential narrators, but they also pose challenges. Such forms of outreach need to make clear that not everyone who steps forward will be asked to participate in an interview, unless a project has unlimited resources. And some people who respond may not, in fact, be able to contribute to the project. Project staff or volunteers might expend considerable time weeding through names of potential narrators, so casting a wide net for participants should be approached with caution, unless a project is designed to be permanent, ongoing, and always ready to interview anyone who makes themselves available, an approach that might not serve a project's purpose.

The names of potential narrators can be put into a pool for consideration. Depending on your project's resources, you'll likely have to make some choices. The most helpful approach is to set priorities, identifying narrators you think are most critical to include and working down the list as resources are available. Although you could identify additional criteria based on the needs of a project, a person's ability to provide information about the interview topics may be the primary factor when choosing narrators. Using this as a guide to match potential narrators to interview topics about which they are most knowledgeable will help organize the project and will ensure inclusion of narrators whose information is most useful.

Project planners generally decide who will be interviewed. Although supporters and others interested in the project will have ideas about potential narrators, people who have been involved in the research and community members engaged in planning are in the best position to know whom to interview, based on project priorities. Names of potential narrators will continue to surface as the project progresses, and the narrator list and priorities could change as a project evolves.

Once possible narrators have been identified, project coordinators begin contacting them, requesting their involvement in the project. This is best done by letter or email, although a telephone call might be appropriate if the individual knows they are likely to be interviewed for the project. Otherwise, a written communication is best because it allows potential narrators to receive a clear explanation of the project and background about their expected involvement.[2] A sample letter, along with samples of other suggested correspondence, is included in appendix B. The designated interviewer usually follows up the letter with a telephone call. This provides an opportunity for the interviewer and narrator to talk informally, allows the interviewer to answer additional questions, and gives the narrator a chance to make a verbal commitment to be interviewed. Some narrators, when first contacted, may be unsure of their ability to contribute effectively to the project. The telephone call can allow the interviewer to address these questions and concerns.

But what about oral history projects that involve communities or individuals who do not have computer access or telephones or who have limited literacy or uncertain citizenship status or who are struggling with the aftermath of a natural disaster or other potentially traumatic or marginalized or vulnerable experiences? Oral historians who are involved in such communities clearly are not going to be contacting potential narrators by letter or email. They are more likely to be working with narrators alongside other community members also involved in the project. Similarly, oral historians engaged in real-time or crisis oral history are, by definition, focused on the immediacy of connecting with narrators, so they likely will use more informal approaches to identify narrators depending upon the realities of the situation.

After the first narrators have agreed to be a part of the project, interviewers should begin narrator-specific research. This step creates the structure for the interview. An interviewer should work on only one interview at a time, selecting or being assigned narrators in priority order from the pool of names.

Narrator-specific research helps structure an interview.

Narrator-specific research involves learning as much as possible about the person to be interviewed and their role in the subject at hand. This may include such details as work history, personal history, family history, political history—anything that gives the interviewer the necessary background to engage the narrator with good project-related questions and appropriate follow-up. Such research also helps build rapport between interviewer and narrator as they co-create the interview. Interviewers can turn to a variety of background materials to become fully informed, particularly if potential narrators are somewhat well known. This often includes online research as well as trips to the historical society, library, or other locations containing resource information. It may also include review of maps, visits to sites that are important to the interview, and additional work with primary sources. As with the general background research, it is important not to become bogged down in the wealth of information that might be available about some narrators. In other cases, it might be difficult to find documented information about a specific narrator. The project's biographical information form can be filled out prior to the interview as a way for interviewers to learn about narrators' backgrounds. If a project involves potentially vulnerable narrators, however, interviewers abide by whatever plans have been made to protect narrators, such as using pseudonyms or limiting access to identifiable biographical details. In any case, narrator-specific research can focus on the context of the narrator's background to give the interviewer as much knowledge as possible.

Unlikely Multidisciplinary Experiment Creates Oral Histories

On college campuses, history departments aren't the only places to find oral history projects. At the University of Nebraska-Lincoln, an unlikely interdisciplinary group of faculty experimented with creating oral histories through an elective course promoted to agriculture majors, journalism students, and anyone else who was interested.

Supported by the university's Rural Futures Institute, the experiment focused on creative civic engagement and community outreach, a reflection of a land-grant university's public mission. Four faculty from the university's College of Agricultural Sciences and Natural Resources, College of Fine and Performing Arts, College of Journalism and Mass Communications, and the Lied Center for Performing Arts created a special topics course that achieved the following over two years:

- Resulted in student-created oral history interviews with more than a dozen Nebraska century farmers whose land had been in their families for one hundred years or more.
- Explored the role of agriculture and rural communities through history, literature, and the arts.
- Involved the production of a new musical, *Catherland*, set in author Willa Cather's hometown, Red Cloud, Nebraska. Written by one of the faculty members and performed in several rural communities, the production gave students a behind-the-scenes look at how professional theater goes from page to stage.
- Led to publication of *Pioneer Farms: A Century of Change*, a collection of excerpts from the oral histories illustrating major themes that emerged from the interviews.

DEVELOP AN INTERVIEW OUTLINE OR GUIDE

Oral history project planners and interviewers often find it useful to think of a three-part research funnel that guides development of the interview content. First, at the mouth of the funnel, is the thirty-thousand-foot view of overarching themes that emerge in the research process. Then, within each theme are topics, or smaller building blocks within the larger theme. And finally, within each topic is the development of specific, focused questions, which often relies on narrator-specific research.

The Oral History Association's publication *Doing Veterans Oral History* offers some clear examples. It suggests that an interview guide developed for an interview with a military veteran might include these overarching themes: "entering military service, daily life in military service, assignments in military service, service in a combat zone, life after military service, reflections about military service."[3]

While those are overarching themes, each one can be subdivided into narrower topics. For example, entering military service might include the following topics:

- Brief description—life before military service
- Entering military service and choice of military branch
- Training[4]

Finally, each of the specific topics can be fleshed out in greater detail with specific questions. Using the same theme and its topics, here are some examples:

- Talk about your life before going into the service. Education? Work experience?

- Describe any family military background/traditions.
  - Any other family members in service? Who? When? Why/why not?
  - Family response to you going into service.

- Tell me about when, why you went into service, and what branch.
  - Enlisted? Drafted? How did it all come about?
  - Recollections about taking the oath?
  - First days in the military.

- Basic training—when and where?
  - Most memorable moments.
  - Particular skills? Special trainings?
  - What did you learn about military life? Experiences that stand out?[5]

The biographical information you collect about individual narrators will guide development of specific questions. In this example, you likely will already have found out the service branch in which the person served as well as training details or particulars of the person's military service. So, while this example includes fairly generic questions, your interview guide for a particular individual might be more detailed. Note, however, that it's not necessary to write questions out word for word. Phrases and keywords are sufficient to help keep you on track as you work through the interview.

Here's another example from a student project aimed at documenting information about one state's century farms, those that had been continuously in the same family for one hundred years or more. The narrators were all men and women who were members of the second or third generation to live on the family farm and who were either children or teenagers during the Great Depression and Dust Bowl years. Overarching themes included original founding of the farm, technological changes in agriculture, and day-to-day life on the farm. Here is an example of topics and selected questions developed within the theme of technological changes in agriculture:

- Farm equipment
  - Transition from horses to mechanized equipment
  - Evolution/adoption of mechanized equipment—bigger size? More expensive? Impact on farming practices?

- Irrigation
  - Suitability of land for irrigation on this farm
  - Availability of water source—impact of Bureau of Reclamation dam building, irrigation canals?
  - Development of center-pivot irrigation technology—cost? Benefits? Suitability for particular land profile? Impact on crop varieties?
  - Water conservation efforts? Impact on farming practices?

- Electricity
  - Life on farm without electricity
  - Impact of creation of Rural Electrification Administration (1935, part of Franklin D. Roosevelt's New Deal)
  - Process for bringing electricity to rural places; when did this farm get it?
  - Impact of having electricity—on agricultural operations? Daily life?

- Hybrid seeds
  - Typical production levels before hybrid seeds
  - Earliest examples of using hybrids—pros/cons? When adopted here?
  - Impact of hybrids on agricultural practices? Farm income?[6]

As with the veterans interview guide, specific questions would be customized to reflect narrator-level research. So questions about using hybrid seeds, for example, would not be relevant for a cattle rancher who did not raise crops. In all cases, the interviewer will want to add follow-up questions that aren't necessarily on the interview guide, depending on how the narrator responds. Also note in both examples that it's not necessary to write questions out word for word. Phrases and keywords are sufficient to help keep you on track as you work through the interview. And when questions are written out as complete sentences, interviewers may be tempted to recite them word for word like a telemarketer, an inappropriate tone for an oral history interview.

The funnel approach of theme-topic-question can become more elaborate depending on the nature of the oral history project, with subtopics and questions for each subtopic. But as a general rule, try to avoid making the interview guide more complex than necessary. Committing to a highly structured question guide can have the unintended consequence of straightjacketing an interview and preventing the narrator from volunteering information that otherwise doesn't seem to fit into the predetermined format.

> An interview guide or outline is the list of topics and notes about questions specific to the narrator's knowledge. The interviewer uses the outline to guide the interview.

As the examples illustrate, many interviewers find that approaching topics chronologically is helpful, since that is often how people remember their experiences. If the questions are likely to include emotionally charged or sensitive topics, it's usually best to plan for those later in the interview, after the interviewer has had a chance to establish rapport with the narrator. The interviewer should use the outline to guide the interview but should be prepared to follow the narrator's train of thought and remain flexible in how and when topics are introduced. Narrators, after all, always have agency over how they tell their own stories.

The interview guide should reflect the purpose of the project. For example, if the focus of an interview is on a person's experiences as a nurse in the Vietnam War, the interviewer probably would not take interview time to ask detailed, in-depth questions about union involvement or farming activities, though the person may have considerable firsthand information on those subjects, too. Similarly, any pre-interview contacts or correspondence with the narrator would make clear that the Vietnam War nursing experiences will be the focus of the interview. Based on what is already known about the designated subject of an oral history project, the interviewer will want to concentrate on eliciting information the narrator can add that fits overall project goals.

The interview guide usually contains as much information as the interviewer needs for the interview. This can include research notes about names, places, dates, or any other details that will help jog the narrator's memory. It's best, however, to stay away from making the guide so voluminous that the interviewer spends more time shuffling notes and looking for details than asking questions and listening to the answers.

Interviewers familiarize themselves with everything in the interview guide and know the reasons for including each topic and how each fits into the overall project structure. They also, however, need to be prepared to hear new firsthand information and ask follow-up questions to clarify anything they don't understand. It's also important for the interviewer to be flexible, because a narrator might want to talk about things in a different order than listed on the interview guide. However the interview unfolds, the guide is a way to ensure all topics have been fully covered. Finally, interviewers should avoid including their own opinions about what they think, either on the interview guide or during the interview. An interviewer's role, however, is not that of a passive audience recording without question whatever a narrator says. Oral history interviews are co-created by knowledgeable, prepared interviewers and narrators identified for their knowledge of the subject at hand. So interviewers aim to pin down information, ask pointed questions, play devil's advocate, and probe beneath the surface for new information about the interview topics.

SCHEDULE THE INTERVIEW

When nearing completion of the narrator-specific research and development of the interview guide, the interviewer can then contact the narrator to schedule the interview, using whatever methods are appropriate. This may be done by telephone but usually is followed up, as appropriate, with a letter or email confirming date, time, and location. The letter typically includes a request for a photograph of the narrator, if available, for the master file.

Oral history projects can include a face-to-face pre-interview or, more commonly, a preliminary telephone contact with potential narrators at this point. This involves a short general discussion with the person about the interview and gives the interviewers a chance to introduce themselves to the narrator, which helps build rapport. Some interviewers like to collect biographical information from the narrator at this point. It also provides an opportunity to answer any further questions about the oral history project and to explain the recording process and the use of the donor form. And it can be a good time to discuss the interview topics and offer examples of the kinds of information the interview will cover. Some oral historians have found that giving narrators lists of specific questions to be asked results in rehearsed responses or even, as some interviewers have found, a narrator who has written out answers that they will then want to just read into the microphone rather than engaging in the back and forth of an oral history interview. Other oral historians have found that

providing more rather than less information about the planned substance of the interview is a better approach and avoids leaving the impression the interviewer will be springing questions on the narrator. Sharing the complete interview guide, however, could lead some narrators to think the interviewer isn't interested in anything that doesn't appear on the guide, even though it might add important details and additional depth to the interview. If your project, however, involves interviewing potentially vulnerable narrators or those who have experienced traumatic events in their lives, sharing a list of questions in advance can prevent narrators from being caught off guard and also can let them indicate if there are things they don't want to talk about.[7] Interviewers generally try to discourage narrators in a pre-interview discussion from launching into telling specific information to be covered in the interview. If that happens and you then ask for the information again in the interview, the narrator often either refers to the earlier conversation rather than answering the question or repeats the story in a less lively way than you heard it initially.

CHOOSE THE SETUP FOR THE INTERVIEW

A face-to-face pre-interview meeting also can serve another important purpose: it allows the interviewer to check out the setting where the interview will take place. Many oral history interviews occur in the narrator's home, a familiar environment that can have a positive effect on the interview. Schools, museums, places of business, libraries, even recording studios are other common interview locations, and each has its own advantages and disadvantages. The goal is to conduct oral history interviews in places where you can control sound (and visual) quality to the extent possible and where the narrator and interviewer will not be interrupted. Business offices, for example, are appropriate places for interviews only if the narrator can prevent telephone or other interruptions. Whatever the setting, it should be a place where the narrator will be comfortable and where the setting itself does not create distractions or make the narrator ill at ease. (See the following checklists for details about the mechanics of setting up an oral history interview.)

Thinking through the setting is an important part of the process, for it can affect the outcome of the interview. As an example, one community embarked on a project documenting the installation of missiles in its vicinity during the height of the Cold War. Because project planners were interested in creating both audio and video recordings, they decided to do most of the interviews in the city library, either in a public studio there or an adjoining reserved room. The same topics and themes were covered in all the interviews, and the choices about who was to be interviewed in which setting were based

Park Ranger Rose Masters interviewing Hiroshima survivor Hisae Genie Obana in June 2017. Genie, born in California and a US citizen, moved to Japan with her parents just before WWII; her sister, also a US citizen, spent the war years in a Japanese internment camp. Manzanar oral history project, Manzanar War Relocation Center (Japanese Internment Camp), Manzanar National Historic Site, California, National Park Service. *NPS Photo.*

primarily on the availability of the narrators. One person specifically did not want to be interviewed on camera at the library, and another would agree only to an audio interview at home. While the setting of an interview is unlikely to be the sole factor contributing to particular narrator behavior or responses, the project leaders noted some curious differences in interview content that seemed to be related to the interview setting. The video interviews in the studio at the public library featured repeated tellings of the more dominant public side of the story expressing support for the missile installations. Interviews in the adjoining room, in which there was no video and only the interviewer and narrator were present, produced a less commonly voiced private side of the story, including expressions of fears for the future. And the narrator who insisted on being interviewed at home recalled active resistance to the missile installation, reflecting what had been a decidedly minority viewpoint in the community and one that even many years after the fact was not widely acknowledged in public.

Did the more public, formal setting, complete with interviewer and camera operator, lend itself to eliciting the popular public narrative about the missile installation? Did a non-threatening home environment with only an interviewer present create a safety zone for the narrator to express an unpopular view? One can never be certain. But the narrators' responses at least suggest that the context in which an interview takes place—including the presence or absence of video—is an important element affecting an interview's content and character.

PRACTICE WITH THE RECORDING EQUIPMENT

Interviewers should be thoroughly trained on using the recording equipment and should practice with it repeatedly before using it for the first time in an interview. They should know how to use it unobtrusively and with confidence and how to handle minor difficulties in the field. Always begin by reading the manual that comes with the equipment. It will help you understand what all the dials,

> Always remember to practice using the recorder before the interview.

switches, and buttons mean and how each works to control the recording process. You will want to know how to set sound levels and how to troubleshoot.

Remember that the microphone is a critical part of the recording process and has capabilities and limitations with which the interviewer needs to be familiar. Some researchers who do other kinds of field recordings focus the microphone primarily on the narrator with less emphasis on hearing the interviewer's questions. But in an oral history interview, the exchanges between the interviewer and narrator are critical to understanding the information that emerges. So it is important to record both speakers, documenting clearly both sides of the interview. This helps future users understand the context of the interview and, thus, the information in it.

If you will be conducting interviews by Zoom or other remote access tools, see chapter 5 for technical considerations to handle in such interviews. Whenever possible, practice a dry-run connection with your narrator so you can troubleshoot any glitches that might arise, and encourage your narrator to use a neutral, uncluttered background if the session will be video recorded.

HEAD OUT FOR THE INTERVIEW

You're almost ready now for the next big step: conducting the oral history interview. All the planning so far is aimed at making the process flow as smoothly as possible. Some oral history projects put interview kits together that include all the necessary tools. Such a kit can include:

- recorder;
- microphone, cables, and microphone stand;
- AC adapter/transformer and extension cord;
- media (it is wise to take more than you could possibly need);
- batteries;
- notebook (often in an easy-to-use "steno" format, six by nine inches);
- pencils;
- folder containing the donor form (two copies—one for the master file and one to leave with the narrator), the interview guide, the biographical information form, and copies of correspondence with the narrator;
- camera to take a picture of the narrator in interview setting (this is necessary for audio interviews and is helpful to add to the master file for video interviews); and

- a package of tissues if the interview participants become emotional.

Also give some thought to your attire. What will make narrators feel most comfortable with interviewers? The Shoah Foundation advises, for example, that interviewers in some cases cover any tattoos, which "carry significant historical meaning in relation to the Holocaust and Cambodian Genocide, for example."[8]

Finally, arrive on time. A prompt arrival will start the process on the right foot. If there has not been a pre-interview meeting, this may be the first time the interviewer and narrator meet, in which case it is even more important not to be late.

Preparation for the interviews is not glamorous. Nor is it as exciting as the actual interview. Without adequate preparation, however, the oral history interview will not fulfill its potential.

CHECKLIST FOR SETTING UP AN AUDIO INTERVIEW

✓ The narrator is in a comfortable spot where they can relax and focus on the interview and where the narrator and interviewer will not be interrupted.

✓ Pay special attention to the audible environment. Be sure that the narrator's chair doesn't squeak or make other noises and that other audible distractions—pets that bark, meow, or chirp; chiming clocks; dishwashers; telephones; lawn mowers; and the like—are minimized. People will tune out such extraneous noises, but recorders will faithfully record them all. Ask the narrator to turn off mobile phones or other devices, and be sure to turn yours off, too. Recognize, however, that in some circumstances creating a recording-studio-quality audio setting is simply not possible, in which case, do your best and stay flexible.

✓ The interviewer should sit no more than about six feet away, facing the narrator. The two should be able to hear each other clearly and maintain eye contact.

✓ Use a table or other sturdy surface next to the interviewer to hold the recorder within easy reach to monitor it and make adjustments as necessary. It is best to position the recorder out of the narrator's direct line of vision so they will focus on the interviewer, not the equipment, but *never* hide it from view. Oral historians do not engage in clandestine recording.

✓ An omnidirectional microphone should be placed no more than two or three feet from and pointed at the narrator. Carry a long enough microphone cable to facilitate the best placement of the microphone and recorder.

✓ If lavalier microphones are used, clip one on the interviewer and one on the narrator, each about ten inches from the speaker's mouth. Remove jewelry, scarves, or jackets made of crisp fabrics. All can cause rustling noises as the speakers move. (For more details about microphone choices, see chapter 5.)

✓ Plug the audio recorder into a wall or floor outlet whenever possible, bringing long extension cords to facilitate this. Be sure to place extension cords in such a way that no one will trip on them.

✓ Carry back-up batteries for the recorder to use in emergencies or where electrical outlets are unavailable or impractical to use.

✓ Decline offers of food or drink. While interviewers will want to be sociable, an oral history interview is not, strictly speaking, a social occasion. Coffee cups, ice in glasses, pop tops on cans being opened, and other food or drink consumption all make noise the recorder will pick up. Narrators will understand if you explain to them that you want to minimize any extraneous noise that might mar the sound quality of the recorded interview.

✓ Do a sound check with the equipment to be sure it is working properly and the voices are being picked up clearly. Keep it simple by asking the narrator to give their name and chatting about something neutral while checking recording levels. Fussing over the equipment can make an interviewer nervous.

✓ Use headphones to continuously monitor the sound, allowing you to identify and correct any problems.

CHECKLIST FOR SETTING UP A VIDEO INTERVIEW

✓ Read and follow the checklist for setting up an audio interview. Many of the considerations for arranging the interview setting are the same for both formats.

✓ Refer to the section of chapter 5 that discusses the questions to consider in determining how or whether video recording will enhance the oral history.

✓ Unless a video interview will take place in a studio or other controlled setting, plan to visit the site in advance, preferably with people who will be operating the camera, microphones, lights, or any other equipment that will be needed for the recording session.

✓ Because a video interview may involve more staff, who generally may be paid, and possibly rented locations such as production studios, consider developing a more detailed interview guide to ensure the best use of a specific block of time. You may not be able to extend the interview even if the narrator has important things still to say, so try to make sure the interview covers all the essentials in the allotted time.

✓ Indoor video interviews should be shot in soft light that appropriately illuminates the setting. Avoid overhead lighting, which results in poor quality video.

The narrator should not sit in front of a window or other source of natural light.[9]

✓ The background setting should not overwhelm the narrator. Studio backdrops, like dark curtains, may sometimes be available, but in a person's home or place of business, try not to place the narrator in front of a blank wall. It may help to add visual depth to the recorded image if you pull the narrator's chair slightly away from a wall or backdrop. In any event, check that items in the background—lamps, potted plants, pictures on walls, and the like—do not appear to be sprouting out of the narrator's head.

✓ Always frame the shot so it is in focus with the narrator centered in the picture and at eye level with the camera, a psychologically and emotionally neutral position. Give the narrator what videographers call "head room" and "look space," meaning the camera is not at too close range.

✓ A head shot from the mid-chest or shoulders is customary; never cut the person visually at the neck, waist, or knees.

✓ If more than one narrator is in the video interview, position everyone so all their faces are clearly visible and so that the interviewer can maintain eye contact with all of them. This is sometimes done using a V format, with the interviewer sitting on the open end facing the narrators.

✓ Narrators should be asked to wear uncluttered clothing in neutral or dark colors. White shirts and blouses reflect light and make filming natural skin tones difficult.

✓ The camera should be placed on a tripod to assure stability and focused on the narrator with little or no change in the camera beyond the essentials to capture movement once the shot has been framed.

✓ Even though the camera has a zoom lens, do not zoom in and out on the narrator. This is a televised interview technique that oral historians do not use. Instead, use the zoom lens for close-ups of photographs or other materials you wish to document as part of the interview.

✓ The interviewer's questions should be heard clearly, but an interviewer generally is not seen, unless the interview is being conducted in sign language. The interviewer should be positioned to look directly at the narrator, with the camera over the interviewer's shoulder. If project coordinators want the interviewer to be seen, a second camera will be needed because one camera always should be on the narrator.

✓ When filming on location, be aware that lighting and background sound elements can change during the video recording, so plan for such possibilities. Always stop the interview if noise from airplanes, highways, farm machinery, or other intrusive sounds occur and wait for conditions to return to normal.

✓ Record video interviews simultaneously on audio equipment to be used for transcribing and as an archival back-up of the interview.

✓ Project planners usually choose to video record interviews when the physical environment illustrates important interview information, so be sure to video record the setting, including specific items or places, before or after the interview.

✓ Still photographs or three-dimensional objects that are to be documented as part of the video process should be propped up on a stand against a black background.

Remember that video interviews, just like their audio counterparts, are primary source documents; they will not look like a scripted, polished documentary. Audio and video interview excerpts often are used effectively in documentaries and other productions, but the interviews themselves should be kept intact and handled as primary source material.

NOTES

1. David Kyvig, Myron Marty, and Larry Cebula include several chapters of helpful, commonsense research guidelines in their book, *Nearby History: Exploring the Past around You*, fourth edition (Lanham, MD: Rowman & Littlefield Publishers, 2019).

2. Pioneering oral historian Martha Ross was fond of telling students at the University of Maryland that initial contact with potential narrators always should be in writing. "Almost no one," she would say, "is standing by their phone waiting to be asked to participate in an oral history interview." So an out-of-the-blue call is likely to be met with uncertainty and confusion, not an ideal way to begin an oral history relationship.

3. Barbara W. Sommer, *Doing Veterans Oral History* (Atlanta, GA: Oral History Association, 2015), 22.

4. Ibid, 23.

5. Ibid, 26.

6. The Pioneer Farms Oral History Project was conducted at the University of Nebraska-Lincoln in 2015 and 2016. Excerpts from the interviews were published in *Pioneer Farms: A Century of Change* (Lincoln, NE: Rural Futures Institute, 2017).

7. For a detailed discussion, see USC Shoah Foundation, "Interviewer Guidelines," University of Southern California, 2021; and Sarah C. Bishop, *A Story to Save Your Life: Communication and Culture in Migrants' Search for Asylum* (New York: Columbia University Press, 2022).

8. USC Shoah Foundation, "Interviewer Guidelines," University of Southern California, 2021, 8.

9. For more information about lighting video interviews, see "The Art of Lighting for Recording Video Oral History Interviews," in *Oral History in the Digital Age*, edited by Douglas A. Boyd, Steve Cohen, Brad Rakerd, and Dean Rehberger (Washington, DC: Institute of Museum and Library Services, 2012), http://ohda.matrix.msu.edu/2012/06/the-art-of-lighting-for-recording-video/, accessed December 6, 2023.

7

The Interview

At last you're ready to begin the interview, the most visible part of an oral history project. Good interviewing techniques are integral to its success. In this chapter, we suggest a model for conducting an oral history interview. While the model reflects a common approach to oral history interviewing, it is certainly not the only approach interviewers might use. Nonetheless, people new to oral history often can gain confidence by using such a guide as they develop their interviewing skills and perfect approaches that work for them. We also will then review additional techniques interviewers find useful and discuss special interviewing circumstances. Keep in mind that oral history interviews are exchanges between specific individuals and are, by definition, unique experiences. Over time, interviewers may adapt

these techniques to what works best for them and for the reality of any given situation.

GETTING THE INTERVIEW UNDER WAY

After you have organized the interview setting, you will want to ask the narrators if they have any questions before the interview begins.

This is a good time to review the language in the donor form and to let the narrators know they will be asked to sign it as soon as the interview is over. Some interviewers also take this time to ask narrators to fill out a biographical information form to keep a record of the person's name, address, and other particulars, as appropriate. (A sample biographical information form is in appendix B.) After an equipment sound check, the interviewer will want to begin with a recorded introduction, such as: *The following interview was conducted with _____ (name of narrator) on behalf of the _____ for the _____ Oral History Project. It took place on _____ (date) at _____ (place). The interviewer is _____ (name).*

The recorded introduction also names and identifies everyone whose voices will be recorded or who is in attendance. Some interviews, for example, rely on translators if interviewers and narrators do not share the same language. In other cases, an elderly narrator, for example, may wish to have a family member be part of the interview. Even if that person isn't expected to play an active role in the recording session, it makes more sense to introduce the participant at the outset rather than having to stop to introduce a new speaker who interjects a comment as the interview progresses. Additional descriptive information about the project may be given as part of the introduction but is not necessary. The introduction should be brief, to the point, and thorough. Adding too much information

---

The Interview Setting

Remember to keep the interview setting as comfortable as possible. This will help the narrator concentrate on the interview.

It is important to establish rapport with the narrator. A sense of trust between narrator and interviewer helps make a good interview.

Listen (and look) carefully for noise sources, such as ringing phones and chiming clocks, that will undermine the sound quality of the interview.

Take a little time with the narrator before beginning the interview to talk and relax.

Always be on time for an interview.

The interviewer should always record an introduction before starting the interview. It should include the following:

- Name of narrator
- Name of interviewer
- Place of interview
- Date of interview
- Name of oral history project
- Name of repository
- Media or track number

This is usually done in the interview setting and is a signal to the narrator that the interview is ready to begin.

ilar introduction should begin each subsequent recording session, even with the same narrator, to avoid orphaned recordings whose identifying features are lost.

As a rule of thumb, the interviews generally unfold in chronological order and are structured to elicit not only facts about the time, place, or event that is the focus of the interview, but especially the narrator's thoughts about and analysis of the subject at hand.[1] Even if an interview focuses on a specific subject or event, the interviewer usually begins with questions about personal background. This should be brief, but it is a good way to start virtually every interview because the questions are easy for the narrator to answer, and it provides a context for evaluating subsequent information the narrator gives. Some interviewers have found that initial questions about a narrator's work experience prove useful in getting a reticent narrator to relax, open up, and talk freely about past experiences. Particularly when dealing with potentially vulnerable narrators, asking about their backgrounds at the outset of interviews also avoids stereotyping or painting them as "one-dimensional victims or heroes" in connection with the subject.[2]

about the expected interview topics could give the impression that the interviewer is not interested in information on other topics that, when brought up, could lead to interesting, important, new, and pertinent information. A sim-

Tracey Williams-Dillard, chief executive officer and publisher of the *Minnesota Spokesman-Recorder*, with interviewer Carson Tomony, in an interview for the Minnesota's Daily Newspaper Environment Oral History Project, 2023. The photo was taken in Williams-Dillard's office, originally the office of her grandfather, Cecil Newman, founder of the paper in 1934. The interviews may be found on the website of the Hennepin History Museum (https://hennepinhistory.org/). *Photographer Chris Juhm. Used with permission.*

Chapter 7

After these background questions, move to the interview topics, beginning with when, how, and why the narrator initially became involved with the subject or event. This sets the stage for the narrator to tell the story from the beginning. Then move to questions about the subject or event. Prompted by open-ended questions, the narrators will talk about what happened, what they did or observed, and what others did.

After listening to the narrator's account, a thoroughly prepared interviewer will be able to explore the information further and attempt to clarify any apparent contradictions with other written or spoken accounts uncovered in the prior research. Exploring contradictions, not necessarily resolving them, can be a key outcome of an oral history interview. Our understanding of the past is enriched by looking at events or actions from different perspectives. Narrators also will sometimes contradict themselves, and if they do, interviewers should strive for clarification by calling attention to the apparent contradictions.[3] Sometimes it will turn out that a narrator simply misspoke. But in other cases, a narrator's response can offer fascinating insights into how the person tries to reconstruct and make sense of the past—one of the multiple layers of meaning that can be embedded in an oral history interview.

Finally, ask the narrators to assess the experience or event. Why did things happen as they did? What did the narrators think about it then? What do they think about it now? Asking for a narrator's analysis and reflections obtains insight into their thinking, another important aspect of oral history. Pragmatically, it also signals that the interview is winding down and provides for a graceful closing.[4]

Interviewers working with one person on a series of life interviews will follow the same process of beginning with questions that are easy for the narrator to answer, then moving to the subject of the interview, and finally assessing the information as each interview session winds down. Life interviews are often organized around specific periods in the person's life. This gives each interview session a focus for both interviewer and narrator.

While an interviewer generally prepares a chronological outline to guide an interview, it's worth noting that not everyone recalls information or recounts stories in chronological order. Adept interviewers are prepared to be guided by whatever approach narrators—as co-creators of the oral history—take to telling their stories. Regardless of the structure in which an interview unfolds, it can be helpful for both interviewer and narrator to be sure that by the end of the interview session they have covered all the themes they intended to document.

Interviewing Tips

Use open-ended questions: "Tell me about . . ." "Describe . . ."

Don't be judgmental or let your own opinions show. The interview is the narrator's time to tell their story.

Use your background research to prompt the narrator as necessary. Reminders of names, dates, places, and events are helpful.

Ask about thoughts and feelings. It is the subjective information that helps make oral history such an interesting primary source.

Don't interrupt the narrator. Wait until they are finished to ask another question.

Be prepared to ask follow-up questions to clarify information.

Don't argue with the narrator's information. If you question its accuracy, politely ask the narrator for greater elaboration. You may find the narrator's story actually sets the written record straight.

Be thoroughly familiar with the research and the topics you intend to pursue. It breaks the rhythm of the interview to be constantly referring to the interview outline or to other notes.

Know how to operate the recording equipment. Practice repeatedly before the interview and always do a sound check before beginning.

Thank the narrator when finished. Follow this with a written thank-you letter.

Land Stories: Farming and Kaua'i Culture

Land Stories, founded by oral historian Angela Zusman, is a collaboration between several local organizations in Kaua'i under the guidance of Hawaiian spiritual adviser Kumu Kauilani Kahalekai. The narrators for this project are individuals with personal lived experience farming or taking care of land on Kaua'i's south shore in the Kōloa and Po'ipū regions. Native Hawaiians tended the land for centuries, creating sophisticated water systems and a farm culture where everyone had the ability to contribute to and benefit from the land. Then came the sugar plantations, creating jobs and changing the landscape of the Hawaiian Islands, starting with Hawaii's first sugar plantation and mill in Kōloa.

Since then, independent farmers, landowners, local government, huis (clubs or associations), billionaires, and others have taken the lead in land management and care. The interviews cover all these areas and will be archived at the Kaua'i Historical Society and Kōloa Public School and Library. A series of public events has been convened to share these stories and create the space for dialogue with the local community. These stories are also being crafted into a curriculum for young people to be taught along with farming practices at Old Kōloa Regenerative Farm, which lies on a former sugar plantation, to pass on valuable history and knowledge to the next generation.

Land Stories is about preserving the cultural wealth of Kaua'i as a basis for building respect and appreciation for one another and the land we share and depend upon. It's about providing our community with a rich history of this precious land and how to care for it. It's about building historical perspective and inspiration for present and future generations to sustain, protect, and care for our beloved 'aina.

This program is funded by a grant from the Hawai'i Council for the Humanities, through support from the National Endowment for the Humanities.

Oral historian and Story For All founder Angela Zusman interviews Daryl Kaneshiro, multigenerational farmer, for the Land Stories: Farming and Kaua'i Culture oral history project. Interviews are archived at the Kaua'i Historical Society and can also be accessed at https://storyforall.org/land-stories-farming-and-kauai-culture/. *Used with permission.*

Oral history interviews generally last from sixty to ninety minutes. An interview that goes on for two or more hours often ends with extreme narrator and interviewer fatigue. If you think you'll need extensive information from a particular narrator, plan for more than one interview session. If only one session was planned but the narrator still has more to say about the subject, it can be helpful to schedule an additional interview if possible rather than extending a session to the point of exhaustion. Keep track of the time during an interview, making sure not to tire out the narrator before covering key points. Judging how much time to spend on personal questions at the beginning and on questions that set up the body of the interview is the interviewer's responsibility and should be carefully considered and thoughtfully addressed.

INTERVIEW GUIDELINES AND TECHNIQUES

Always keep the ethics of the situation in mind. An oral history interview is not a casual two-way conversation, a social call, or a heated debate over the interpretation of the past. Narrators are entitled to respect for their stories.

Rely on open-ended questions. They elicit the most information. Examples are: "What were you told?" "How did you celebrate Christmas?" "Tell me about . . ." "Describe . . ." The importance of asking open-ended questions cannot be overemphasized. As oral historian Donald A. Ritchie points out in his book *Doing Oral History*, third edition, asking open-ended questions empowers narrators "to relate to and interpret their own stories. . . . The interviewer may be asking the questions, but the narrator is actively shaping the course of the interview rather than responding passively." Open-ended questions enable the narrator to "to talk broadly, ranging as far and wide as possible," volunteering whatever information they consider relevant to the topic at hand.[5]

Use neutral, not leading, questions. Asking the narrator "Why don't you like living here?" will not result in as complete an answer as the more neutral prompt "Tell me about living here." Questions beginning with *how, what, when, why, where,* and *who* are often used to introduce a subject or to follow-up an initial statement. They can help clarify an answer and can elicit further information. Some scholars have noted that within every question lies a clue to its answer, something oral historians need to keep in mind as they frame questions.[6] An interviewer, for example, might be tempted to think that "How do you like living here?" is a more neutral version of "Why don't you like living here?" It's certainly less inflammatory, but still not as neutral as "Tell me about living here."

Ask only one question at a time, not a smorgasbord of questions that will puzzle the narrator. If clarification is needed, make sure your elaboration does not lead the narrator to believe you expect a particular type of answer.

Avoid the temptation to share your personal agreements or disagreements with the narrator's views. Your opinions on the subject are not the focus of the interview. Some narrators, believing the purpose of the interview is an equal exchange of views like that encountered at a roundtable discussion or cocktail party, will try to draw an interviewer's opinions into the exchange. If that happens, an interviewer might satisfy the narrator's curiosity by one of several neutral responses like: "I never thought of it that way," "That's very interesting," "I can see your point," or "I can tell you're really passionate about this." Often, such replies prompt the narrator to elaborate even further. If a narrator presses for the interviewer's views, it may occasionally be necessary for the interviewer simply to explain forthrightly that the purpose of an oral history interview is to document the narrator's views, not the interviewer's. Note, however, that in some oral history projects in which community members are deeply engaged in project development and planning as well as serving as interviewers and narrators for the project, it may be useful for people serving as interviewers to be interviewed themselves before interviewing others. That way, all participants' information and perspectives can be adequately documented.

Keep your focus on the narrator. Don't show off your knowledge. Your background research is intended to help you draw out the narrator, but bragging about what you know is likely to have the opposite effect. Likewise, it's never advisable to pretend to know more than you do. If a narrator says something you don't understand, despite your background research, always follow-up by asking for clarification or more details.

Listen carefully without interrupting the narrator. The goal in an oral history interview is to collect in-depth answers by posing focused, clearly stated, open-ended, neutral questions.

If the narrator insists on telling a rehearsed story, listen politely and let them finish. Then go back and ask additional questions, focusing, for example, on specific details, that will get the narrator to go beyond the rehearsed performance.

Concentrate on what the narrator is saying. Take notes as necessary and appropriate and wait until the narrator has finished speaking. Then ask follow-up questions for clarification or to develop new information that did not emerge in the research process.

Watch for hints, such as pauses or slight changes in voice, that indicate the narrator may have additional thoughts or feelings to describe, and ask respectful follow-up questions. Sometimes narrators may indicate their feelings about subjects being discussed through body language. These are non-verbal responses to questions, such as pointing a finger, leaning toward the interviewer, leaning away from the interviewer, crossing the arms and legs, shifting or moving noticeably, breaking eye contact, and talking slower or faster than normal. You will want to be aware of these clues and respond to them as necessary. It is sometimes helpful to respectfully mention a non-verbal response and ask the narrator to discuss their feelings in more depth. Additionally, when interviews are not video-recorded, relevant observations about a narrator's non-verbal behaviors can be included in an interviewer's notes as part of the documentation of the interview context.

Use information identified through background and narrator-specific research to help facilitate a smooth interview. This may be as simple as supplying the correct date or place for an event or the name of someone connected with the event. Providing such information saves the narrator the frustration of trying to remember specifics or the possible embarrassment of giving incorrect information. It also indicates the project is important enough to have interviewers who are thoroughly prepared.

It helps to ask the narrator to put an event or memory into the context of time and place as much as possible. This may be done by encouraging the narrator to think in terms of people and places that have ties to the interview topics. For example, one narrator, when asked to think about a specific subject in this way, closed his eyes and asked the interviewer what year he should put himself back to. This helped him put the memory into context. Another technique is to ask the narrator to describe what a place or event from the past looked like. For people with keen visual memories, this can be an important memory-jogging technique. Likewise, scents, sounds, and even recollections of weather conditions can prompt memories for some narrators. Use the list of names and dates as necessary to help the narrator put events in context.

Photographs, maps, drawings, and three-dimensional objects are useful aids, although careful verbal descriptions of each will have to be given in audio interviews. The interviewer might say, for example: "So in this photo Great Uncle Joe is the second from the left wearing a bowler hat." In a video-recorded interview, if a narrator has photographs or other objects pertinent to the interview, the videographer may be asked to film the materials while the narrator describes each of them.

Remember to ask for specifics of place names, names of people, and dates or context. Sometimes the narrator's story is so interesting, you can forget to ask for these details.

Try to establish where the narrator was and what their connection to the story was at each major point. This will help differentiate firsthand information from accounts given by others.

Avoid asking questions beyond the narrator's expertise or about things they will not know firsthand. Narrators should not be made to feel they're being put on the spot or expected to talk about matters beyond their knowledge.

When a narrator uses acronyms or jargon that the general public is unfamiliar with, ask for explanations, descriptions, spellings, or translations, as appropriate. Your research or specific knowledge may mean you understand what the narrator is saying, but others listening to the interview or reading the transcript may not share this knowledge. This can be especially important with military or other government jargon and acronyms that fall into disuse and whose translations can be difficult to recover.

Use body language and eye contact to encourage the narrator's responses. Smiles and nods are often effective. Silence—even uncomfortable silence—is also an effective tool to elicit information.[7] When the narrator finishes responding to a question, resist the temptation to jump right in with a follow-up or a new topic. Some narrators simply need a few moments to continue gathering their thoughts. Additionally, a natural tendency to want to fill silences in conversation may induce the narrator to add something more without verbal prompting. Repeated verbal encouragement by the interviewer, such as "uh-huh," is intrusive and lowers the sound quality of the interview.

Discourage requests to turn off the recorder. Only information given during the recorded interview will become part of the historical record. If narrators ask you to stop the recorder, it helps to see if you can determine what concerns they may have that affect their willingness to speak on the record. But if they request repeated breaks in the recording, you might need to reconsider whether they are having second thoughts about participating in the project. Halting the interview for further discussions or clarifications with the narrator about options for closing the interview transcript might be useful. You will have to be prepared to make these decisions on the spot. Oral historian Donald A. Ritchie has suggested that if a narrator specifically refuses to discuss particular topics, that should be noted in the interview files.[8]

Take breaks as needed. Oral history interviews can be intense. And for some participants, just sitting in one place for an extended period can be difficult. Use your judgment about when to take a short break to allow time to stretch, leave the room, get a drink of water, or quickly review the topics to be covered in the next part of the interview. If a narrator becomes too tired to continue effectively, determine whether you can return for another interview session at a different time. Be sensitive to such situations and handle them graciously.

Use a notebook to keep track of follow-up questions, additional points to make, or other interview needs. This will help keep you organized and will allow you to continue to concentrate on the narrator.

Also use your notebook to keep a running list of proper names mentioned in the interview. It is a good idea to ask the narrator to review the list and correct any spelling errors at the end of the interview. Always double-check spellings if possible. Sometimes interviewers won't know for sure whether Aunt Ann spelled her name with or without an "e." The list of proper names should be kept in the master file, with a copy given to the interview processor.

Keep track of the time. Make sure you don't extend the interview past a reasonable limit.

Immediately label all the recording media. Include the oral history project name, the name of the narrator, the name of the interviewer, the date, and, if appropriate, the media number (for example, "one of three generated in the interview").

Take a photograph of the narrator in the interview setting. This is the general practice for both audio and video interviews; such photos become part of the permanent record of the interview.

Sign the donor form with the narrator. More sessions may be planned with the narrator, but each recorded interview needs its own signed donor form.

TROUBLESHOOTING THE ORAL HISTORY INTERVIEW

Narrators sometimes will not immediately give long answers to questions. In such cases, it helps to wait before asking the next question, making sure they are not considering an additional comment. If nothing is forthcoming, it may be that the narrator is not interested in or comfortable with the question, and you might try switching to a different topic or approach. It also may be that the narrator isn't sure what kind of additional information you might find interesting, in which case a follow-up question might open the floodgates. Careful listening and genuine curiosity are the keys to asking follow-up questions. The point of the interview, after all, is to learn something new that is not already part of the public record.

As the interview progresses, the narrator, understanding the direction of the questions, may anticipate several points on the interview guide and cover them with

John Schooley and interviewer Emily Dean with the signed donor form after an interview in the University of Wisconsin-Madison Oral History Program's "Dow 50 Project" (https://www.library.wisc.edu/archives/archives/oral-history-program/uwohp-and-outreach/dow-50-story-gathering-project-powered-by-ohms/). The interviews were conducted at the Madison (Wisconsin) Public Library, the university's partner on the project. *Image by Troy Reeves, held at the UW-Madison Archives. Used with permission.*

one answer. Interviewers who aren't paying attention can make the embarrassing mistake of simply referring to their interview guide and asking about the next point, even if the narrator has already addressed it.

Some people habitually answer with short sentences or one or two words. Try to ask questions that elicit as much information as possible, but remember that each narrator is unique and treat the situation respectfully. Verbally interpret non-verbal responses, especially in audio interviews. A brief "I see that you nodded *yes* to my question" will help clarify the situation.

On the other hand, some narrators talk a great deal. A good interviewer is prepared to keep the interview focused on the topics at hand in a polite and gentle manner, recognizing that some narrators might have a wide variety of experiences that go beyond the specific focus of the particular oral history project. In such cases, clarifying the interview's and project's focus is an important element to emphasize when first contacting potential narrators. Although it is generally better to avoid unnecessarily interrupting unusually talkative narrators, interviewers should be prepared to ask a question at an appropriate moment, such as when the narrator changes the subject.

At times, interviewers may arrive as scheduled only to discover that narrators have changed their mind about participating for any of a variety of reasons—the narrator's health is not good, the time scheduled for the interview is not good, the narrator is unexpectedly busy, the health of family members is not good, and the like. Interviewers should remain flexible, review the situation, and come up with a solution, which may simply mean rescheduling the interview.

Narrators also might be unwilling to be interviewed for a variety of other reasons. The topics to be covered, while important to the project, may be irritating or difficult for the narrator to discuss. In some cases, talking about past events or people to whom the narrator was close can bring about emotional reactions. Be prepared for these eventualities. Oral history interviews, while sometimes difficult, offer narrators a chance to tell their stories fully and to contribute information about experiences that are important to them. Often, allowing the narrator a moment of silence or sadness before moving on to happier memories allows you to complete the interview successfully.

The Shoah Foundation, whose volunteers routinely interview people who have experienced torture, sexual violence, and other traumatic events that are hard to hear about, reminds its interviewers that they are not responsible for their narrators' sadness. If an interviewer shows extreme discomfort during the interview, the narrator might start censoring their story, shut down altogether, or feel obligated to take care of the interviewer.[9]

In such situations, interviewers also should take care not to respond to a narrator's account of a tragic experience by saying something like: "I can imagine how you feel." Instead, follow oral historian Sarah C. Bishop's advice and say: "I'm so sorry that happened to you."[10]

ENDING THE INTERVIEW

Ending an interview is an art in itself. Oral history interviews are intense and can involve revelation of extremely personal information. To help the narrator wind down, the interviewer might ask a few introspective questions while giving the narrator an opportunity to add any thoughts or information that might not have been covered elsewhere. Be sure to thank the narrator before the recorder is turned off.

After signing the donor form, which should be done after every interview session, the interviewer may want to sit and talk for a little while to help the narrator unwind. This often depends on how tired the narrator is and the interviewer's schedule. This is the time to ask the narrator exactly how to record their name on project files, unless some other arrangement has been made to use pseudonyms. Sometimes, this is the time for the coffee or tea you couldn't accept during the interview. A measured packing up of interview equipment also allows for after-interview comments and discussion. Another good end-of-interview activity is to review, as appropriate, the spelling of proper names jotted down during the interview. While a good exercise for interviewer and narrator, it also provides helpful information for people processing the interview. If this isn't done at the end of the interview, you will want to call the narrator as soon as possible to review and check this information.

Narrators often have photos, other archival material, or artifacts related to the information discussed. If so, they may want either to give the items to the repository holding the oral history project materials or to loan them for copying (especially in the case of photographs or historic documents). If project planning calls for taking this information at the time of the interview, carefully inventory all materials, signing and giving one copy of the inventory to the narrator while keeping the other with interview records. If the materials are to be identified for future consideration, the interviewer will still want to look them over and write a description for project coordinators or take a picture of them with a smartphone. See appendix B for sample inventory forms.

Sometimes, during discussions after the interview, a narrator remembers something pertinent to the interview. If possible, you should try to record this information, even if it means unpacking the recorder and setting it up again. As an alternative to this, you can take thorough notes and ask the narrator to schedule another interview session. At the very least, carefully write down the information and include it in the interview master file. Such information also could be added as a footnote to the interview transcript.

Finally, be prepared to answer any additional questions the narrator might have about the project repository, accessibility, and future use of the interview, even though a complete review of those matters should already have taken place. If full transcription is to be done, let the narrator know they will receive a copy to review and correct before it is put into final form. It is also a good idea to offer the narrator a personal copy of the interview media and a copy or copies of the transcribed interview, explaining when they will be sent.

In the case of particularly emotional interviews in which narrators have described unusually harrowing situations—a common occurrence in social justice and crisis interview work—interviewers need to try to keep their own emotions under control so the focus of the interview remains on the narrator and their story. But afterwards, interviewers also need to take care of themselves to avoid vicarious trauma or compassion fatigue, which in extreme cases can lead to losing sleep, feeling guilty or helpless, or having persistent nightmares. Some options for self-care in such situations include debriefing with others involved with the project, journaling, playing calming music, spending time in nature, or engaging in creative activities you enjoy. Turning to "alcohol or other numbing substances" is not a good idea, nor is sharing details with friends and family.[11] Projects that include narrators who have experienced trauma can plan in advance to make sure interviewers and others have access to emotional support they may need.

SPECIAL INTERVIEWING CONSIDERATIONS

VIDEO INTERVIEWS

The techniques and guidelines listed in this chapter apply to all oral history interviews, whether they are audio or video recorded. But video interviewers should keep in mind the special points related to the physical set-up, as outlined in chapter 6, as well as these additional considerations.

Remember that a video-recorded oral history interview is not a polished documentary program ready for use on television or online. It is a video version of an audio interview. As such, its focus is on collecting the information as the narrator tells it. Although the video adds a more formal touch to the process and allows for documenting visual aspects of the narrator's information, narrator and interviewer should not feel constrained by the presence of the camera. The narrator should be free to start and stop talking in a relaxed manner, including false

starts. Do not abandon the use of silences or pauses, though they are more noticeable because of the camera.

More time constraints can affect the use of video compared to audio if recording is done in a studio or on location. It can be easier for the audio interviewer to go a little beyond the allotted one or one and a half hours if the situation calls for it, while camera and studio time are usually rented by the hour and may be tightly scheduled. Because of this, the interviewer should keep an even closer eye on the time during a video interview, making sure to cover the most important or critical information the narrator is in a position to provide. Video interviews conducted outside a studio may allow the same flexibility as an audio-only interview.

LONG-DISTANCE INTERVIEWS

Before the COVID-19 pandemic shut down all manner of in-person social engagement in March 2020, oral historians generally were wary of conducting oral history interviews by telephone or by using software applications for internet voice and video calls. The consensus was that telephone calls inhibited the ability of an interviewer to develop personal rapport with a narrator and made it impossible to read body language and verbal cues, like sarcasm or facetiousness, all of which may affect understanding a narrator's meaning. Likewise, video connections like Skype and Zoom, while adding the face-to-face element lacking in a telephone interview, sometimes suffered from impaired audio and video quality and lost connections, adding another wrinkle to the oral history process. It's also worth noting that an overreliance on remote interviewing can unintentionally limit the range of narrators to those who can afford or have access to appropriate computer resources and who live in areas with sufficient broadband connections, phenomena that became only too apparent as schools attempted to switch to remote learning during the pandemic. Despite shortcomings, however, as the pandemic wore on, many people became more comfortable using remote options like Zoom to keep in touch with friends and family, even those living nearby.

In any case, recording a long-distance interview with a narrator who has unique information to contribute to an oral history project is far better than not interviewing the person at all. Sometimes limited funds prevent traveling to a narrator's location, or a narrator's infirmity or other considerations may make a face-to-face interview impossible to arrange. Whenever remote interviews are planned, it's a good idea to practice with your equipment in a trial run to be sure the connections will result in an appropriate quality voice recording. One positive aspect of a long-distance interview may be that the interviewer will feel less constrained about taking notes to keep track of follow-up questions and the like, for the notetaking is unlikely to be a distraction the way it might be in person. See chapter 5 for more details about conducting remote oral history interviews.

EMAIL INTERVIEWS

We have just one recommendation about the advisability of conducting email interviews: don't. An email exchange is, by definition, not an oral history interview. It is a written exchange of information, even more impersonal than a telephone interview. Sending written questions and reading written responses incorporates none of the spontaneity of a spoken exchange and involves no opportunity for the interviewer to take non-verbal cues from the narrator. Moreover, the interviewer cannot even be certain who is providing the answers to the questions.

Having said that, however, one striking exception to this advice is worth noting. Interviewer Esther Ehrlich and playwright and performance artist Neil Marcus created a remarkable interview for the Artists with Disabilities Oral History Project at the University of California, Berkeley, Regional Oral History Office, communicating by voice, computer instant messaging, and gestures. Marcus was a child when he was diagnosed with dystonia, a severe neurological disorder that made it difficult for him to speak and to control his body. To conduct the interview, two computers were set-up side by side so Marcus could type responses to Ehrlich's questions, in addition to offering verbal responses from time to time. The interview sessions, six in all totaling sixteen hours, also were videotaped.[12] The critical point here is that Ehrlich and Marcus were engaged in a face-to-face exchange, a defining element of oral history. Use of the computer, as well as their voices, was simply the medium that made the process work, just as sign language may be the appropriate medium in an oral history interview with a deaf or hearing-impaired narrator.

In the absence of such unique circumstances, don't entertain the fiction that an email exchange is an oral history interview. It may be an exchange of information, even historical information, but it is not oral history. If for any reason information gathered from someone in this way is included in an oral history collection, its origins should be clearly defined and explained.

INTERVIEWS WITH MULTIPLE NARRATORS

It is usually best to interview one person at a time and to have as few people in the room as possible during the process. An interview is an intense situation because of the degree of concentration required by both the interviewer and the narrator, and narrators tend to be more comfortable with fewer people around, although some cultures may require or encourage witnesses or observers. Sometimes oral history interviews may require the presence of an interpreter if the narrator and interviewer do not share the same language. But in such cases, while multiple people may be present, the focus is still on gleaning information from just one narrator.

If you are interested in interviewing several people together, consider using video. Think carefully, however, about what this interview will produce. Despite the ideal give-and-take that having several people in a group seems to offer, what generally happens is that one person dominates or the narrators contradict one another enough to bog down the interview. Sometimes, even if people disagree with one another, they won't say so for fear of offending or being ridiculed by the more outspoken members of the group. Sometimes, it might be part of an oral history project's goal to document those kinds of exchanges within a group, in which case the interviewer should make clear at the outset that it's okay for the narrators to engage in a lively give-and-take. But whatever the purpose, it takes an experienced interviewer to keep an interview with multiple narrators moving along effectively.

Whatever the possible disadvantages, the exchanges in a multiperson interview can illuminate the narrators' process of remembering, which, in itself, can yield important insights.[13] For example, interviewers sometimes will encounter situations in which husbands and wives have assumed both partners are expected to participate in a scheduled oral history interview. While the phenomenon of one person dominating the interview may well result, it is also possible that the couple may help each other remember details or spark responses that otherwise would not have occurred.

If interviewing several people together is necessary because of time or other constraints, it is critically important for the interviewer to establish some method of carefully tracking who is speaking if the interview is not video recorded. Many voices sound similar when recorded, and without a running list of the order in which people spoke, or a rule that everyone introduces themselves when beginning to talk, a person—or speech recognition program—trying to transcribe such a multivoice interview session may become hopelessly lost.

Getting groups together and recording their conversations, prompted by an interviewer or group leader, has enjoyed certain popularity at gatherings like college reunions and other similar events. But these might more accurately be called recorded group discussions, not oral history interviews, unless the session has some pre-planned research-based structure, the participants all sign deeds of gift, and the recording is processed and archived in such a way that the information is available to others.

INTERVIEWS WITH MULTIPLE INTERVIEWERS

Discussions about the most effective ways of working with multiple narrators in an interview are an important part of the practice of oral history. Less well known is the use of multiple interviewers in an interview. This can happen in many situations—in some, it may be required, while in others, it often is a choice made during the project planning process. Either way, it involves a somewhat complex arrangement of deciding who does what and when while giving a narrator plenty of opportunity to respond to questions and follow-up questions.

When considering using multiple interviewers, think through why and how this step will benefit a project. Overall, what impact can or will multiple interviewers have on community engagement in project planning and development and on interviewer-narrator interactions? How does the plan describe what each interviewer brings to the project and how each will benefit the project? What does each co-interviewer bring to the project and to an interview? Consider also the relationships among the interviewers—do they know one another, or will they be meeting through work on the project? What are the plans for handling each situation? Does each interviewer clearly understand their role and the roles of the others? Does everyone on the team understand the purpose of using an interviewing team and the reasons each person has been asked to be a part of the team? What do the co-interviewers bring to the project, and what does each add to the interview? Also, for the narrators, how did each respond to being told there would be multiple interviewers, and what questions did they have? What about matching interviewers and narrators? What impact does using multiple interviewers have on this step? What about diversity among narrators and interviewers? How do narrators with diverse ethnic, racial, gender, and age backgrounds respond to interviews with multiple interviewers? What about interviewers from diverse backgrounds—how do they respond to being part of an interviewing team, and what do they need to know about the project and the interviews?

Answers to these questions are critical when working with multiple interviewers in an interview. For example, in the HIV-AIDS Caregivers Oral History Project, questions from each co-interviewer—on provision of public health care and administration of health care broadly defined to include food and shelter—strengthened the interviews. Firsthand input from the co-interviewers in working with health care providers, food providers, and housing providers as narrators provided access to additional depth of information. The oral historian on the team guided the work in meeting the Oral History Association "Principles and Best Practices." Team discussions on the purpose of the project and the types of questions that each would ask

were part of the planning process. Confirming how each co-interviewer understood their role and their purpose as part of an interview team supported smooth-running interviews that benefited from a co-interviewer process.[14]

Others have successfully used co-interviewing to help teach oral history to students. A roundtable discussion at the 2023 Oral History Association meeting explored this question, offering examples of the benefits of co-interviewing as an educational tool. Benefits include giving students a hands-on opportunity to learn about interviewing from an experienced oral historian.[15]

TRAUMATIC EVENT INTERVIEWING

Oral history projects that adopt a social justice framework or that seek to document emerging crises are highly likely to involve narrators who have experienced traumatizing situations. Some examples cited in this chapter suggest how such narrator experiences can affect the ways in which they tell their stories.

Beginning with the idea stage of the interview life cycle, projects that expect to involve potentially vulnerable narrators should keep in mind the challenges such interviews might present for narrators as they tell their stories as well as interviewers who listen to them. As project planning moves forward, participants can give careful thought to the best ways to support all participants and achieve project goals. Of foremost concern, of course, is the welfare of narrators, who *never* should be pressed to participate. The Shoah Foundation, Voices of Witness, and Oral History Association publications like the *Oral History Review* are among the resources to consult for information about interviewing narrators who have experienced trauma. As more oral historians engage in such work, more research and information will become available on practical ways to deal with challenges associated with traumatic event interviewing. So before embarking on such a project, it's advisable to seek the most recent available information on appropriate ways to proceed.

CROSS-CULTURAL INTERVIEWING

Community engagement is the key to success in oral history projects involved in cross-cultural interviewing. Using a social justice framework in particular, projects that focus on vulnerable communities may include outsiders who don't share the language or customs of the community planning a project. In such cases, the community may welcome outsiders to an oral history project if the outsiders demonstrate an openness to learn and if they exhibit respect for the community.

But even in community-engaged oral histories where everyone—even the outsiders—speaks the same language, they all may not share the same cultural customs.

What, for example, are the cultural practices regarding handshakes or other forms of greeting? What about making eye contact? Do people speak slowly or rapidly? Are there cultural differences in how people treat silences in conversation? How close do they stand to each other? To strangers? In an increasingly multicultural world, community engagement creates opportunities for everyone involved to learn—and teach—about cultural differences and similarities, which can enhance opportunities for co-creating valuable oral history interviews.

WRAPPING IT UP

Narrator and interviewer must sign the donor form after all interviews, regardless of whether they are in audio, video, or remote formats. As noted in chapter 4, under federal copyright law, the words on the recording are protected by copyright and may not be used without the person's permission.

Send a thank you note to the narrator as soon as possible after the interview. It should thank the person for their time and reinforce the importance of the information given. See the sample in appendix B.

Although there is no substitute for thorough research and careful preparation before conducting oral history interviews, we offer this caveat: Be prepared to be flexible.

The late Arlington County, Virginia, librarian Sara Collins recalled an occasion where an elderly woman came to Arlington on a "last" trip to her hometown and wanted to visit the school she had attended from 1913 to 1915. Collins opened the building, which had since become the Arlington Historical Museum, and an interviewer from the library's oral history program rushed over, recorder in hand. The result was a priceless account of the woman's school days, in which she recalled the arrangement of classrooms, described the daily routine of fetching coal and water, and talked about teachers and classmates she remembered. Flexibility and an experienced interviewer combined with a willing, articulate narrator to capture an unplanned firsthand account of a long-ago era.

Oral history interviews are as unique as the people who give them. Interviewing techniques and narrator responses may vary, but a well-prepared interviewer can elicit from a willing narrator much information important to the overall project. It is not always easy. The interview can be an intense experience for both interviewer and narrator, but the results are well worth the effort.

A FINAL NOTE

The discussion in this chapter of the many permutations oral history interviews might reflect serves to emphasize yet again the importance of oral historians documenting all aspects of their work. While the focus of an oral history project might be on the immediate creation of a final product for public consumption—an exhibit, theatrical performance, political advocacy, doctoral dissertation, and the like—what sets oral history apart from other forms of information-gathering is the safeguarding of the interviews a project creates and a process for making them available, as appropriate, for researchers or others to use. And future users—especially those who come to an oral history collection years after all the original participants are long gone—are entitled to know the details about how and why a project evolved as it did. Such documentation is critical for future users of oral history material to decide how they want to make sense of it. Next-generation oral historians, for example, might not agree with decisions today's project planner or interviewer might make, but at least they need to know *why* such decisions were made and can take that into account as they consider an earlier project's outcomes.

Project master files, for example, should include the following:

- A project might seem to have a strong visual component but was recorded only in audio. Future users should be informed that a restricted budget led project planners to choose a less expensive form of recording as a trade-off to interview more narrators and rely on verbal descriptions of visual elements.
- A project that relied heavily on group interviews should explain why that option was chosen and how interviewers were trained to manage a complex group of narrators.
- Projects that involve multilingual participants need to include a clear explanation of how translators were selected or trained and how transcripts were verified for accuracy.
- A project likely to include crisis interviewing or the participation of potentially vulnerable narrators must document how interviewers were trained to deal with traumatic stories or traumatized narrators.
- Projects that use pseudonyms or otherwise retain narrators' anonymity need to explain why and indicate any other ways in which narrators' identities were protected.
- If the recordings reflect problems with audio or video quality or if there are otherwise unexplained interruptions, document the reasons so future users will not just assume the work was sloppily done.

Ideally, all such documentation will be done as a project evolves. It's a critical part of the oral history process and is a gift from today's oral historians to those who delve into your work tomorrow.

NOTES

1. Australian oral historian Katie Holmes has observed that in life history interviews in particular, narrators "rarely tell their life story in purely chronological form. They often revisit episodes previously discussed, circling back to add further information and detail either as they recall them or on closer questioning from the interviewer." While not essential to the chronology of a person's life, returning to a previously discussed point "helps communicate a sense of self and the meaning of the event." See Katie Holmes, "Does It Matter If She Cried? Recording Emotion and the Australian Generations Oral History Project," *Oral History Review*, 44 (winter/spring 2017): 68.

2. Voice of Witness, "Voice of Witness Ethical Storytelling Principles," https://voiceofwitness.org/ethical-storytelling-principles/, accessed December 6, 2023.

3. Some oral historians suggest that interviewers are sometimes too reluctant to engage with their narrators or challenge narrators' assertions, resulting in a "deferential politeness" rather than a lively and informative dialogue. See Linda Shopes, "'Insights and Oversights': Reflections on the Documentary Tradition and the Theoretical Turn in Oral History," *Oral History Review*, 41 (summer/fall 2014): 265.

4. The description of a model interview format is based on the teaching of pioneering oral historian Martha Ross, a past president of the Oral History Association.

5. Donald A. Ritchie, *Doing Oral History*, third edition (New York, NY: Oxford University Press, 2015), 82.

6. Alice Hoffman, retired labor historian and a past president of the Oral History Association, made this point in response to a panel discussion at the 2006 Oral History Association conference in Little Rock, Arkansas, noting that "within every specific question is hidden its answer."

7. Canadian oral historian Alexander Freund has raised ethical questions about how interviewers can manipulate narrators by the use of silence, inducing them to divulge information they never intended to share, in the inherently unequal power relationship of an interview setting. Freund suggests that oral historians should explore how oral history practice fits into a larger social and cultural context, including the centuries-long practice of asking people about themselves, from the evolution of confession in the Roman Catholic tradition to the rise of psychoanalysis and the contemporary "mass culture of confession" promulgated by celebrities like Oprah Winfrey and the explosion of personal story sharing on social media. See Alexander Freund, "Confessing Animals: Toward a *Longue Duree* History of the Oral History Interview," *Oral History Review*, 41 (winter/spring 2014): 18–26.

8. Ritchie, *Doing Oral History*, third edition, 88.

9. USC Shoah Foundation, "Interviewer Guidelines," University of Southern California, 2021, 43–48.

10. Sarah C. Bishop, *A Story to Save Your Life: Communication and Culture in Migrants' Search for Asylum* (New York: Columbia University Press, 2022).

11. USC Shoah Foundation, "Interviewer Guidelines," 50–51.

12. "Lives of Artists with Disabilities Documented in Oral Histories," *Oral History Association Newsletter* (spring 2007): 3, https://digitalassets.lib.berkeley.edu/roho/ucb/text/marcus_neil.pdf, accessed December 6, 2023.

13. Bethan Coupland, "Remembering Blaenavon: What Can Group Interviews Tell Us about 'Collective Memory'?" *Oral History Review*, 42 (summer/fall 2015): 277–99.

14. HIV/AIDS Caregivers Oral History Project, University of Minnesota Libraries, Minneapolis, Minnesota, https://archives.lib.umn.edu/repositories/13/resources/2123, accessed February 24, 2024.

15. "Does More Equal Better? A Roundtable Discussion on Co-Interviewing Models in Oral History," 57th Annual Meeting of the Oral History Association, Baltimore, Maryland, chrome-extension://efaidnbmnnnibpcajpcglclefindmkaj/https://oralhistory.org/wp-content/uploads/2023/10/OHA-Final-Program-2023.pdf, accessed February 24, 2024. See also Minnesota Pandemic Oral History Project, Hennepin History Museum, https://hennepinhistory.org/minnesota-pandemic-oral-history/, accessed February 24, 2024; and Minnesota's Daily Newspaper Environment, Hennepin History Museum, Minneapolis, Minnesota.

8

Preservation

What now? You've recorded an interview. What are the recommended ways to preserve the recording and keep its information accessible? Preservation and access, stewardship of the interviews, help ensure the interview information will be available for a long time.[1] This chapter covers preservation steps including initial care for an interview, contact with a repository, and transcribing guidelines. Chapter 9 covers steps that support ongoing access.

When thinking about providing care for oral histories, several terms often are used. Repository is a common term; archive is another term that often is used. Oral historian and archivist Nancy MacKay described the distinctions between the two. A repository refers to a place—physical or digital—where historical materials are kept and cared for; it can include libraries, museums, research centers, and corporations, among others, some of which may have an archive. Both a repository and an archive feature institutional stability and a controlled physical environment designed to keep the materials in it free of damage from blight and safe from intruders. In addition, an archive uses a standard record-keeping system for tracking metadata and has a trained staff, a preservation management plan, and a public space in which to access and use materials such as oral histories.[2] Throughout this manual, we use the term repository as the broadest and most inclusive term referring to a permanent place to hold oral histories, and we encourage oral historians to work with trained archival staff whenever possible.

STEWARDSHIP

What is stewardship? Basically, it is the responsibility of caring for something that has value and is worth preserving. Specifically, for oral histories, stewardship is the responsibility of caring for oral histories, including information documenting their creation, and for providing responsible and ethical access to them. It further extends to providing this information while meeting oral history standards and adhering to repository guidelines and policies.

Caring for interviews has always been an important part of the practice of oral history, but the digital age with its worldwide access options has expanded this need. It includes, but is not limited to, documenting who the interviewer and narrator are, interview purpose, interview setting, interview technology, interview interactions, community engagement, and substance and meaning of the interview information. Beginning with a brief discussion of oral history standards, we'll explore each of these areas of responsibility.[3]

STANDARDS

Standards guide all parts of the oral history life cycle, including preservation and access. They not only support this, but also serve as a reminder of the need for documentation of the context in which oral histories were recorded as a support for ongoing access and use.[4]

The "Principles and Best Practices" of the Oral History Association are an example of the standards, as are

> Oral history refers to both the interview process and the products that result from a recorded spoken interview (whether audio, video, or other formats).
>
> Oral History Association, "OHA Core Principles," https://oralhistory.org/oha-core-principles/, accessed November 24, 2023.

the "Best Practices for Community Oral History," a list of community-based best practices in the *Community Oral History Toolkit*. The statements help remind oral historians of the importance of transparency when working in communities and of the role of stewardship in this process.[5]

Oral history associations throughout the world, such as the Oral History Society in the United Kingdom, provide additional examples of standards that support appropriate and effective access to interview information. Taken together, the organizations and their standards help remind us of the importance of oral history in documenting the ongoing history of our times and the role that stewardship plays in providing future generations access to this history.[6]

COMMUNITY ENGAGEMENT

The *Community Oral History Toolkit* begins with a definition of community. Drawing on the definition in the Oral History Association pamphlet *Using Oral History in Community History Projects*, it states that community is any group of individuals bound together by a sense of shared identity. The importance of stewardship to a community is underscored in the "Best Practices for Community Oral History Projects," also from the *Community Oral History Toolkit*. The "Best Practices" include the direction to "cast a wide net to include community." As this best practice is further described: Make sure all appropriate community members are involved in your project and have an opportunity to make a contribution. Community members know and care the most about a project at hand, and the more closely they are involved in every aspect of it, the more successful it will be.[7]

Information about community engagement can cover many points. Who participated in community engagement, and what were their roles? What did they represent in the community, and how did this contribute to a project or set of interviews? For purposes of stewardship, confirm careful and thorough documentation of community engagement and its contributions as part of the oral history preservation step.

Key stewardship issues for community engagement also include making decisions about requests for access to interview information. Access decisions balance requests for availability with individual privacy concerns. Information about the purpose and expectations for use of interviews are critical components in these decisions. They often are made on a case-by-case basis and are guided by available information about an interview. With guidance from oral history standards and repository policies, stewardship includes caring for this information and, drawing on many sources including insights this information can provide, making decisions

about access that can have an impact on an individual and a community.[8]

INTERVIEWER AND NARRATOR

Oral historians have documented basic biographical information about narrators for years. The purpose is to tell future users of the interviews just who the narrator is. Stewardship reminds us to include, and to provide care for, details about both a narrator's and an interviewer's background, interests, and relevance to the purpose of an interview. It also includes development of materials based on this information that provide ethical user access to an interview.

Questions about documenting narrators from potentially vulnerable populations can come up. When thinking about this, putting the needs of the narrator first is important. Look over the sample forms in the appendices to this manual and answer as many questions about a narrator as possible without putting them into a difficult or challenging position.

Documenting who the interviewer is also is important. With the recognized importance of the roles of interviewer and narrator as co-creators of an interview and increasing digital age access to interview information, responsible stewardship includes documentation of an interviewer's background and experience and inclusion of this information in project materials for a repository.

INTERVIEW PURPOSE

As participants, based on a project's mission statement, narrators and interviewers have firsthand knowledge about the recording and purpose of an interview. A clear and well-documented understanding of purpose helps provide a foundation for its ongoing use. Written correspondence including printed-out emails, notes from conversations, insights provided by the interviewer in interview notes, and information on project forms all help document an understanding of the purpose for doing an interview. Stewardship includes care for all documentation. And guided by oral history standards and repository policies, it includes the steps needed to make this information available to users of the oral histories.

Oral history forms can help guide this step. Look over the examples of the forms in the appendix and document as much information about the overall context of the interview situation and the roles of the interviewer and narrator as possible, again keeping situations involving narrators from potentially vulnerable populations in mind. Provide this information to cataloguers; it is useful in developing descriptions of the materials that will aid future researchers.

Douglas A. Boyd, John A. Neuenschwander, and Sarah Milligan discuss oral history care and access at the Kentucky Oral History Commission, Frankfort, Kentucky, 2013. *Kopana Terry, photographer, used with permission.*

INTERVIEW STATUS

Standard oral history theory describes interviews as co-created sources. Interviewer and narrator share authorship of an interview. For legal purposes, oral historians recognize shared authorship by interviewer and narrator as joint owners of interview copyright.[9] Legal release agreements signed by narrator and interviewer provide context for oral history materials. Stewardship covers responsibility for care for this documentation and its ethical inclusion in outreach materials.

When asked to do an oral history interview, it is not uncommon for a narrator to suggest they just don't know enough. Even though most narrators know more than enough, documenting this first response and any subsequent narrator responses provides insight into a narrator's frame of mind for purposes of ongoing access and use.

Stewardship includes confirming the signing of an up-to-date legal release agreement for each interview and making sure an original signed agreement is kept as part of the documentation for each oral history.

INTERVIEW CIRCUMSTANCES

Preserving information about the general circumstances of an interview is another area of stewardship. Interview circumstances can include background on why an interview was done, why and how a narrator was selected to do an interview, interviewer and narrator expectations for an interview, and general comments about an interview.

Oral history interviews are recorded for many reasons. Careful documentation about the purpose helps users of interview information better understand an interview, the topics covered (or not covered), and the questions asked (or not asked). Often this information is provided by an interviewer after an interview is completed. Stewardship helps preserve the interview information and provide ongoing ethical access to it.

Oral history projects often include narrators who represent various sides or perspectives of interview topics. Documentation of why and how the perspectives were identified and why and how the narrators representing each were chosen is part of providing context for oral history materials. Stewardship covers responsibility for care for this documentation and its ethical inclusion in outreach materials.

INTERVIEW SETTING

Documenting information about an interview setting is another stewardship responsibility. An interview setting can be in a narrator's home, a museum or library, a recording studio, or any appropriate place that serves the needs of a project, allows for good recording quality, and is agreed on by the narrator and interviewer.

Information about an interview setting includes its location, how the space was organized, the narrator's response to it, and factors that have an impact on the quality of the recording. This setting can have an unintended or subtle impact on an interview; for example, a narrator in a comfortable or familiar setting may be more open about discussing interview topics, while a narrator in a more public setting, such as a recording studio, could offer more formal responses. Sound and light conditions, even if not noticed by interview participants during an interview, can have an impact on future use as well as care and migration decisions. These are broad, basic, general examples, but each calls attention to the importance of

carefully and thoroughly documenting an interview setting and the narrator's response to it.

INTERVIEW TECHNOLOGY

Technical questions—questions about recording equipment and media—are some of the most-discussed among oral historians. Usually, this discussion focuses on an interview. The need for information about technical questions does not, however, end at the end of an interview. Turning off the recorder signals the beginning of curatorial needs, including documenting the recording equipment and media used in an interview.

Combining rapid development of digital age technology with the basic premise that oral histories are recorded to provide ongoing access to the interview information emphasizes the need for stewardship. Documentation of technical information can be invaluable for oral history archivists and curators. The type of recording equipment used in an interview with brand name and details, the type of media used in the recordings with brand name and size, the formats in which the recordings were made, and information about the number of copies made and the formats of each—all

---

Oklahoma State University Library, Oklahoma Oral History Research Program, Impressions from the Pandemic: Oklahomans Reflect on COVID-19

The Impressions from the Pandemic: Oklahomans Reflect on COVID-19 oral history project documents, preserves, and makes accessible many aspects of the COVID-19 experience in Oklahoma. The project was funded in part by an American Rescue Plan grant from the Institute of Museums and Library Services, a funding source that supported museum and library services in addressing community needs created or intensified by the pandemic. As Project Director Sarah Milligan described it, the project captured impressions, in-depth recollections, and analytical reflections of a diverse group of Oklahomans who were affected by the pandemic, including perspectives from individuals who weren't the focus or public face of the disease.

Through this project, more than forty individuals were interviewed about their experiences during the first two years of the pandemic. Narrators, representing a variety of occupations, geographic locations, and positions in the community, included educators, parents, policy-shapers, service and health industries workers, and student interviewers who participated in the early part of the project. In addition to the interviews, the project also included a presentation by a researcher working on rumor, belief, and vaccine hesitancy and its impact on the pandemic and development of a podcast highlighting the impact of the pandemic on the lives of the narrators. The interviews are available through Oklahoma State University Edmon Low Library. For more information about the project, contact the Oklahoma State University Library's Oklahoma Oral History Research program or visit the "Impressions from the Pandemic" website.[1]

NOTE

1. Oklahoma State University Edmon Low Library Oklahoma Oral History Research Program, Impressions from the Pandemic: Oklahomans Reflect on COVID-19, https://library.okstate.edu/search-and-find/collections/digital-collections/impressions-from-the-pandemic-oklahomans-reflect-on-covid-19, accessed November 15, 2023.

---

provide a repository with the information it needs to support ongoing access to oral histories and help with future migration needs and decisions.

INTERVIEW INTERACTIONS

Oral histories are not conversations with more or less equal exchanges of information. Nor are they scripted questions and answers. Rather, they are carefully planned and developed interviews designed to capture information from a knowledgeable source about an event, time period, or way of life. Often, the probing questions asked in an oral history interview probably would not be asked or discussed in the course of general conversation.

A clear description of the narrator-interviewer relationship provides a repository with information it needs for informed interview access. This information can include documentation of the expectations for the interview as well as its ongoing access by both interviewer and narrator. Do both participants understand the purpose of the interview? Were there expectations about topics to be covered or not covered? If so, did they have an impact on the interview, and what was it? Do both participants understand the expectations for its placement in repository collections? What about expectations for distribution? Do they understand the possibilities for outreach on the internet, the potential worldwide access it offers? Caring for all documented information about expectations for use of an interview can help guide ethical, ongoing access to its information.

Information about an interview also can include insights that help users better understand its basic content. An interview recorded for the Library of Congress Veterans History Project offers an example. In this interview, the narrator was noticeably uncomfortable with questions about his service, but when the interviewer changed to questions about what his service meant to him, his answers went into lively depth and detail. Information documenting this interaction can help future users better understand the interview content.

Interview interactions also can cover a narrator's reaction after completing an interview. For example, in separate interviews with a husband and wife about events they had experienced together half a century earlier, the husband was pleased with his interview and the information he had provided. His wife was pleased with her interview, too. She also commented that she learned things from her husband's interview that she had not known before. Including this information as part of interview documentation can help future users understand the interaction and the information in the interview. Interview interactions are both spoken and unspoken. Unspoken interactions also have an impact on interview content. For example, a narrator may be tired or distracted or less

than willing to fully answer some questions, as was the man who lost interest when an invited colleague arrived toward the end of his interview. On the other hand, a narrator may take actions that indicate a positive response. In one case, a woman, in a first meeting with an interviewer who graduated from the same college, wore a dress in their school colors to welcome the interviewer. This opened an avenue of shared background and trust in narrator-interview interaction that had a positive impact on interview circumstances and content. Documenting these and other interactions can help future users of interviews better understand their full content.

Interviewer-narrator trust can have an impact on interview content and the quality of an interview. It is based on mutual understanding—informed consent—about the purpose and disposition of an interview and the access/user policies of the repository. Stewardship responsibilities include caring for all information about informed consent and making accurate and thorough information about interviewer-narrator trust available to users of oral histories.

SUBSTANCE AND MEANING OF THE INTERVIEW INFORMATION

Information related to the substance and meaning of interview information goes to the heart of the practice of oral history. It involves an understanding of memory and all the steps involved in doing oral history.

For purposes of stewardship, documenting all available information about an interview helps support an understanding of its meaning. Answering the question "why is this interviewer asking these questions of this narrator at this time and this place about this topic" is a basic part of this documentation. Supported by the responsibilities of stewardship, the answers to this question can help build a foundation for ongoing use of interview information.

Overall, stewardship is a critical part of oral history access. Its work is based on an understanding of the importance of a repository holding and caring for oral histories and on the availability of thorough and accurate information about each interview. Stewardship cannot provide answers to all questions, but responsible documentation of all parts of oral histories can help build a foundation for informed discussion and ongoing decisions related to their ongoing use.[10]

PRESERVATION OF ORAL HISTORIES

In the years prior to the digital revolution, recording and preservation media were the same for oral historians. Oral histories were recorded on tapes that were then preserved by a repository as the primary source document. With the coming of the digital age, preservation of oral histories changed. Some projects, following original guidelines with new forms of media, have continued to maintain the media as recorded and to label it with an acid-free marker showing the project name and date. As with the earlier forms of the recordings, ongoing access to playback equipment is critical in this situation. Next, regardless of the type of recording media, a cardinal rule of oral history comes into play. Follow the LOCKSS principal: *lots of copies keep stuff safe.* Make at least two copies of your interviews and keep them in two separate places. This protects them from inadvertent loss. If no other audio exists, make a copy of the audio portion of video footage. Follow the guidelines for storing and backing up data files given in chapter 5.

Store the interview recordings on an external hard drive, a dedicated computer, or in the Cloud—or on several of these options. Make another copy on a flash drive for ongoing access as you work with preservation steps. Consider converting the flash drive copy to a compressed version of the recording for future access purposes, but maintain the original uncompressed format on the hard drive, computer, and Cloud copies.

This is the time to check for the possibility, however remote, of potentially defamatory statements in the interview. These sometimes can slip past the most astute interviewer. If found, refer to the information in chapter 4 and check immediately with your contact person at the repository about how to handle the situation.

WORKING WITH A REPOSITORY

Nancy MacKay, in her books *Curating Oral Histories from Interview to Archive* and the *Community Oral History Toolkit*, has described the steps involved in cataloging oral histories for preservation and access. The role of oral historians, as discussed in this chapter, is to be as accurate and careful as possible in providing information about the oral histories to those working on the cataloging step. These guidelines are reinforced by the Oral History Association's "Principles and Best Practices" and its "Archiving Oral History: Manual of Best Practices."[11]

In certain cases, oral historians question the placement of oral histories in repositories. Because the placement most often involves transfer of copyright, which some interviewers and narrators do not recommend in specific instances, the recommendation is to hold onto interview recordings and make well-researched and carefully planned alternate decisions. When using this model, it is always helpful for project planners, community engagement personnel, interviewers, and narrators to work together to confirm careful long-term plans for ongoing access to the interview information.

When oral history project deliverables are handed over to a repository, here is a quick overview of what to expect. The information is from two archivists working at medium-sized archives in a metropolitan area of about 750,000 people. The archivists recommend oral history project personnel provide:

- information that helps provide access to the interview information including an index or full transcript, one copy printed on acid-free paper for archival preservation and one printed as a researcher access copy;
- individual folders containing printed information for each narrator including a fully signed legal release agreement, a copy of the interview guide used during the interview, correspondence, and any other support materials;
- an external hard drive containing:
  - interview recordings in archival formats (as an example, WAV for audio, MOV for video) and access formats, such as M4A and MP4;
  - completed copies of all project forms documenting interview context and suggested project and individual interview keywords;
  - digital copies of interview transcripts; and
  - copies of project research or research products, such as a project timeline;
- stewardship information that is as complete and accurate as possible, realizing that archives staff will verify each signature and all descriptive information and metadata and will correlate all information, including suggested keywords, to conform with the organization of its cataloging program; and
- openness to various options for letting the public know about the oral histories, such as blogs, and how oral historians can help in this part of the process[12]

WHAT ABOUT PHOTOGRAPHS?

Photographs are some of the most common materials to be given to an archive as part of an oral history collection. When including photographs, check with a representative of the archive about the formats they work with. For more recent collections, most use common digital formats and have recommendations on what will work best with their collections. It may also be helpful to ask about older formats such as glass plates negatives, black-and-white glossies, color photos, and slides.

ADDITIONAL CONSIDERATIONS

Although standards and guidelines are the baseline for working with repositories, they may not apply to all projects. There are exceptions, many related to working with potentially vulnerable populations or when placing an interview in a public repository may pose a danger for a narrator or a project. For example, most oral history projects include the full name of each narrator on recordings and transcripts and on legal release agreements written to allow unrestricted access to interview information. However, if these situations put a narrator in a difficult or dangerous position, steps to protect a person and a project can include the following:

- Use either no name or a pseudonym to identify a narrator.
- Exclude identifying information, but, if possible, include information that can help document interview context.
- Work with a repository to close access to project materials for a stated period of time.

These steps can help protect and provide ongoing access to oral histories.

PROJECT FORMS AND OTHER POST-INTERVIEW TASKS

The period shortly after the interview can be a busy one for the interviewer. This is the time to finish housekeeping tasks:

- Make sure all signatures are on the donor form and it is filed with interview materials.
- Make sure the narrator and interviewer biography forms are as complete as possible. They often are filled out as part of the interview process; now is the time to check them over and fill in any missing information.
- Complete an interview summary form. This is an initial interview preservation step. It covers documentation of the circumstances of the interview and the information needed for its full curating. The form includes an interview summary that can be reused to help catalog the interview as well as to develop finding aids and publicity. It also is a helpful place to list interview keywords and proper and place names mentioned in an interview.[13]
- Check the photo and memorabilia form. This form contains information about photographs, scrapbooks, and other materials pertaining to the interview. If a narrator has agreed to allow donation or use of materials, the interviewer should develop an itemized list of these materials before leaving the interview. Follow the instructions on the form and provide as much detail in the descriptions of the items as possible.

You may also want to check other project forms, such as the potential narrator forms, at this time. They are designed to help maintain access to information that can be a help for future interviews.

This is the time to write up notes about the interview. The notes may be included as part of an interview summary form or developed separately. The interviewer's information and insights help future users of the oral history information understand details about interview context and content. Notes can include comments about the setting, the narrator's reactions to the interview, the narrator's health or other issues that could affect the interview, and speech patterns such as regular use of filled pauses (ums and ahs) or of phrases in more than one language. Notes do not need cover pages; often bullet points are sufficient, but make them as thorough and detailed as possible to provide appropriate context.

This also is the time to check the spelling of proper names on the list made during the interview and to make a copy of this list for the transcriber to use when transcribing the interview. And, of course, if this has not already been done, write a thank-you letter to the narrator.

INDEXING

Oral historians have several options for helping preserve interview content. In addition to making copies of an interview recording, options include developing an index and doing a full transcript. These may be done with co-creators of an interview or by oral historians working with repository personnel.

Through use of new technologies, development and use of oral history indexing has grown and changed dramatically in the twenty-first century. Leading the way have been uses of forms of artificial intelligence such as computer-generated speech management that use indexes to provide access to specific spots in a recording; this is based on preserved recordings while allowing, as engineer and oral historian Douglas Lambert states, "end users to browse interviews as a multimedia experience."[14]

Development and use of indexing, based on availability of preserved, web-based oral history content, uses organization of thematic content, multimedia environments, and electronic linkages to achieve the level of access. As technology has advanced, oral historians preserving collections have developed systems of practices, forms, and vocabularies for applying its advances to use of indexes. Through use of these systems, researchers and users of oral history information can now, drawing on descriptive titles, synopses, and keywords, use indexes to work from a collection-level search to something as specific as a particular segment in a time-coded interview. There is no one set of practices on how to do this; organizations, using the technology, develop indexes and systems that fit the needs of their institutions. One of the best-known of the systems that use preserved, time-coded oral histories to provide levels of access is the aptly named Oral History Metadata Synchronizer. Developed through the Louis B. Nunn Center for Oral History at the University of Kentucky Libraries, it is an open source system that provides web-based access to interview information through use of an index, as well as a transcript, by connecting a text search term to a corresponding place in an interview recording. This, and other, advances in indexing systems serve as models for use of preserved oral history recordings while supporting advances in access to the voices on the recordings.[15]

TRANSCRIBING

Transcribing interviews is an often-discussed part of the oral history process. Questions about transcripts generally cover access to and use of interview information. Oral historians view the recording as the primary source document, but both the interview and transcript as a part of the oral history. As Donald A. Ritchie commented in the third edition of *Doing Oral History: A Practical Guide*: "Archivists generally consider the audio or video recording, being the original and verbatim record, the primary document. Looked at another way, one is a record of what was said and the other—the transcript—represents the intended meaning of what was said."[16] Oral historian Nancy MacKay expanded on this statement when she wrote that a transcript documents the intellectual content of an interview and preserves this content on paper—"the most reliable preservation medium." It also, through the electronic version, provides a text-searchable option.[17]

Ideally, the goal for oral history projects is preservation of the information on the recordings. Digital migration techniques offer the possibility of continuing access to recordings, although the reality may not always be cost-effective. When printed on acid-free paper and kept in archival conditions, transcripts are archival and reference tools that support continuing, accurate access to interview information.

Decisions about transcribing are part of the planning process. Some projects elect to transcribe only parts of

Not all products labeled "acid-free" will be safe to use when caring for oral history materials. Some commercial products, while technically free of acid when developed, may develop acids later. Acid-free materials have a pH between 7.0 and 10.0 and a lignin content of no more than 1 percent.

interviews, but oral historians discourage this as it can impose artificial access limits on use. Regardless of the decisions, transcribing can be time-consuming and transcripts can be expensive to create, requiring as many as eight hours of processing time (including all transcribing steps) for each hour of interview time if done manually. This is not said as a deterrent to transcribing, only as a guide to help when working with this step in the oral history life cycle. Transcribing apps cut down considerably on development time, but the time needed to audit-check them remains.[18]

Transcribing Suggestions

Develop a transcribing guide to maintain consistency in transcribing formats.

Make sure you spell all words accurately. Check the spelling of all proper and place names.

Add full names and titles in brackets the first time they are mentioned. Example: [Senator John] Doe.

Listen carefully. If you can't understand a word or phrase after checking it three times, indicate [unclear] on the transcript. Check with the interviewer about missing words or phrases. Sometimes the interviewer or the narrator can fill in the missing information.

Use a time code in the left margin of the transcript. This will help readers find the spoken information.

Transcribing apps are growing in use and accuracy. Here are some tips for their role in oral history stewardship:

- Clearly identify all speakers.
- Carefully audit-edit the transcripts to ensure accuracy in spelling, speaker identification, and speech.
  - Check for basic transcribing errors; for example, even with high-quality audio, a sentence: "And I grabbed on to that and hung on tight and here I am" could sound to transcribing apps like: "And I go out grabbed I got out and I went right in here, I am." Correcting errors in apps requires hands-on transcribing and careful audio checks for accuracy.
  - Check the spelling of proper and place names, including capitalizations; apps can default to the most common spellings.

- Check for the spelling of homophones—words that sound alike but have different spellings and meanings, such as write and right or to, too, and two.
- Check and maintain consistency in use of numbers—when to spell them out and when to use numerals.
- Check sentence structure and punctuation; transcripts are working with vernacular speech which may show up as unusual variations on the written page.

Troy Reeves, oral historian at the University of Wisconsin-Madison Archives & Records Management Services, commented on the practicality of working with transcribing apps when he said, "We use AI [artificial intelligence/transcribing apps] almost exclusively to create a draft transcript, because the technology now creates a good enough draft. But, we still have staff, primarily our students, audit/edit the transcript to get it as accurate as possible. And, we now put a statement at the beginning of all our AI-drafted transcripts, letting researchers know how it was created and why; when they doubt what they see in the text, they should review the audio."[19]

In terms of time commitment, it is helpful to plan for thorough audit-checking for all transcripts; this can take hours for each hour of recording. Involve narrators when possible; often they can decipher seemingly indecipherable words or phrases. They also can add explanations or details that enhance the meaning of the interview information. Following these tips and Troy Reeves's information can help produce an accurate transcript. Accuracy takes time, which should be planned into a project from

Consider giving a copy of the recorded interview and a bound copy of the transcript as a gift to the narrator.

the beginning and respected during the preservation step in the oral history life cycle.

After completion of a transcript, ask the narrator to review it. When doing this, it helps to remember that a transcript of spoken words will not read like a written document; resist the urge to edit. The goal is to have a clean, accurate document that is faithful to the spoken recording.[20]

Try not to skip narrator review, even if narrators have limited eyesight or difficulty reading. In such situations, take the transcript to the narrator and slowly read it through, allowing the narrator to indicate necessary corrections.

When all corrections have been made, develop an index. Finally, create a title page listing narrator, name of project, date of interview, and copyright information. And, at this point, many projects, in addition to providing the transcript to a repository, send a completed copy to a narrator.

THE PARTS OF AN ORAL HISTORY

The definition of oral history used in this publication states the term refers both to the process and product. When defining materials that make up oral history products, include the following—each supports or contributes to an understanding of the interview and its information:

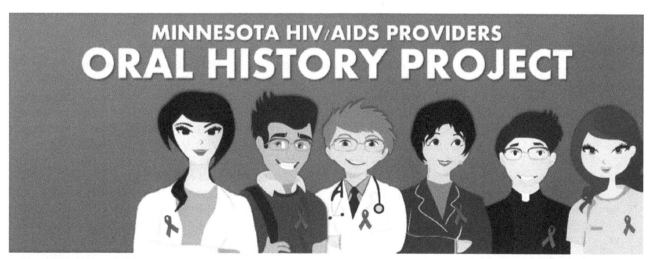

The HIV-AIDS Care Providers Oral History Project began with the goal of recording information about care for an unknown and deadly disease for medical educational purposes. Through the process, it created a study collection of thirty-five oral histories held in the University of Minnesota Libraries Jean-Nickolaus Tretter Collection in Gay, Lesbian, Bisexual and Transgender Studies, University of Minnesota, Minneapolis, Minnesota. *Image used with permission from the HIV Care Providers Oral History Project, Minneapolis, Minnesota.*

- interview recordings in archival and access formats
- the original signed donor or legal release form and all other project forms relating to the interview
- the audit-checked transcript with the interviewer's and narrator's comments
- all recorded interview media
- the abstract and interview log
- the transcript in its final form, printed on acid-free paper, in an acid-free folder and acid-free container, and a computer file copy
- the interviewer's question guide and notes taken in preparation for the interview
- all completed forms with the project name as it will be recorded in repository records and the narrator's name as it will appear in the public record
- a correctly spelled list of proper and place names mentioned during the interview
- correspondence between interviewer and narrator, including notes of telephone conversations and copies of email messages
- a photograph of the narrator, often taken in the interview setting, clearly labeled with the narrator's name, the date of the interview, and the project name
- a bibliography of project and interview preparation sources
- an index to the interview

Most of these materials may be turned over to the repository in electronic form. But in addition, turn over the original, signed copy of the donor form and one copy of the transcript, both printed on acid-free paper. These are permanent records that benefit from being in the most stable forms possible.[21]

NOTES

1. For more information, see the Society of American Archivists, "Archivists Toolkit," https://www2.ar chivists.org/groups/collection-management-sec tion/archivists-toolkit, accessed November 24, 2023; Nancy MacKay, *Curating Oral Histories: From Interview to Archive*, second edition (New York, NY: Routledge, 2016), offers a helpful step-by-step guide for working with repositories on long-term care for oral history materials. See also Cyns Nelson, *Oral History in Your Library: Create Shelf Space for Community Voice* (Santa Barbara, CA: Libraries Unlimited, 2018).

2. MacKay, *Curating Oral Histories: From Interview to Archive*, second edition, 22.

3. For additional information, see Barbara W. Sommer, *Practicing Oral History in Historical Organizations* (New York, NY: Routledge, 2015): 85–94.

4. Oral History Association, "Principles and Best Practices," https://oralhistory.org/princi ples-and-best-practices-revised-2018, accessed November 24, 2023.

5. Mary Kay Quinlan, Nancy MacKay, and Barbara W. Sommer, "Best Practices for Community Oral History," in *Introduction to Community Oral History*, volume 1 (New York, NY: Routledge, 2013), 12–13.

6. Oral History Society, http://www.ohs.org.uk/, accessed November 24, 2023. See also the list of international oral history associations on the Oral History Association website, http://www.oralhistory.org/ regional-and-international-organizations/, accessed November 24, 2023.

7. Mary Kay Quinlan, Nancy MacKay, and Barbara W. Sommer, *Introduction to Community Oral History*, volume 1 (New York, NY: Routledge, 2013), 10, 11.

8. Mary Larson, "Steering Clear of the Rocks: A Look at the Current State of Oral History Ethics in the Digital Age," *Oral History Review*, 40:1 (winter/spring 2013): 36–49. See also John A. Neuenschwander, "Major Legal Challenges Facing Oral History in the Digital Age," in *Oral History in the Digital Age*, edited by Doug Boyd, Steve Cohen, Brad Rakerd, and Dean Rehberger (Washington, DC: Institute of Museum and Library Services, 2014), http://ohda.matrix.msu .edu/2012/06/major-legal-challenges/, accessed November 24, 2023. See also Cyns Nelson, *Oral History in Your Library: Create Shelf Space for Community Voice* (Santa Barbara, CA: Libraries Unlimited, 2018).

9. John A. Neuenschwander, *A Guide to Oral History and the Law*, second edition (New York, NY: Oxford University Press, 2014), 15, 66–69.

10. Much information has been written about the meaning and interpretation of oral history. This section focuses on steps that can be taken to support access, laying the groundwork for ongoing opportunities for interpretation and use. For a discussion about the types of questions that can help support accurate insight and interpretation, see Linda Shopes, "Questions to Ask," *History Matters: The Survey Course on the Web*, https://historymat ters.gmu.edu/mse/oral/, accessed November 24, 2023. See Linda Shopes, "Insights and Oversights: Reflections on the Documentary Tradition and the Theoretical Turn in Oral History," *The Oral History Review* 41:2 (summer/fall 2014): 257–68, for further discussion on meaning and interpretation. For more information, see Nancy MacKay, "Curating for the User," in *Curating Oral Histories: From Interview to Archive*, 147–54.

11. Oral History Association, "Archiving Oral History: Manual of Best Practices," https://oralhistory.

org/archives-principles-and-best-practices-complete-manual/, accessed November 24, 2023.

12. Michele Pollard, archivist, Hennepin History Museum, Minneapolis, Minnesota, conversation with Barbara W. Sommer, June 14, 2023. Mollie Spillman, curator/archivist, Ramsey County Historical Society, St. Paul, Minnesota, conversation with Barbara W. Sommer, June 13, 2023.

13. MacKay, *Curating Oral Histories*, second edition, 106.

14. Douglas Lambert, "Oral History Indexing," *Oral History Review*, 50:2 (September 2023): 169–70.

15. Lambert, "Oral History Indexing," including case studies of a number of indexing systems, 169–92. "Oral History Metadata Synthesizer: Enhance Access for Free," https://www.oralhistoryonline.org/, accessed December 2, 2023. See also MacKay, *Curating Oral Histories*, second edition, 107–10; Doug Boyd, "OHMS: Enhancing Access to Oral History for Free," *Oral History Review*, 40:1 (winter/spring 2013): 95–106.

16. Donald A. Ritchie, *Doing Oral History: A Practical Guide*, third edition (New York, NY: Oxford University Press, 2015), 54.

17. MacKay, *Curating Oral Histories*, second edition, 102, 110. See Teresa Bergen, *Transcribing Oral History* (New York, NY: Routledge, 2019).

18. For more information on transcribing, see Bergen, *Transcribing Oral History*.

19. Troy Reeves, email to Barbara W. Sommer and Mary Kay Quinlan, February 23, 2024.

20. In the context of transcript preparation and review, oral historians comment on the distinction between transcribing (the verbatim record of the interview) and editing (preparing a transcript for further use, such as publication). For more information, see MacKay, *Curating Oral History*, second edition, 100–06. See also Linda Shopes, "Transcribing Oral History in the Digital Age," in *Oral History in the Digital Age*, edited by Doug Boyd, Steve Cohen, Brad Rakerd, and Dean Rehberger (Washington, DC: Institute of Museum and Library Services, 2012), http://ohda.matrix.msu.edu/2012/06/transcribing-oral-history-in-the-digital-age/, accessed August 2, 2017.

21. For access examples, see Columbia University Libraries, Oral History Office, "Oral History Archives," http://www.columbia.edu/cu/lweb/indiv/oral/offsite.html, accessed November 24, 2023; The British Library, Bodleian Libraries, "Collection Guide: Oral History"; University of Oxford, "Oral History-Guide to Resources: Great Britain," https://libguides.bodleian.ox.ac.uk/oralhistory/greatbritain, accessed November 24, 2023; The Bancroft Library, University of California Berkeley, "Oral History Center," https://www.lib.berkeley.edu/visit/bancroft/oral-history-center, accessed November 24, 2023.

9

Access

In 2007, when oral historian Alistair Thomson identified the impact of technology through the digital revolution as a paradigm transformation facing oral historians, discussions about what this new digital world meant were in the early stages.[1] As oral historians have continued their work, the impacts of the digital age have increasingly been identified, questioned, analyzed, and discussed, with a growing recognition that the pace of change itself poses challenges. What are the ethical guidelines governing respectful and accurate use of interview information and of a narrator's voice, image, and words, particularly when evolving technology makes it possible to alter, virtually seamlessly, those fundamental elements of an oral history? How do we, as oral historians, determine what is respectful and, as importantly, what is accurate? These are ongoing access questions, amplified by digital age possibilities for outreach and use—or misuse.

In the midst of this change, oral historians also recognize that much about the practice of oral history access remains constant. The need for careful planning, recording interviews that stand the test of time, and the importance of providing a stable, long-term environment with clear and accurate finding aids and documentation of interview content and context have not changed.

Use of the internet has become a major factor in the work of oral historians. Although not a repository, the internet has quickly become an effective outreach tool. Whether used to post full oral histories, oral history excerpts, complete oral history collections, or finding aids, its reach is global. Through the internet, oral histories have moved out of the repository and are now accessible worldwide.

Use of the internet also raises many questions. What are the ethical implications of worldwide access? How do

oral historians use blogs and podcasts in disseminating information about oral history? How protected is oral history content on the internet, and how protected should it be?[2] How do oral historians define and document a full understanding of the information in an interview? These access and use questions go to the heart of the practice of oral history.

Overall, the future for access to oral histories in the digital age is open, and the possibilities for its use are limited only by the imagination. But the opportunities do not absolve oral historians from thoughtfully and responsibly dealing with the questions as well. Development of sources of information, such as the *Oral History in the Digital Age* website, with its information on topics ranging from access to video, provide oral historians with sources to help navigate answers to these questions.[3] Articles in *The Oral History Review*, as well as in archival, history, and public history publications, also explore questions related to legal and ethical uses of oral history. This information has helped ease oral historians into a thoughtful and careful use of oral histories in the digital age.

In this chapter, we'll review the access stage and responsibilities for oral historians. The various steps and responsibilities may sound mundane, but they are necessary actions for effective and ethical ongoing use of interview information. With hundreds of thousands of oral histories in repositories, additional oral histories being added around the country and the world every day, and through ever-growing options for digital age access and use, access steps provide a model for documenting information about an interview that can help guide its ongoing use. In this chapter, we'll focus on steps that support access to oral histories. We also will review outreach options that can support ongoing access.

CENTER FOR ORAL AND PUBLIC HISTORY
PRESENTS

OUTSPOKEN:
A COPH
PODCAST

EPISODE TWENTY-FOUR:
DOROTHEA LANGE'S CALIFORNIA: 1935-1942

Illustration for a podcast from the Lawrence de Graaf Center for Public and Oral History, California State University, Fullerton, California. *Used with permission.*

Pass the Word: A Project of the Kentucky Oral History Commission

As another example of oral history access, the Kentucky Oral History Commission began recording and collecting oral histories in 1976 as a project for the US bicentennial. It is now an active state-supported commission administered by the Kentucky Historical Society that funds and provides access to oral histories from across the state.

Pass the Word, a website developed by the commission and maintained by Kentucky Historical Society staff, provides a single access point to oral histories from repositories throughout the state. The commission describes it as a "roadmap for users," showing available interviews and the repositories where they may be found. Repositories are encouraged to keep their entries up to date. All repositories meet the standards of the Oral History Archival Accreditation program, a state program developed by the commission to ensure that repositories holding oral history collections have the capacity and resources to preserve them and make them accessible.

The oral histories listed on the website range from the Civil Rights Movement in Kentucky Oral History Project, a major statewide initiative by the commission, to state and local projects focusing on such topics as the rights of women, on veterans, on arts and culture in the state, on Indigenous history, and on local history. Oral histories are treasures; according to the commission, the oral histories accessible through the *Pass the Word* website "embody the unbridled spirit of Kentucky."

For information about the *Pass the Word* website, contact the Kentucky Oral History Commission, the Kentucky Historical Society, and visit the website at https://passtheword.ky.gov/.

A REPOSITORY

In this book, we refer to repositories as places to provide ongoing preservation and access.

As discussed in chapters 3 and 8, when working with a repository to provide care for oral histories, start this discussion at the beginning of the oral history planning process and follow through during the preservation step. A partnership with a repository can help ensure effective long-term care of and access to oral history materials.

As a reminder, what are the basic features to look for in a repository? Oral historian Nancy MacKay identified the key characteristics in her book, *Curating Oral Histories: From Interview to Archive*, second edition. They include:

- institutional stability;
- control of the physical environment, including light, heat, and temperature;
- ability to protect the materials from damage; and
- skill and expertise in providing access to the interview information.[4]

The importance of the stability in preservation and access that repositories can provide is critical to ongoing access. In some instances, however, placement of oral histories in a repository may not be possible. If that's the case, think carefully about other options for ongoing access and care for oral histories that may be available to project co-creators and community members. Consider information about preservation of oral histories covered in this chapter and incorporate all that are applicable.

PHYSICAL AND VIRTUAL REPOSITORIES

The digital age has opened up possibilities for access to oral histories. At the most basic, it offers both physical and digital options. Physical repositories, with a defined space or place in a building, are the traditional form. The Library of Congress American Folklife Center Veterans History Project is an example of an oral history project housed in a physical repository and archive, in this case in the Library of Congress in Washington, DC. Physical repositories provide access to the materials in their collections, including oral histories, in both original and electronic formats. For example, access to the materials held in the collections of the Veterans History Project is available at its physical location in the Library of Congress and through the Veterans History Project website. Digital repositories, on the other hand, do not have a defined physical space. They store their collections on

> A virtual archive is a "true archive in a digital format."
> —Oral historian Nancy MacKay

servers and provide access to the material through an established URL. Densho: The Japanese-American Legacy Project is an example of a digital repository.[5]

When working with repositories, look for options for ongoing access to the interview information. What are repository procedures for maintaining media in formats no longer widely available? What about digitizing analog recordings? Does the repository have an ongoing migration plan in place, including digitizing (transferring analog to digital), refreshing (recreating files on new software-hardware systems), reformatting (moving files to software-hardware systems with different specifications), and migrating (moving data between media)? Technological advances including digitizing analog recordings and recording in born digital (interviews that are created and exist only in digital formats) emphasize the importance of a migration plan as a critical factor for ongoing access to the recorded interviews.

The original recording, regardless of type of media, is the primary source document; the recommended archival standard is to maintain ongoing access to it, including maintenance of equipment to provide that access. It is helpful to confirm that repository policies, both physical and digital, conform to these guidelines.

MAKING AND KEEPING RECORDS

When turning oral history materials over to a repository, make sure the information about the interviews is accurate and complete. Fill in all forms, maintaining consistency and accuracy in the name of each narrator. Provide information that can help a repository develop accurate and useful finding aids. Be available to continue to answer questions when needed.

Generally, this information provides documentation about the content and context of an interview. For example, information on a biographical form provides a repository with information that can contribute to a more complete finding aid. Information on an interview information form includes as clear a statement as possible defining ownership of interview information, the names—unless circumstances prevent this—of interviewer and narrator, the technical characteristics of an interview, the physical environment of an interview, proper and place names mentioned in an interview, a summary of interview content, and suggested keywords.[6]

Project co-creators will want to make sure the interviews and all related oral history materials are turned over to the repository as quickly as possible. Documentation of context, used to help provide full and accurate use of oral histories, brings the oral history life cycle full circle. Following through on work that began in the planning process, through the care it represents in supporting accurate use of accessible oral histories and documentation of as full an understanding of interview context as possible, helps fulfill an honoring of a narrator that is at the core of the work of oral historians.

A finding aid for the Brooklyn Historical Society Bedford-Stuyvesant Restoration Corporation (New York) oral histories illustrates this process. Accessed through the Center for Brooklyn History, a search begins with a short history of the center's oral history program along with a list of its accessible oral histories. A portal accessed from this webpage introduces documentation about content and context of the oral history interviews and projects in the center's collections. A click on the name of a specific set of interviews, for example the Bedford Stuyvesant oral histories, leads to detailed information about the oral histories—their purpose, scope and content, historical background, names of interviewers and others involved in the project, lists of subjects, genres, topics, places mentioned in the interviews, related materials, and a note about oral history, all providing increasingly in-depth information about interview content and context. Accessing each of the narrators in these oral histories opens information about interview content, biographical background, and a link to the audio recording and an index or transcript. The result is a comprehensive set of information, designed in a user-friendly format, that introduces a researcher to the full set of oral histories in the library's collection, includes information about content and context of the interviews, and provides access to the oral histories.[7]

WEBSITES

The proliferation of digital materials makes use of the internet relatively easy. Do not, however, confuse access with long-term storage. The internet has expanded access to oral history collections, but it is not a repository.[8] Again, oral history standards and repository policy guidelines are important considerations here. Many projects maintain oral history collections in a designated repository and carefully and thoughtfully use websites as tools for access outreach.

Websites provide an opportunity to offer wide access to oral history information. You will want to decide

Oral history refers to both the interview process and the products that result from a recorded spoken interview (whether audio, video, or other formats).

Oral History Association, "OHA Core Principles," https://oralhistory.org/oha-core-principles/, accessed November 24, 2023.

whether or how to use a website for your oral histories. A discussion of legal and ethical issues related to use of the internet in oral history and public history publications can help provide guidelines for this process.

A word about websites. Although there are permanent digital repositories on the internet developed for long-term preservation of digital materials including oral histories, websites offer a different type of internet access. Websites are a webpage or series of webpages about a specific topic and accessed through a single network address. They are not always designed to be permanent, but to highlight and call attention to specific information at a specific time; URLs that provide access to the websites can change. With that, keep in mind that websites provide some of the most frequent options for access to oral histories. Their use can support a repository and the oral histories it holds by providing information about oral history, access to a project and its audio and video recordings, a blog or blogs about oral history topics, and an option for online contact with repository personnel. As an example, see the Samuel Proctor Oral History Program in the College of Liberal Arts and Sciences at the University of Florida. The site provides access to information about the program and its dozens of oral history projects including the Mississippi Freedom Project and the Native American History Project with its work on a long-time partnership with the Poarch Band of Creek Indians in Alabama.[9]

PUBLICATIONS

Oral historians are tapping into the immense possibilities of access in the digital age with publications as well. *Australian Lives: An Intimate History*, by oral historians Anisa Puri and Alistair Thomson, offers an example. This book, published both in a traditional softcover format and in an e-version, uses digital technology in the e-version to hyperlink oral history recordings to the text, allowing readers to hear the voices of the narrators included in it. In *Oral History and Digital Humanities: Voice, Access, and Engagement*, essays edited by oral historians Douglas A. Boyd and Mary A. Larson explore developments in the practice of oral history through a review of projects that represent advances in the use of digital technology.[10]

ARTIFICIAL INTELLIGENCE AND ORAL HISTORY

Oral historians, like everyone involved in technology-driven pursuits, often are on the lookout for evolving tools that will enhance their work. Thus, reel-to-reel tape recorders gave way to cassettes, which, over time, have given way to digital audio recorders, video recorders, and smartphones as tools to record interviews.

Advances in computing technology have likewise made way for methods to curate, access, and readily analyze oral history materials.

As in many technology-dependent fields, when the prevailing technology seems to make a quantum leap, practitioners exhibit a range of reactions. Some are like a Labrador puppy cavorting around the backyard eagerly searching for the freshest new squirrel scent. Others resemble the rural blacksmith in the 1920s firing up his forge and hammering horseshoes because he can't believe the automobile is here to stay. Still others meander through the middle of such a continuum or experiment their way into an approach that seems to work.

The takeaway? Oral history best practices regarding the latest developments in artificial intelligence are far from settled. And the rapid pace of technological change suggests that experimentation—and lively discussions—will be ongoing. Oral historians may despair of ever managing to keep up with the pace of change, but they may take solace in knowing that organizations like the Oral History Association, the Oral History Society in the United Kingdom, the International Oral History Association, and other professional organizations of historians and oral historians serve as ongoing sources of information and advice on best practices, including those for access, as artificial intelligence tools evolve.

NOTES

1. Alistair Thomson, "Four Paradigm Transformations in Oral History," *The Oral History Review* 34:1 (winter/spring 2007): 49-70.
2. John A. Neuenschwander, "Major Legal Challenges Facing Oral History in the Digital Age," in *Oral History in the Digital Age*, edited by Doug Boyd, Steve Cohen, Brad Rakerd, and Dean Rehberger (Washington, DC: Institute of Museum and Library Services, 2014), https://ohda.matrix.msu.edu/2012/06/major-legal-challenges/, accessed November 24, 2023.
3. *Oral History in the Digital Age*, https://oralhistory.org/oral-history-in-the-digital-age/, November 24, 2023.
4. Nancy MacKay, *Curating Oral Histories: From Interview to Archive*, second edition (New York, NY: Routledge, 2016), 22.
5. Library of Congress, American Folklife Center, Veterans History Project, https://www.loc.gov/programs/veterans-history-project/about-this-program/, accessed December 3, 2023; Densho Digital Repository, https://ddr.densho.org/, accessed December 3, 2023.
6. MacKay, *Curating Oral Histories*, second edition, 24, 113-20.
7. For more information, see the Brooklyn Public Library, Center for Brooklyn History, Oral History Collections, https://oralhistory.brooklynhistory.org/, accessed November 15, 2023.
8. MacKay, *Curating Oral Histories*, second edition, 79.
9. University of Florida, College of Liberal Arts and Sciences, Samuel Proctor Oral History Program, https://oral.history.ufl.edu/, accessed November 15, 2023.
10. Anisa Puri and Alistair Thomson, *Australian Lives: An Intimate History* (Clayton, Australia: Monash University Publishing, 2017), e-version: http://publishing.monash.edu/books/al-9781922235787v.html, accessed November 14, 2017; Douglas A. Boyd and Mary A. Larson, eds., *Oral History and Digital Humanities: Voice, Access, and Engagement* (New York, NY: Palgrave Macmillan, 2014).

10

Oral History Outcomes

Your oral history project has now come full circle—from idea to plan, interview preparation, interview, preservation, and access. Perhaps you've created a web presence—minimalist or elaborate—for your project where anyone, from serious scholar to accidental visitor, can delve into the interviews or any other information you've decided to share. The project may be "done" from your perspective. But the magic of oral history is that it can live on, virtually indefinitely, if you've followed the steps outlined in this book. Moreover, the first-person information you've collected is more than just a compilation of isolated stories. Done well, it contributes to the raw material of history and may help lay the foundation for social change. If you've given your oral history project an online presence—even if it's limited to making basic catalog and interview abstract information available—you've made it possible for curious site visitors as well as serious scholars to explore previously unavailable information. But many oral history projects, inspired by anniversaries, advocacy, or aging family members, begin with a goal not only of archiving interview materials for posterity but also of creating something tangible in the present based on the information collected in the interviews. Transforming interviews into tangible outcomes can take myriad forms, limited only by your imagination.

Oral history materials are frequently used to:

- create museum exhibits or, in some cases, entire museums;
- contribute to curricula in post-secondary and graduate programs;
- provide opportunities for original research in academic, community, public history, and educational settings;
- document and interpret historic sites;

- provide raw materials for poetry, songs, dances, theatrical presentations, and performances of all kinds;
- document and inspire banners, quilts, and other three-dimensional objects;
- narrate neighborhood tours;
- create blogs, podcasts, video documentaries, and other audio-visual programming;
- contribute to natural resources management and cultural preservation;
- support genealogy or family research;
- document community history, particularly including the perspectives of historically underrepresented or marginalized groups;
- inspire or buttress community organizing and other social activism and advocacy;
- serve as a method for gerontologists and others who work with elderly people to engage in life review or other therapeutic techniques;
- preserve vanishing languages;
- enliven the study of history in elementary and secondary classrooms; and
- contribute primary sources of information for scholarly articles, books, dissertations, and the like.

It is beyond the scope of this manual to describe in detail how to create a museum exhibit, a podcast, a theatrical performance, or a community-organizing effort using the content of oral history interviews. But creating any such tangible outcomes relies first on teasing out the historical meanings embedded in the interviews.

INTERVIEW CONTENT

To begin the process of teasing out those meanings in interviews, revisit the project's original purpose or mission statement. Why did you do it in the first place? What were you trying to find out? If you're working with interview materials created by others, you will have to rely on the project background information that accompanies the interview collection to contextualize the interview content.[1] And now, what are you going to *do* with this new information that is now part of the historical record? And just who is the audience you hope to reach with whatever tangible outcome you envision? The answers to those questions will help you determine what you're looking for as you engage with your recordings or transcripts.

Independent scholar and oral historian Valerie Raleigh Yow has suggested that analyzing and interpreting oral history material begins with looking for patterns, topical categories, and turning points in a narrator's life or in their involvement in the subject at hand.[2] Well-crafted

Marie Ilene O'Gara, age five, and her father, W. H. O'Gara, prepare to fly in a barnstormer's plane at Laurel, Nebraska, circa 1920. After World War I, barnstormers took to the skies offering plane rides, usually for a fee, to anyone daring enough to give it a try. This family photo is an example of the memorabilia that can surface during oral history interviews. Ilene recalled that her mother strongly objected to the escapade, but she and her dad went anyway. Decades later, as a young woman, Ilene took flying lessons with a group of friends. She and others who had not yet soloed for their licenses were grounded during World War II.
Family photograph, used with permission of Ilene's daughters, Ann, Mary Kay, and Nancy Quinlan.

Chapter 10

keyword searches, highly structured content analysis, or subjective but systematic observation of interview content can help identify recurring themes that may help develop post-interview products based on oral histories.

Another useful approach that can help make sense of interview material is analogous to the yardstick journalists use to assess the newsworthiness of issues or events. So in reviewing oral history interview content, you might look for *timeliness* of the information. For example, does something about the past time, place, or situation have particular relevance today? You might consider the *impact* of the past events. Little-known actions in the past can have long-lasting effects, which oral history interviews can illuminate. What is the *proximity* of the oral history information to your current circumstances? Community oral history projects typically will include intensely local content, but there also might be psychological if not geographical proximity. For example, a project documenting the evolution of teachers' experiences in inner-city schools might resonate with school communities everywhere, not just with those in the city where the oral histories took place. Are there particular *oddities or deviations from the norm* that emerge in the oral history interviews? Familiarity with what's already on the historical record about the subject will help you differentiate the unusual from the commonplace or expected information in the oral history interviews. And finally, are there examples of *conflict or controversy*? Exploring past times, places, and events almost inevitably requires exploring conflict, controversy, or even mystery. And searching oral history interviews for such information can be a fruitful way to identify content for use in post-interview products or presentations.

Oral historians sometimes find that even when working with interviews they helped create, subsequent close reading and listening reveal new insights—and raise new questions—they didn't previously perceive. Returning to the initial focus of the project may help identify key themes that emerge in the interviews, creating the skeleton of an outline for a publication or other product. But the initial focus may be insufficient in reflecting the array of information the interviews contain.

For example, the Pioneer Farms Oral History Project cited in chapters 3 and 6 set out to focus on the early years of farms that had been in the same family for a century or more, day-to-day life on the farm, and the impact of major changes in agricultural technology, including farm equipment, irrigation, and hybrid seeds. What emerged in the narrators' discussions of daily life on the farm, however, was additional detail about community life, churches, and schools, topics narrators raised in their answers to open-ended questions but that were not initially a theme expected from the interviews. Even the topic of how major changes in agricultural technol-

ogy affected the farm families yielded some surprises. The impact of improved seed varieties, access to irrigation, and technologically advanced farm equipment are widely acknowledged, and interviewers wanted to know how those developments affected the narrators' farming operations. What came as a surprise to one interviewer, though, was a narrator's identifying improved weather forecasting as the most important technological change affecting agriculture.[3]

Sometimes, interviews intended for a fairly narrow purpose may yield an untold breadth of information, as people involved in one oral history project learned. When the Cushman Motor Works closed the foundry at its scooter manufacturing plant in Lincoln, Nebraska, in 1959, only Charlie Botts could say what it was like to be the first Black man to move from foundry work—the toughest, hottest place at Cushman—to a job in the tin shop as a welder and sheet metal finisher.[4] The plant itself is long gone, but an oral history interview with Botts opens a window into a time and place in the history of race relations in Lincoln as well as work in the factory, which was the initial purpose of the centennial celebration interview. The union-sponsored interviews at Cushman, in fact, resulted in a collection of information that went far beyond what its planners initially intended. They sought to celebrate work by union members on the factory floor. But they also documented stories that contribute to a deeper understanding of race relations,

All those who use oral history interviews should strive for intellectual honesty and the best application of the skills of their discipline. They should avoid stereotypes, misrepresentations, and manipulations of the narrator's words. This includes foremost striving to retain the integrity of the narrator's perspective, recognizing the subjectivity of the interview, and interpreting and contextualizing the narrative according to the professional standards of the applicable scholarly disciplines. Finally, if a project deals with community history, the interviewer should be sensitive to the community, taking care not to reinforce thoughtless stereotypes. Interviewers should strive to make the interviews accessible to the community and where appropriate to include representatives of the community in public programs or presentations of the oral history material.[1]

NOTE

1. Oral History Association, "Best Practices," https://oralhistory.org/best-practices/, accessed November 24, 2023.

the role of women in the labor force beginning in World War II, changing trends in education, corporate history, workplace health and safety issues, and the globalization of manufacturing, among other themes that emerged from the interviews. In short, it matters that the interviews, created for a specific, short-term purpose, contain information whose value to future generations is unknowable.[5]

INTERPRETING CONTENT

Oral historian Linda Shopes has suggested that "it is fair to assume that many interviews—perhaps the majority—include errors and interpretations that don't square with other available evidence, that are inaccurate in some way, or generally seem 'off.'"[6] Narrators may conflate multiple events into one and be just plain mistaken on chronologies, dates, names, and other demonstrable facts. In one family history, an aunt described witnessing a speech by Charles Lindbergh during his nationwide tour in 1927,

following his record-setting solo airplane crossing of the Atlantic Ocean. Other family members noted that she wasn't even in town when Lindbergh appeared there and couldn't possibly have seen him. But by some estimates a quarter of the nation's population did see the aviator while he was on the tour celebrating his stunning achievement. So the woman's account associating herself with it tells us more about the importance of Lindbergh's status as a hero than it does about the literal accuracy of her claim.[7]

Shopes suggests that oral historians seeking to publish interview materials should use footnotes or other interpretive devices to correct factual errors and misremembered or invented experiences by presenting other evidence and offering alternate interpretations or explanations of the narrator's statements.

Clarifying or elaborating interview content can be an important element of providing context for interviews, particularly as people involved in oral history projects seek to create tangible outcomes for contemporary work. But some oral historians express concern about focusing on

DeGonda Family, ca. 1916. L-R back row: Gion Rest (John) DeGonda, Giachen Antoni (Jacob) DeGonda. L-R front row: Onna Maria Turte (Mary Dorothy) DeGonda Freiberg, Rosa Martina (Rose) DeGonda Simonett, (Maria Aloisa) Louisa DeGonda Joerg. Family history research, including oral histories, helped uncover this photograph of a Swiss Romansch immigrant family, including co-author Barbara Sommer's great-grandmother, Louisa DeGonda Joerg. The history of Romansch immigration to the United States often is absorbed into broader Swiss immigration patterns. The Romansch people are from eastern Switzerland and are ethnically Rhaetian and Roman. Their language, also called Romansch, is a modern form of Latin spoken in the Roman Empire and is an official language of Switzerland. This family photograph helps document Romansch immigration and settlement patterns. It was taken in a Romansch settlement in central Minnesota about fifty years after the family's 1866 arrival in the United States with their widowed mother, Onna Maria (Anna Mary) Muggli DeGonda. *Family photograph, used with permission from Richard C. DeGonda.*

oral history interviews as documents that convey specific nuggets of information. Canadian oral historians Anna Sheftel and Stacey Zembrzycki note: "We often listen to our interviews to try to understand how our narrators construct memories and narratives of their own lived experiences; we look for patterns, connections, silences, and other hard-to-index material—we are as interested in form as in specific content."[8] From that perspective, following the tortoise rather than the hare—moving slowly, steadily, carefully through a recording or a transcript— contributes to a more nuanced understanding of the complexity of a narrator's story than can be achieved by identifying discrete topics or themes.

Still other oral historians have explored the value of revisiting interviews conducted years ago in light of access to new sources of information and new insights into how memory works.

Australian oral historian Alistair Thomson interviewed Fred Farrall, an Australian World War I veteran, in the 1980s in a project that turned into a book, *Anzac Memories*, which focused on Farrall's war experiences and subsequent struggles with shell shock, his involvement with the pacifist movement, and other aspects of his post-war life, including his radical activism.[9] (Anzac is shorthand for the Australian and New Zealand Army Corps, established in World War I.) In an updated edition of *Anzac Memories*, Thomson had access to wartime letters Farrall wrote to family members that, among other details, changed the oral historian's understanding of when Farrall developed his pacifist views. Thomson also had access to newly released Australian World War I pension and medical records that painted a far more complex picture of Farrall's medical and mental health history and his evolving anti-war sentiments.

Farrall's medical files were more than four inches thick and were dated from 1920 to 1981, with significant gaps during several periods, but they indicate he suffered everything from trench foot and associated disabilities to shell shock, then known widely as war neurosis, which more commonly today would be called post-traumatic stress disorder. Above all, the files show Farrall became a persistent and effective advocate for himself, Thomson found. Additionally, Thomson notes that new theories and perspectives on the effects of trauma, memory, and mental health add new insights to his efforts to make sense of Farrall's wartime experiences. Moreover, Thomson says, his own life experiences have intervened since he was a novice oral historian writing the first edition of *Anzac Memories* decades ago: "I've been lucky enough to revisit Fred's story long after his death, guided by new sources and new ideas. I wish I could now ask Fred about these conclusions, and I can imagine a robust discussion. It's a discussion Fred started for me in the 1980s which, through oral history, continues after his passing."[10]

Thomson's insights into his evolving understanding of Fred Farrall's story illustrate a critically important characteristic of oral history: It is always an exchange and a collaboration between two specific individuals. That exchange may occur in real time, as the interview is recorded. Or it may occur many years later, when the interview is separated from its origins by time and place and by the nature of the exchange itself, in which the disembodied narrator speaks only in a recording or in words on a page (or computer screen) to a more mature oral historian who conducted the interview years before or to a student who wasn't born when the original interview took place.

BLOGS AND PODCASTS

Blogs and podcasts are often seen as part of an organization's outreach or marketing strategy. They are developed to call attention to the organization.

Blogs, webpages with a specific focus that are regularly updated, are a useful tool for oral historians. They differ from an organization's informal Facebook updates, for example, in their careful and coordinated design and their planned and regulated placement of information. They can be used to disseminate up-to-date information about the practice of oral history, collections and publications related to oral history, and thoughts and analysis about interviews and the information in them. When developing an oral history blog, consider the information you want it to feature, include descriptive information about the oral history project collection that the interviews are drawn from, and insert a statement about working to the standards of the Oral History Association.[11]

Podcasts, digital files produced for downloading from the internet, are developed as a series of programs, usually thirty to sixty minutes long, with installments added regularly. They can help disseminate information about oral history and oral history projects through posting complete interviews or stories about projects including interview excerpts. Podcasts are audio but can have a visual component such as a series of photographs; they are similar in format to a radio show but can be accessed on demand as streamed or downloaded as content on computers, smartphones, and tablets. They are available through various apps; YouTube is one of the most common. When researching or developing oral history podcasts, look for and include information about the project the interviews were drawn from, the context in which the interviews were planned and recorded, confirmation the work was done according to Oral History Association standards, and where (archives or libraries, for example) the interviews are held and how they can be accessed. For examples of podcasts based on oral histories, see "Our Streets, Our Stories," Brooklyn Historical Society and the Brooklyn Public Library in New York, and "A Sense of Place – Oral Histories," a project of the National Park Service.[12]

Whatever strategy you choose to assess the information that emerges in an oral history, it is important to remember that the *words* from an interview are not, by themselves, sufficient. Nor should they always be taken at face value.

ORAL HISTORY OUTCOMES

Oral historians increasingly have been inspired to document times, places, and events not in the distant past but that may be as recent as the day before yesterday, motivated often by a desire to effect meaningful social change. While it may be difficult to draw a direct line of impact between a particular oral history project and subsequent change, such projects can help lay the groundwork. Voice of Witness, for example, a California-based non-profit organization, uses oral history to amplify "the voices of people impacted by—and fighting against—injustice."[13] It does so by publishing books based on oral histories with people from marginalized, disenfranchised, or otherwise ignored communities and by working extensively with educators to develop oral history-based curricula that enable people to further grassroots storytelling. Other social justice oral history work includes that of award-winning scholar Sarah C. Bishop, whose book *A Story to Save Your Life: Communication and Culture in Migrants' Search for Asylum* uses wide-ranging interviews to document stark realities of the US asylum system.[14] Policymakers are unlikely to be inspired to reform the US immigration system based solely on Bishop's book. But the in-depth information her work documents through interviews surely contributes to the accumulation of knowledge about this complex issue that may inspire lasting change. Still other oral history work focused on social justice and civic engagement, like that of the University of Florida's Samuel Proctor Oral History Program, uses oral history fieldwork to connect students with both the past and present. Under the leadership of former director Paul Ortiz, students participating in the Mississippi Freedom Project have conducted more than two hundred interviews dealing with civil rights activism and organizing in the Mississippi Delta. And in a less prominent undertaking, the program has had a real-time impact through a partnership with the university's College of Medicine in which students participating in a required geriatrics medicine clerkship are immersed in oral history to learn how to listen and talk to older patients, an often-marginalized population.[15]

Such examples represent merely the tip of the proverbial iceberg of oral historians' efforts to take on work that makes a difference now. But there's an ongoing magic to creating oral histories: whenever oral historians use well-planned and ethically carried out interviews to document and contextualize a time, place, event, or way of life, whether recent or long ago, they are keeping alive the firsthand experiences and knowledge of times and places that otherwise may fade from public memory. When those memories fade, the storehouse of human knowledge is likewise depleted. The steps detailed in the preceding chapters suggest an approach that not only makes it possible to create oral histories that you can use now, for an immediate purpose, but that also will make it possible for students, scholars, and the just plain curious to open a window onto a time and place outside their realm of experience and come away enriched, and perhaps inspired to take action, in ways you may not even be able to imagine. Your oral histories, in other words, may be motivated by specific, tangible social, political, or other goals. But they also are your gift to the future. And the history you document today in the expectation of effecting change in real time also will forge a link between a soon-forgotten past and generations yet unborn, enriching the lives of those who tell the stories today as well as those who will hear them, learn from them, and, perhaps, be inspired by them, in years to come.

NOTES

1. Working with interview materials you created offers an advantage over working with oral histories created by others because you know the context in which your interviews were conceived and carried out. If you ever try to work with oral histories whose creators neglected to document the interview purposes and circumstances in detail, you'll understand why this manual stresses the importance of providing such documentation.
2. Valerie Raleigh Yow, *Recording Oral History: A Guide for the Humanities and Social Sciences*, third edition (Lanham, MD: Rowman & Littlefield, 2015), 3–15.
3. Becky Boesen, Deepak Keshwani, Mary Kay Quinlan, and Petra Wahlqvist, *Pioneer Farms: A Century of Change* (Lincoln, NE: Rural Futures Institute, 2017).
4. Interviews with Charlie Botts and others who worked in the Cushman foundry also illustrate how oral history interviews seldom can stand alone and, indeed, are useful largely in conjunction with background information from other sources. For example, determining exactly when the foundry closed required sleuthing that involved consulting newspaper archives, corporate archives, and aerial photographs in addition to the recollections of current and retired workers. See also Mary Kay Quinlan and Barbara W. Sommer, *The People Who Made It Work: A Centennial*

History of the Cushman Motor Works (Lincoln, NE: Cushman Motor Works, 2001).

5. Laurie Mercier and Madeline Buckendorf, *Using Oral History in Community History Projects* (Carlisle, PA: Oral History Association, 2007).

6. Linda Shopes, "After the Interview Ends: Moving Oral History Out of the Archives and into Publication," *Oral History Review*, 42 (summer/fall 2015): 302.

7. In *The Death of Luigi Trastulli* and in other works, Italian scholar and oral historian Alessandro Portelli has shown the importance of going beyond the question of whether oral histories are literally true, but also to examine the *meanings* one can derive from narrators' accounts.

8. Anna Sheftel and Stacey Zembryzcki, "Slowing Down to Listen in the Digital Age: How New Technology is Changing Oral History Practice," *Oral History Review*, 44 (winter/spring 2017): 102.

9. For a detailed account of the evolution of *Anzac Memories*, see Alistair Thomson, *"Anzac Memories Revisited: Trauma, Memory and Oral History," Oral History Review*, 42 (winter/spring 2015).

10. Ibid, 29.

11. For examples of oral history blogs, see the Oral History Review blog, https://oralhistoryreview.org/, and the Oral History Society blog, https://www.ohs.org.uk/blog/.

12. Oral History Association, "Principles and Best Practices," https://oralhistory.org/principles-and-best-practices-revised-2018/, accessed November 24, 2023; Brooklyn Public Library and the Brooklyn Historical Society, "Our Streets, Our Stories," https://open.spotify.com/playlist/37i9dQZF1DWVbd3jrep6hf, accessed November 24, 2023; National Park Service, "A Sense of Place–Oral Histories," https://www.nps.gov/subjects/oralhistory/podcasts.htm, accessed November 24, 2023.

13. Voice of Witness, https://voiceofwitness.org/about/, accessed February 25, 2024.

14. Sarah C. Bishop, *A Story to Save Your Life: Communication and Culture in Migrants' Search for Asylum* (New York: Columbia University Press, 2022).

15. Samuel Proctor Oral History Program, https://oral.history.ufl.edu/, accessed February 25, 2024.

Appendix A

ORAL HISTORY ASSOCIATION PRINCIPLES

OHA Principles

Principles for Oral History

Adopted October, 2018

For OHA Best Practices and related statements, see
https://oralhistory.org/best-practices/, accessed 12/28/2023

For OHA Guidelines for Social Justice Oral History Work, see
https://oralhistory.org/guidelines-for-social-justice-oral-history-work/,
accessed 12/28/2023

- Introduction
- Core Principles of the OHA
- OHA Statement on Ethics
- Best Practices
- For Participants in Oral History Interviews
- Archiving Oral History (Adopted October 2019)
- Guidelines for Social Justice Oral History Work (Adopted 2022)
- Glossary

These documents replace the OHA's previous Principles and Best Practices, which were revised and adopted in 2009.

Introduction

The History behind Our Work, 1966-2009, by Sherna Berger Gluck[1]

Credit: Oral History Association.

This 2018 version of the Oral History Association's Principles and Best Practices, like each one before it for the past fifty years, is a product of its time. Since the initial 1968 Goals and Guidelines was issued, the theory and practice of oral history in the US has become more complicated and nuanced, influenced by both the expanding base of its practitioners and shifting intellectual paradigms in a host of disciplines. The trajectory of the theory and practice of oral history itself has moved apace in what Alistair Thomson has identified as four paradigmatic shifts, each of which is reflected in the various revisions of OHA's standards and guidelines.[2]

Despite differences in focus, the early stage of the oral history movement in the Anglophone world focused on oral history as data, what Thomson referenced as "the renaissance of memory as an historical source.[3] Reflecting this thinking, the Goals and Guidelines adopted in 1968 by the academic historians and archivists who founded the OHA displayed an empirical/positivist bent, with underlying assumptions about objectivity.[4] While the basics remained unchanged, in 1979 an Ethical Guidelines document was adopted that basically provided a useful checklist to help those engaged in the various stages of oral history process.[5]

With the increased visibility of a new and more diverse generation of oral history practitioners both inside and outside the academy, and the growing influence of cultural studies and feminist practices, oral history took a new turn in the 1980s. As a coeditor of one of the earliest anthologies noted: "Now a debate emerged in the profession over the purpose of oral history: was it intended to be (1) a set of primary source documents or (2) a process for constructing history from oral sources?" [6] These kinds of debates, fueled by the work of a new generation of oral historians in both the US and Europe, flourished during the late 1970s and early 1980s, reflecting what Thomson called "post-positivist approaches to memory and subjectivity."

As early as 1979, then president of OHA Waddy Moore had taken note of the changing nature of oral history, suggesting that a proverbial corner had been turned and that the OHA was ready to enter what he called "the second stage of self analysis."[7] Nevertheless, it was not until 1988-1990 that the next (third) of Thomson's paradigmatic shifts was evidenced in public OHA thinking: "the subjectivity of oral history relationships – interdisciplinary approaches."

Under the stewardship of immediate past president Donald Ritchie, four committees were formed in 1988, charged with revising the 1979 Evaluation Guidelines. In the course of their work, it became apparent that a new statement of principles was needed, and following the adoption of the 1989 Ethical Guidelines, a new committee was convened. The newly crafted Principles and Standards adopted in 1990 broke new ground. For the first time, the interactive and subjective nature of oral history was introduced; sensitivity to the "diversity of social and cultural experiences and to the implications of race, gender, class, ethnicity, age, religion, and sexual orientation" was specifically referenced; and ethical concerns were extended to include concern for the interviewee's community

By and large, the 1990 Principles and Standards and Ethical Guidelines stood the organization in good stead until the approach of the new millennium, when the vast implications of the digital revolution could no longer be ignored. Responding to the new challenges it posed, and engaging with the fourth paradigm transformation ("the digital revolution in oral history"), a Technology Update Committee drafted new guidelines that were adopted at the 1998 OHA conference and were incorporated into what became the 2000 edition of the OHA Standards and Evaluation Guidelines.[8]

Rather than respond to a paradigmatic shift, a committee was convened in 2008 to work on streamlining the OHA standards and guidelines, which, as Donald Ritchie noted, had become unwieldy and "more of a mini-manual than a statement of core principles."[9] Additionally, the various documents had not yet fully spoken to the changing constituency of the organization. The new revision, which for the first time used the terms *narrator* and *interviewee* interchangeably, was adopted at the 2009 Louisville conference.[10]

The regular reassessment of the values/principles and practices of oral history over the past fifty years has demonstrated a responsiveness of OHA to the paradigm shifts in oral history and in the various disciplines from which we draw insights. It has also helped to keep oral history practitioners sensitive to the impact and ethical implications of social and technological changes. -For those who have spent countless hours on revising these documents over the past fifty years, it has been a labor of love and a commitment to promote the highest standards of our craft.

2018 Principles and Best Practices Overview, by Troy Reeves and Sarah Milligan

For the development of this iteration of the Oral History Association's Principles and Best Practices, OHA President Todd Moye (2017-2018) convened a task force of twelve members under our stewardship, with an intentional inclusion of backgrounds from historical societies, community organizations, independent scholars, and academic historians from diverse geographical regions, with representation from a variety of age, gender, and racial demographics, and experience.

We worked to blend the large committee work with a combination of video chats, email correspondence, and small group work, initially talking through reactions to the historical documents, bringing inspiration for various logistical and language approaches from related fields, and finally settling on priorities for what could be accomplished over the course of a year. We also grappled with what this document could and should be as a text living on the Web with a multitude of targeted audiences, most with their own specific need for direction. Early in the process, we decided to think of this less as a single statement of Principles and Best Practices, but rather a suite of statements and guides addressing multiple perspectives and needs.

We identified four core documents to prioritize from our initial discussions with the task force members: (1) a core values statement defining our foundational beliefs, (2) a best practices statement to outline the work of an oral historian, (3) an ethics document to define ethical work in our field, and (4) a decoding document for participants interested in understanding their rights in ethical oral history work. There are definitely more documents that should go into this suite, and as we have worked through this process and received feedback from our task force and other OHA members, we have compiled recommendations for the OHA executive council of work that needs to continue in the coming year(s).

Moreover, this version of our principles and practices, among other things, reaffirms not only respect for narrators and their communities, but also the importance of being attentive to those who are especially vulnerable; it reemphasizes the dynamic, collaborative relationship between interviewer and narrator, with a commitment to ongoing participation and engagement and sensitivity to differences in power, constraints, interests and expectations. These principles have been incorporated into four documents listed above (Core, Ethics, Best Practices, and Participant's Rights), as well as a glossary to help define more deeply some of our terms.

Two final things to conclude: First, as noted above, there is more that could and should be done. During one phone call, we referred to this work as "scaffolding." While we will take pride in, and responsibility for, our efforts, we understand, even relish, seeing the additions that our work will inspire and bring forth. Last, we feel the best idea in these documents comes from the Ethics piece, which asserts that the ideas in it "represent the beginning of the path toward becoming an ethical oral historian, rather than its culmination." So, too, all the thoughts and ideas in all the other documents serve as the starting points to becoming an oral historian.

We are more than grateful to the task force members—Ryan Barland, Doug Boyd, Adrienne Cain, Sherna Berger Gluck, Erin Jessee, Calinda Lee, Rachel Mears, Martin Meeker, Tomas Summers-Sandoval, Liz Strong, Sady Sullivan, and Anne Valk—who remained engaged throughout the year of this work and who volunteered their time and expertise to ensure these documents represent who we strive to be as oral historians.

---

[1] Gluck's introduction draws on both Don Ritchie's excellent, earlier "History of the Ethical Guidelines" (https://oralhistory.org/wp-content/uploads/2009/10/History-of-the-Evaluation-Guidelines.pdf) and her experiences as a 2018 OHA Principles and Best Practices Task Force member.

[2] Alistair Thomson, "Four Paradigm Transformations in Oral History," *Oral History Review* 34, no.1 (Summer/Fall 2006): 49-70. For a longer historical account of oral history, see Rebecca Sharpless, "The History of Oral History,"

in *Handbook of Oral History*, ed. Thomas Charlton, Lois Myers, and Rebecca Sharpless (Lanham, MD: AltaMira, 2006).

[3] Thomson, "Four Paradigm Transformations," 51.

[4] In reporting on the adoption of Goals and Guidelines in 1969, the leadership of OHA noted "an opportunity and obligation on the part of all concerned to make this type of historical source as authentic and useful as possible"; *Oral History Newsletter* 3, no. 1, 1969.

[5] The Ethical Guidelines document came out of a gathering of OHA leadership at Wingspread Conference Ground in Racine, Wisconsin. See Ritchie, "History of the Ethical Guidelines."

[6] David Dunaway, "Introduction: The Interdisciplinarity of Oral History," in *Oral History: An Interdisciplinary Anthology*, 2nd ed., ed. Dunaway and Willa K. Baum (Walnut Creek, CA: AltaMira, 1996), 8-9.

[7] Waddy Moore, editorial, *Oral History Newsletter*, Spring 1978

[8] Participants at the Buffalo meeting where the technological update was adopted recall the long, spirited—and sometimes testy—discussion that took place in two separate sessions. After the first lengthy discussion, the committee was sent back to incorporate the changes that had been suggested, and following another long discussion, the new guidelines document was adopted.

[9] Ritchie, "History of the Ethical Guidelines."

[10] The question of what to call the person being interviewed had been debated from the inception of the OHA, and although no consensus emerged from the 1967 discussion, the default designation until 2009 became *interviewee*; *Oral History Newsletter* 1, no. 1, 1967. Because there was insufficient opportunity to reach consensus on the revised document, it was dubbed a beta version—that is, still in process.

OHA Core Principles

The Core Principles of the Oral History Association

1. The Oral History Association, in both its national and regional professional organizations, brings together practitioners from a variety of communities, backgrounds, and academic and professional fields, including many who might not label themselves oral historians. Nevertheless, whether motivated by scholarly research questions, political or social change goals, efforts to preserve history, pedagogical aims, or any other purpose, oral history practice shares common principles. This document lays out some of those guiding principles, keeping in mind the diverse practices of those involved in the collection, interpretation, use, and preservation of oral history.

What is Oral History?

2. Oral history refers to both the interview process and the products that result from a recorded spoken interview (whether audio, video, or other formats). In order to gather and preserve meaningful information about the past, oral historians might record interviews focused on narrators' life histories or topical interviews in which narrators are selected for their knowledge of a particular historical subject or event. Once completed, an interview, if it is placed in an archive, can be used beyond its initial purpose with the permission of both the interviewer and narrator.

3. The value of oral history lies largely in the way it helps to place people's experiences within a larger social and historical context. The interview becomes a record useful for documenting past events, individual or collective experiences, and understandings of the ways that history is constructed. Because it relies on memory[1], oral history captures recollections about the past filtered through the lens of a changing personal and social context.

4. The hallmark of an oral history interview is a dynamic, collaborative relationship between the interviewer and the narrator. While interviewers pose questions based on research and careful preparation, narrators shape

the interview based on what they deem to be relevant, meaningful, or appropriate to share. Despite the fluid nature of the interview process, an oral history is grounded in thoughtful planning and careful follow-through of the agreed-upon process.

Guiding Principles

5. The oral history process, from the interview stage through preservation, use, and access, must be guided by respect for narrators and the communities from which they come. This means a commitment to an <u>ethical process</u> and to honoring diverse cultural values, ways of knowing, and perspectives.

6. The interview process must be transparent, with ongoing participation, consent, and <u>engagement</u> among all parties from the first encounter between interviewer and narrator to the creation of end products.

7. Oral history practitioners must be sensitive to differences in power between the interviewer and the narrator as well as divergent interests and expectations inherent in any social relationship. These dynamics shape all aspects of the oral history process, including the selection of people to interview, research questions, personal interactions during the interview, interpretations, decisions on preservation and access, and the various ways that the oral history might be used.

8. To the greatest extent possible, both the narrator and the interviewer must be protected from harm, particularly those who are <u>vulnerable communities</u>. This means that certain lines of inquiry or public access to completed interviews might be precluded. Any stipulations should be considered before the beginning of the oral history process with the understanding that they can be renegotiated as the project proceeds.

9. Whenever possible, an oral history interview and its accompanying documentation should be preserved and made accessible to other users. Oral history practitioners must be clear on the various ways the interview might be preserved, made available, and used. Likewise, narrators must grant explicit permission to make their interview public, and when possible, should

be given an opportunity to establish parameters for preservation, access, and use.

10. While oral historians are bound by laws covering <u>copyright</u>, and in some institutions might be bound by regulations governing research involving <u>living human subjects</u>, their responsibilities also go beyond these official rules. They should conduct themselves <u>ethically and thoughtfully</u> and be vigilant about the possible consequences to narrators and their communities of both the interview process and the access/use of completed interviews.

---

[1] The intersection of oral history and memory is well documented. To explore this concept more, please see the Oral History Review: <u>https://academic.oup.com/ohr</u>

OHA Statement on Ethics

Oral historians have ethical obligations that are both specific to oral history methodology and shared with other methodologies and practices, ranging from anthropology to archival work. Ethics encompasses the principles that should govern the multiple relationships inherent in oral history. Everyone involved in oral history work, from interviewers and narrators to archivists and researchers, becomes part of a web of mutual responsibility working to ensure that the narrator's perspective, dignity, privacy, and safety are respected. This statement draws upon the decades of thoughtful work concerning the appropriate way to engage with humans as participants in research projects.

Here we offer general principles for practicing oral history in an ethical way. These points represent the beginning of the path toward becoming an ethical oral historian, rather than its culmination.

Preparation & Communication

Oral historians strive to become fully informed about oral history theory, methodology, and ethics. They work to become informed of oral history practices, including how narrators and interviewers should be treated equitably, with care and respect. One way to help ensure fair treatment is to create a beginning-to-end process that works for everyone involved. This process[1] should entail, at minimum, four points:

1. Prior to beginning the interview, the interviewer obtains the narrator's informed consent, which means, most generally, documenting the knowing agreement of the narrator to participate in the process and overall project, as described in "The Core Principles of the Oral History Association."
2. The interviewer clearly communicates the goals of the project, the potential risks of participating in it, and the proviso that, once accessible[2], the oral history can be used[3] in any number of ways, by any number of potential users. While oral historians strive to protect the narrator, they are careful, at every point in the process, not to make promises that they cannot keep.
3. The interviewer provides the narrator, whenever possible, with the opportunity to review and approve the interview (recording and/or transcript) prior to using the interview, depositing it in an archive, or otherwise making it accessible to the public.
4. While developing this process, oral historians should conduct preliminary research about the topics they intend to study and be comfortable with the recording technology they intend to utilize.

Collaboration: The Oral History Interview

The interview is at the heart of the oral historian's work and thus requires extra attention to ensure that the encounter meets ethical standards.

Oral historians should consider the goals of the research project and seek narrators who are able, collectively, to present a variety of points of view. When contacting potential narrators, interviewers should clearly and plainly share the project goals, explain the interview process, and describe what will happen to the interview after it is completed.

Power operates in every human engagement, and no less so in oral history interviewing. Ethical oral historians take care to give serious reflection to power differentials, implicit bias, potential areas of disagreement, and other instances in which their positions do not align with the narrator. Choice of interview strategy, such as possible topics covered, the language in which the interview is conducted, or question phrasing, should be part of the consideration. Oral historians recognize the differences that might exist between themselves and the narrator; they consider how these differences might impact the way a narrator shares memories; and they strive to treat each narrator equitably and do their best to listen with empathy.

During the course of the interview itself, oral historians attempt to minimize potential harm to the narrator, communicate the narrator's right to refuse to answer questions, and honestly describe their institutional, professional, political, and other affiliations, as well as obligations and demands. They continue to safeguard the trust implied by the oral history process and to work through competing interests in fair and impartial ways.

After the interview, oral history ethics strongly recommends that the narrator be given the opportunity to review the interview (recording and/or transcript) and approve what was said for public release or other use. This step sets oral history apart[4] from other[5] methodologies in that it ensures the narrator's account enters the public record[6]; and that future researchers who wish to draw upon these accounts can access them in their entirety–not just excerpts that may lack important context. The interview should not be made public until the narrator, as the original recording's copyright holder, has provided formal authorization to do so.

Stewardship: Preservation and Access

Oral history is unique, in part because the collaboration between interviewer and narrator results in a historical document for posterity. In most instances, the interview and supporting material[7] is made available to the broader public through deposit in an archive, distribution online, and/or any number of other methods for providing public access. Because of this, ethics calls for narrator review and approval.

There are many valid options for managing the review process; thus, ethical oral historians plan ahead and develop a process that works in their specific context, while adhering to the principles outlined here. Options for narrator review include the right to delete, restrict, and/or redact portions of an interview; the ability to add clarifications and correct mistakes; and the choice to keep the interview closed to the public until a set date or to decline to release it to the public in the first place.

Oral historians should establish a clear procedure[8] (including dates or a timeline) for finalizing, archiving, and releasing the interview to the public. This step communicates to the narrator that the process has been completed and that the interview is (or will be) preserved and made accessible to the public.

Oral historians should promote equitable access to the final interview (recording and/or transcript) and attempt to make these materials accessible in a timely manner. Oral historians and their archivist partners clearly document relevant metadata so that future users will know easily who was interviewed, when and where the interview was conducted, and other key pieces of data about the interview. As the interview is prepared for preservation, decisions about description, categorization, and access should respect the personhood and desired privacy of the narrator. Moreover, oral historians should educate themselves about legal concerns such as libel, invasion of privacy, and other issues that might endanger the narrator.

One goal of the agreed-upon oral history process is that it allows the narrator to make an informed decision about whether to participate in a project and to make the interview public. An ethical oral history process assures that the narrator is fully informed about the many possible uses of the oral history once it is publicly available.

Using Oral Sources [9]

The core of the oral history process concludes once the narrator has approved the interview and, in most instances, plans have been made for it to be preserved and made available to the public. Still, scholars and other users of oral sources, including oral history interviews, should educate themselves about discipline-based resources and ethical guidelines that detail issues in more depth. Oral historians who intend to use the oral sources that they create or oral sources created by others should endeavor to use the oral histories honestly and respectfully. This means users of oral sources should provide analyses, including when edited or excerpted, that remain true to the words and meanings offered by the narrator and take care to not quote words out of context or otherwise contort the original meaning. Users may arrive at conclusions that diverge from those offered by a narrator, but conclusions should be derived from evidence properly cited.

---

[1] We recommend that this process be fully documented in writing and that signatures of all participating parties be obtained and preserved in project records. However, we recognize that limitations of time, language, literacy, and other factors may make this recommendation unfeasible; in those cases, we recommend both the communication of the goals and risks associated with the project along with interviewee informed consent be recorded prior to the beginning of the interview.

[2] The ultimate plan for what happens with the interview once it is completed should start before a narrator is approached about participation, and well-before an interview is conducted. For full transparency and strong project planning, the process for care and access of the recorded interview should be mapped out in the early stages of the process.

[3] For example: printed publications (monographs, pamphlets, journals), text in museum & web-based exhibits, examples used in pedagogy (both K-12 & higher ed), performances (plays, ballet, opera, monologues), others

[4] What also sets it apart: The oral historian's unique responsibility and skill in co-creating, co-representing, and co-interpreting.

[5] such as interviewing methodologies that are journalistic, anthropological, folkloristic, sociological, or linguistic

[6] whether the plan is to share within a family group or with the public at large, it is important to have a plan there is a plan for long-term care of, and access to, (whatever that means for the project) the recorded interview.

[7] Transcript, images, artifacts, indexes etc...

[8] We recommend reviewing the Society of American Archivists' Core Values Statement and Code of Ethics: https://www2.archivists.org/statements/saa-core-values-statement-and-code-of-ethics.

[9] We recommend users of oral sources consult various discipline-based ethical guidelines. For example: the American Historical Association's Statement on Standards of Professional Conduct; the American Anthropological Association's Principles of Professional Responsibility; the American Sociological Association's Code of Ethics; and the Society of Professional Journalists' Code of Ethics.; The Society of American Archivists' Core Values Statement and Code of Ethics; The American Folklore Society 's Statement on Ethics.

Appendix B

SAMPLE ORAL HISTORY FORMS

The following pages provide examples of forms that oral history project coordinators and administrators may find useful.[1]

SAMPLE DONOR FORM WITH COPYRIGHT LANGUAGE

(also called Legal Release Agreement. Note: This form is sometimes modified to provide a separate form for narrator and for interviewer.)

DONOR FORM
The mission of the _____ (oral history project) is to document the history of __ _____. The major part of this effort is the collection of oral history interviews with knowledgeable individuals.
Thank you for participating in our project. Please read and sign this donor form to release your interview for future use. Before doing this, read it carefully and ask questions you may have about its terms and conditions.

AGREEMENT

I, _____ , narrator, donate and convey my oral history interview dated _____ to the _____ (oral history project/repository name). In making this gift, I understand that I am conveying all rights, title, and interest in copyright to the oral history project/repository. I also grant the oral history project/repository the right to use my name and likeness in promotional materials for outreach and educational materials. In return, the oral history project/repository grants me a non-exclusive license to use my interview through my lifetime.

I further understand that I will have the opportunity to review and approve my interview before it is placed in the repository and made available to the public. Once I have approved it, the oral history project/repository will make my interview available for research without restriction. Future uses may include quotation in printed materials or audio/video excerpts in any media, and availability on the internet.

NARRATOR	INTERVIEWER
Name (print) _____	Name (print) _____
Signature _____	Signature _____
Date _____	Date _____

SAMPLE RECORDING EQUIPMENT OPERATOR/PHOTOGRAPHER DONOR FORM (ALSO CALLED LEGAL RELEASE AGREEMENT)

Note: If a recording equipment operator and/or a photographer participate in an interview, each must sign a form for each interview.

I, _____ (name of interviewer/recording equipment operator/photographer—circle one), hereby give to the _____ (repository) as a donation this interview recorded on _____ (date). With this gift, I hereby transfer to the _____ (repository) legal title and all literary rights to the interview, including copyright.

I understand the _____ (repository) may make the interview available for research and use as it may determine, but it may not be broadcast, cablecast, or electronically published for commercial purposes without my written consent.

Interviewer/Recording Operator/Photographer

_____
(one signature per form)

Address _____

City, State, Zip _____

_____

Date _____

Form filled out by_____

Date_____

SAMPLE PROJECT DESIGN STATEMENT

PROJECT DESIGN STATEMENT
GENERAL
PROJECT NAME
PARTNER or GRANTING INSTITUTION
GOALS
MISSION STATEMENT
PROJECT CO-CREATORS
COMMUNITY ENGAGEMENT CONTACTS
ADVISORY COUNCIL MEMBERS
PROJECT CONTENT
FOCUS
SCOPE
PROJECT TOPICS
SOURCES/RESEARCH
PROJECT MANAGEMENT
DURATION
PROJECTED NUMBER OF NARRATORS
EQUIPMENT (type, media)
SPACE NEEDS—ADMINISTRATION, INTERVIEWS
BUDGET
COMMUNITY RESOURCES
REPOSITORY/LONG-TERM CARE PLAN
ONLINE ACCESS FOR INTERVIEWS (website, blog, podcast)
Submitted by and Date
Revised by and Date

SAMPLE PHOTOGRAPH AND MEMORABILIA FORM

PHOTOGRAPH/MEMORABILIA FORM	
PROJECT NAME	
OWNER (of photograph/memorabilia)	
Name	
Address	**Phone/Email**
ITEM	
Type	**Quantity**
Detailed Description (describe item and circumstances of learning about it)	
Associated Dates	
Physical Condition	
Owner Instructions for Use, Loan, Gift	
RETURNED/DISPOSITION	
Items Returned By (name)	
If Gift, Disposition of Item	
If Loan, Reason for Return and Date of Return	

OWNER	INTERVIEWER
Name (print)	**Name (print)**
Signature	**Signature**
Date (item identified)	**Date (item identified)**
Date (item returned to owner or donated)	**Date (item returned to owner or donated)**

SAMPLE LETTER OF AGREEMENT, INTERVIEWER

Note: This form could be used for paid and volunteer interviewers.

I, _____, interviewer for the _____
Oral History Project, understand and agree to the following statements:

- I understand the goals and purposes of this project and understand I am representing the _____
  _____ (project sponsor, co-creators) when I am conducting an interview.
- I have participated in oral history training sessions and am familiar with the recording equipment.
- I understand the legal and ethical considerations regarding the interviews and will communicate them to and carry them out with each narrator I interview.
- I am willing to do the necessary preparation, including background research, for each interview I conduct.
- I will treat each narrator with respect, and I understand each interview will be conducted in a spirit of openness that will allow the narrator to answer all questions as fully and freely as they wish.
- I am aware of the need for confidentiality of interview content until such time as the interviews are released for public use and I will not exploit the narrator's story.
- I understand my responsibilities regarding any archival materials or artifacts that the narrator may want to include in the interview process.
- I agree to turn all interview materials over to the designated personnel in a timely manner and to help facilitate all necessary processing steps.

_____ Date: _____
(Interviewer)

_____ Date: _____
(Designated Project Co-Creator)

SAMPLE LETTER OF AGREEMENT, TRANSCRIBER

Note: This form may be helpful for use with transcribers, both paid and volunteer.

I,_____, a transcriber or a transcript audit-checker for the
_____ Oral History Project, understand and agree to the following statements:

- I will provide full, accurate, verbatim transcripts.
- I will follow the transcript format, making sure each transcript clearly identifies the narrator, interviewer, place and date of the interview, and copyright status.
- I will follow the full transcribing process, including:

    ○ Developing a draft transcript (typed or through use of a transcribing app)
    ○ Audit-checking the draft transcript
    ○ Returning the draft for review
    ○ Finalizing the draft
    ○ Printing the final copy on acid-free paper if requested
    ○ Providing an electronic copy

- My work will be done in _____ (word processing program) unless otherwise specified.
- I understand the interviewer will provide a list of proper and place names to facilitate accurate transcribing.
- I understand the narrator will have thirty days to review a transcript and return for corrections. After that time, the transcript will be considered complete.
- I understand the need for confidentiality of interview content until such time as the interview is released for public use and I will not exploit the narrator's story.
- I will turn all materials, including copies of the interview recordings and transcripts, over to designated personnel immediately upon completing the transcribing work.

_____ Date: _____
(Transcriber)

_____ Date: _____
(Designated Project Co-Creator)

SAMPLE NARRATOR BIOGRAPHY FORM

Note: A narrator biography form provides background information for future users. Be aware of any specific narrator privacy needs when using this form.

NARRATOR BIOGRAPHY FORM	
PROJECT NAME	
FULL NAME	**CONTACT (TELEPHONE, EMAIL ADDRESS)**
OTHER NAMES KNOWN BY	**YEAR/PLACE OF BIRTH**
PLACE OF RESIDENCE	**YEARS IN THE COMMUNITY**
OCCUPATION	**EDUCATION**
RELEVANCE TO THE PROJECT	
RELEVANT BIOGRAPHICAL INFORMATION (AS IT RELATES TO THE GOALS OF THE PROJECT) *Fill in information relevant to the project with sensitivity to narrator privacy needs.*	
FAMILY (full name, date of birth, relationship to interviewer)	
COMMUNITY ACTIVITIES (include activity, date, and significance to the project)	
INTERESTS	
INFLUENCES	
LIFE MILESTONES	
Completed by	**Date**

SAMPLE INTERVIEWER BIOGRAPHY FORM

Note: An interviewer biography form provides background information for future users. Be aware of any specific privacy needs when using this form.

INTERVIEWER BIOGRAPHY FORM	
PROJECT NAME	
FULL NAME	**CONTACT (TELEPHONE, EMAIL ADDRESS)**
OTHER NAMES KNOWN BY	**YEAR/PLACE OF BIRTH**
PLACE OF RESIDENCE	**YEARS IN THE COMMUNITY**
OCCUPATION	**EDUCATION**
RELEVANCE TO THE PROJECT	
RELEVANT BIOGRAPHICAL INFORMATION (AS IT RELATES TO THE GOALS OF THE PROJECT) *Fill in any information relevant to the project with sensitivity to interviewer privacy needs.*	
FAMILY (full name, date of birth, relationship to narrator)	
COMMUNITY ACTIVITIES (include activity, date, and significance to the project)	
INTERESTS	
INFLUENCES	
LIFE MILESTONES	
Completed by	**Date**

SAMPLE INTERVIEW SUMMARY FORM

Note: This form is a first oral history interview processing step.

INTERVIEW INFORMATION FORM	
PROJECT NAME	**INTERVIEW ID#**
NARRATOR	**INTERVIEWER**
NAME (as it will appear in the public record)	**NAME**
CONTACT (address, telephone number, email)	**CONTACT (address, telephone number, email)**
OTHER NAMES NARRATOR KNOWN BY	
INTERVIEW DATE	**INTERVIEW LENGTH**
RECORDING MEDIUM _____ digital audio _____digital video	
DELIVERY MEDIUM (check all that apply) ____sound file ____sound card ____CD ____DVD ____ external hard drive ____flash drive	
TECHNICAL NOTES (make/model of recorders and microphones, formats recorded in)	
INTERVIEW NOTES (physical environment, narrator's response to interview request, narrator's response to interview, setting, sound quality, interruptions)	
DATE DONOR FORM SIGNED _____	
PROPER NAMES (personal and place names with proper spelling, dates if mentioned)	
KEYWORDS	
SUMMARY OF INTERVIEW CONTENT	
COMPLETED BY	**DATE**

SAMPLE POTENTIAL NARRATOR FORM

Note: This form helps keep track of additional potential narrator names as they come up.

_____
(project name)

Name: _____

Address:

_____

_____

Telephone (home): _____ Telephone (work): _____

Email: _____ Fax: _____

Preliminary Narrator Background Information (Describe why this person was suggested
as a narrator and what types of information they have about oral history project topics):

Form filled out by_____

Date_____

SAMPLE INTERVIEW TRACKING FORM

Note: The suggested steps on this form help keep track of an oral history project and its interviews. Fill out one form for each interview.

INTERVIEW PROGRESS FORM		
PROJECT NAME	**INTERVIEW ID#**	
NARRATOR	**INTERVIEWER**	
NAME	**NAME**	
CONTACT (address, telephone number, email)	**CONTACT**	
INTERVIEW DATE		

DATE COMPLETED	TASK	NOTES
	Log interview recording and assign an interview ID#	
	Interview Scheduled (date and place)	
	Interview Recorded (date)	
	Interview Donor Form Signed (date and type)	
	Thank Narrator	
	Log Donor Form	
	Log Interview Summary	
	Copy Recording (store copy in separate location)	
	Label Recording Media	
	Transcribe Interview (use transcribing app or transcriber, identify which option used)	
	Check Facts and Verify Spelling of Proper and Place Names	

DATE COMPLETED	TASK	NOTES
	Audit-check Transcript (date and checker)	
	Narrator's Review (date and comments)	
	Complete Interview Forms	
	Artifacts and Memorabilia (note if any identified)	
	Assemble All Project Materials	
	Deliver Completed Oral History to Repository (name of repository or info about alternate placement and handling)	
	Prepare Oral History for Website	
	Archive Oral Histories	
	Celebrate	

SAMPLE CORRESPONDENCE: INITIAL CONTACT LETTER

Date: _____

Dear _____ (narrator)

    I am writing to you on behalf of the _____ oral history project. Through this project, we hope to collect information about _____ (project purpose).

    We would like to talk to you about being interviewed as part of this project. All interview information will be _____ _____ (identify disposition).

    One of our project members will call on you soon to talk about this with you and to ask your permission to be interviewed.

    Thank you.

Sincerely yours,

Project Co-Creator
_____ Oral History Project

SAMPLE CORRESPONDENCE: INTERVIEW CONFIRMATION LETTER

Date: _____

Dear _____ (narrator)

    Thank you for agreeing to be interviewed for the _____ oral history project. I (we) will come to interview you on _____ (date) at _____ (time and place).

During the interview, we will talk about:

List topics to be covered, such as:

- Your background
- Your memories of how you first heard about (topic)
- Your memories of getting started with (topic)
- Your memories of highlights involving (topic)
- Your memories of difficulties involving (topic)
- Your final thoughts and assessment of (topic)

    As part of the interview, I will ask you to give your permission for use of your interview (note: and your copyright if applicable) to the _____ (repository or alternate situation). A copy of the interview will be given to you and your family.

    Thank you.

Sincerely yours,

Interviewer
_____ Oral History Project

SAMPLE CORRESPONDENCE: THANK YOU LETTER

Date: _____

Dear _____ (narrator)

Thank you for your oral history interview for the _____ oral history project on _____ (date). The information you gave in your interview was very helpful and will be kept at the _____ (repository or alternate situation).

A copy of the interview has been made for you and your family. I am delivering it with this letter.

Thank you again for your time and your information.

Sincerely yours,

Interviewer
_____ Oral History Project

NOTE

1. The forms in this manual are modeled on those included in the *Community Oral History Toolkit*. Nancy MacKay, Mary Kay Quinlan, and Barbara W. Sommer, *Community Oral History Toolkit* (New York, NY: Routledge, 2013).

Appendix C

SPECIALIZED CARE GUIDELINES

The need for care of oral histories begins when the recorder is turned off and continues through the lifetime of their access and use. Care guidelines may change, but the need for care remains constant.

The Minnesota State Archives at the Minnesota Historical Society developed "Electronic Records Management Guidelines." The recommendations for care are wide-ranging; this list of standard care steps includes storage environment recommendations from the guidelines that are applicable to oral histories:[1]

- Make copies of all recordings; maintain one copy as recorded as the archival master; make another copy as a user access copy.
- Print archival masters of all paper materials on acid-free paper. Store the archival masters in acid-free folders and acid-free containers.
- Store the storage devices holding electronic copies of oral histories in acid-free boxes on archival shelving; label archival masters as such.
- Take care to make sure players are available for the recordings.
- Protect the oral histories from dust, dirt, and water.
- For server rooms containing dedicated RAID-ready (Redundant Array of Inexpensive Disks) hard disk drives such as those used to hold electronic copies of oral histories, maintain storage conditions at sixty-five to seventy-five degrees Fahrenheit at 35 to 45 percent relative humidity.
- For paper materials including transcripts, maintain storage conditions at sixty-five to seventy degrees Fahrenheit at 40 to 50 percent relative humidity.

If your collections include analog recordings that have been digitized but are retained as archival masters, keep the following storage guidelines in mind:

- For analog recordings in long-term storage, maintain conditions as close to fifty degrees Fahrenheit and 30 percent humidity as possible, but not below this level; allow the audio and video tapes to acclimate to room temperature before use.

If your collections include analog audio or video tapes, CDs, or DVDs still in use, keep these storage guidelines in mind:

- For analog recordings in use, maintain storage conditions at sixty-five to seventy degrees Fahrenheit at a relative humidity of 40 to 50 percent with optimum conditions toward the lower end of this range.
- For CDs and DVDs, maintain storage conditions at sixty-two to sixty-eight degrees Fahrenheit at about 40 percent relative humidity.[2]

What about care policies? What procedures should a repository have in place to prevent loss and damage to oral history materials, including documentation about their creation? Generally, access policies include the following:

- A collections access policy identifying the copyright holder, user policies and procedures, permission process for use of materials, and copyright citation guidelines
- A collections access form with a place for name and contact information of user, review of collections access policy information, and place for signature and date
- A master list of all interviews and all related oral history materials
- A master (non-circulating) file for each interview

- Non-circulating, acid-free transcripts with working copies available for users
- Separate storage for non-circulating archival masters with working copies available for users
- A designated person or position responsible for curatorial care of a collection
- Supervision of access to collection including designated user areas that are separate from collections storage areas
- Use of oral history materials allowed only in designated user areas
- Policies for protection of media when handled
- Policies for use and control of researcher copies of recordings and transcripts
- Standard building surveillance systems including general alarms

For more detailed information on care and maintenance standards, check with your state historical society, your library, a university archive, the Society of American Archivists, and resource websites such as *Oral History in the Digital Age*.

NOTES

1. For the complete set of information, see Minnesota State Archives, Minnesota Historical Society, "Electronic Records Management Guidelines," https://www.mnhs.org/preservation/state-archives/help#guidelines, accessed November 18, 2023; see also Douglas A. Boyd, "The Digital Mortgage: Digital Preservation of Oral History," in *Oral History in the Digital Age*, edited by Douglas A. Boyd, Steve Cohen, Brad Rakerd, and Dean Rehberger (Washington, DC: Institute of Museum and Library Services, 2012), ohda.matrix.msu.edu/2012/06/the-digital-mortgage/, accessed November 18, 2023.
2. For more information, see Nancy MacKay, *Curating Oral Histories: From Interview to Archive*, second edition (New York: Routledge, 2016), 39–44, 57, 129, 139–43.

Appendix D

SAMPLE TRANSCRIBING GUIDE

When planning to transcribe, consider developing guidelines for format and stye. For example:[1]

- Transcript title page format. This should include the narrator's name, project name, interview date, and copyright information. Many also include the interviewer's name.
- Transcript format. This should include the first-page heading, format for identifying the interviewer and narrator, pagination, line spacing (for draft transcripts and the final document), and font (typeface) style including use of bold and italics.
- A stylistic approach regarding use of paragraphs. Some oral historians prefer a narrator's comments be presented in one long paragraph, regardless of change in subjects. Others prefer that an extremely long statement be broken into shorter blocks for ease of reading. Paragraphs in oral history transcripts generally are not indented.
- Guidelines for spelling, abbreviations, numbers, and honorifics. What about spelling of proper names and procedures for ensuring accuracy? (Was it John Smith or Jon Smythe who was prominently mentioned?) The need to check for correct spelling holds true for interviews done with family members as well. Was Great-grandma's name spelled Anne, Ann, or Anna? Pronunciation is not always a guide; a name may be pronounced in one way (Anna or—phonetically—Ahna) while spelled in another way (Anne).
- Guidelines for identifying people by full names and places by full location. If a full name is not stated, include the full name in brackets the first time a person is mentioned. When a town name is mentioned, include the name of the state in brackets when first mentioned.
- Guidelines for standardized punctuation. Where should a transcriber insert commas? What about the use of ellipses, dashes, brackets, parentheses, and quotation marks? Transcribers follow accepted guides and standards; it is helpful to choose a standard style and to have a style manual available as a reference for your project.
- A stylistic approach for use of language. How do you want to handle false starts (which can indicate thought process), filled pauses (ums, ers, ahs), Freudian slips, abrupt changes in subject, and grammatical errors? The goal in transcribing is a truthful representation of the spoken word that respectfully represents the narrator.
- A stylistic approach for persistent mispronunciations, grammatical errors, vernacular speech, and regional speech patterns. Transcripts reflect the interview as accurately as possible, but carefully think through the implications of attempting to replicate in writing mispronunciations, dialect, and the like, which almost always can be seen as pejorative. On the other hand, some narrators may specifically request that an interview be transcribed exactly as spoken for cultural reasons.[2]
- An approach and strategy for transcribing indecipherable words. Even the most carefully recorded interview can yield such words or phrases. What is the process you want your transcribers to follow? How will these be handled in the audit-checking and narrator-review process? Transcribers generally listen to a word or phrase at least three times before indicating it is indecipherable. Indecipherable phrases are identified in transcripts by a bracketed statement; narrator review of the transcript can be a help in deciphering these phrases.

- An approach for inserting descriptive information. This kind of information usually is enclosed in brackets. Examples include [laughs], [pounds table], and [phone rings]. This convention also is used for noting a break in the interview [general discussion] and for noting mechanical failings or sound intrusions. Example: [noise from jet landing at nearby airport can be heard].
- An approach for handling interviews in another language or for interviews that contain words or phrases from another language. Ideally, transcribers of interviews in another language will be fluent in the language. Standard guidelines call for fully transcribing an interview in the language as recorded as well as providing a translation into the dominant language.
- An approach for handling information that may be culturally sensitive, sacred, confidential, or narrator-restricted. Here the ethical standards described in chapter 4 should be clearly and carefully taught to all project transcribers. Project leaders will want to specify guidelines that conform to these standards.
- The use of footnotes or endnotes, both explanatory and reference, to provide additional information or enhance clarity. The style manual will be helpful here.
- A suggested format for developing transcriber's notes documenting the details of the transcribing process for future users.

NOTES

1. The Minnesota Historical Society Oral History Office, "Transcribing, Editing, and Processing Guidelines," provides samples of transcript format: https://www.mnhs.org/sites/default/files/library/research/oral-history/transcribing_guidelines.pdf, accessed November 18, 2023. The "Style Guide" from the Baylor Institute for Oral History covers a comprehensive list of transcript style guidelines from abbreviations to word lists: https://www.baylor.edu/old/2021-02/_oralhistory/doc.php/14142.pdf, accessed November 1, 2023.
2. Julie Cruikshank wrote of Yukon elders in Canada who spoke English as a second language and wanted their interviews transcribed exactly as spoken so people in the future could "hear" them. For more information, see Julie Cruikshank, *The Social Life of Stories: Narrative and Knowledge in the Yukon Territory* (Lincoln, NE: University of Nebraska Press, 1998; paperback 2000), 16.

Appendix E

SELECTED SOURCES

Many oral history sources are available in print form or on the World Wide Web. Included here are readers, anthologies, guides, and manuals as well as several websites and links to various oral history associations. Many of the publications have extensive bibliographies. For more information, also consult your local library, historical organization, and the Oral History Association.

SELECTED ORAL HISTORY PUBLICATIONS

Bishop, Sarah C. *A Story to Save Your Life: Communication and Culture in Migrants' Search for Asylum*. New York: Columbia University Press, 2022.

Boesen, Becky, Deepak Keshwani, Mary Kay Quinlan, and Petra Wahlqvist. *Pioneer Farms: A Century of Change*. Lincoln, NE: Rural Futures Institute, 2017.

Boyd, Douglas A., and Mary A. Larson, eds. *Oral History and Digital Humanities: Voice, Access, and Engagement*. New York, New York: Palgrave Macmillan, 2014.

Bryson, Anna, and Seán McConville, assisted by Mairead McClean. *The Routledge Guide to Interviewing: Oral History, Social Enquiry, and Investigation*. New York, NY: Routledge, 2014.

Cave, Mark, and Stephen Sloan, eds. *Listening on the Edge: Oral History in the Aftermath of Crisis*. New York: Oxford University Press, 2014.

Charlton, Thomas L., Lois E. Myers, and Rebecca Sharpless, eds. *Handbook of Oral History*. Lanham, MD: AltaMira Press, 2006.

Charlton, Thomas L., Lois E. Myers, and Rebecca Sharpless, eds. *History of Oral History: Foundations and Methodology*. Lanham, MD: AltaMira Press, 2007.

Dunaway, David K., and Willa K. Baum, eds. *Oral History: An Interdisciplinary Anthology*, second edition. Walnut Creek, CA: AltaMira Press, 1996.

Frisch, Michael A. *A Shared Authority: Essays on the Craft and Meaning of Oral History and Public History*. Albany, NY: State University of New York Press, 1990.

Grele, Ronald J., ed. *Envelopes of Sound: The Art of Oral History*, second edition. New York, NY: Praeger, 1991.

Lanman, Barry A., and Laura M. Wendling, eds. *Preparing the Next Generation of Oral Historians: An Anthology of Oral History Education*. Lanham, MD: AltaMira Press, 2006.

MacKay, Nancy, Mary Kay Quinlan, and Barbara W. Sommer. *Community Oral History Toolkit*. New York, NY: Routledge, 2013.

MacKay, Nancy. *Curating Oral Histories: From Interview to Archives*, second edition. New York, NY: Routledge, 2015.

MacKay, Nancy, ed. *Practicing Oral History* series. New York, NY: Routledge, ongoing.

Mahuika, Nepia. *Rethinking Oral History & Tradition: An Indigenous Perspective*. New York, NY: Oxford University Press, 2019.

Neuenschwander, John A. *A Guide to Oral History and the Law*, second edition. New York, NY: Oxford University Press, 2014.

Perks, Robert, and Alistair Thomson, eds. *The Oral History Reader*, third edition. New York, NY: Routledge, 2016.

Portelli, Alessandro. *The Death of Luigi Trastulli and Other Stories: Form and Meaning in Oral History*. Albany, NY: State University of New York Press, 1991.

Ritchie, Donald A. *Doing Oral History: A Practical Guide*, third edition. New York, NY: Oxford University Press, 2015.

Ritchie, Donald A., ed. *The Oxford Handbook of Oral History*. New York, NY: Oxford University Press, 2010.

Shopes, Linda, et al., eds. *Palgrave Studies in Oral History* series. New York, NY: Palgrave Macmillan, ongoing.

Sommer, Barbara W. *Hard Work and a Good Deal: The Civilian Conservation Corps in Minnesota*. St. Paul, Minnesota: Minnesota Historical Society Press, 2008, reissued in paperback 2022.

Thompson, Paul, and Joanna Bornat. *The Voice of the Past: Oral History*, fourth edition. New York, NY: Oxford University Press, 2017.

Wheeler, Winona, Charles E. Trimble, Mary Kay Quinlan, and Barbara W. Sommer. *Indigenous Oral History Manual: Canada and the United States*. New York, NY: Routledge, 2024.

Whitman, Glenn. *Dialogue with the Past: Engaging Students and Meeting Standards through Oral History*. Walnut Creek, CA: AltaMira Press, 2004.

Yow, Valerie Raleigh. *Recording Oral History: A Guide for the Humanities and Social Sciences*, third edition. Lanham, MD: Rowman & Littlefield, 2015.

ARTICLES

Baum, Willa. "The Other Uses of Oral History," *The Oral History Review*, 34:1 (winter/spring 2007).

Barnett, Teresa, ed. "Special Section: Looking Back, Looking Forward: Fifty Years of Oral History," *The Oral History Review*, 43:2 (summer/fall 2016): 315-91.

Boyd, Doug. "OHMS: Enhancing Access to Oral History for Free," *Oral History Review*, 40 (winter/spring 2013).

Coupland, Bethann. "Remembering Blaenavon: What Can Group Interviews Tell Us about 'Collective Memory'?" *Oral History Review*, 42 (summer/fall 2015): 277-99.

Douglass, Enid A. "Oral History and Public History," *The Oral History Review*, 8:1 (January 1980).

French, Lindsay. "Refugee Narratives; Oral History and Ethnography: Stories and Silence," *Oral History Review*, 46:2 (summer/fall 2019): 267-76.

Freund, Alexander. "'Confessing Animals': Toward a *Longue Duree* of the Oral History Interview," *Oral History Review*, 41 (winter/spring 2014): 18-26.

Frisch, Michael A. "Commentary: Sharing Authority: Oral History and the Collaborative Process," *Oral History Review*, 30:1 (winter/spring 2003).

Funderburk, Alissa Rae. "Oral History Narrator Compensation Alternatives," *OHA Newsletter* (spring 2023).

Garcia, Fanny Julissa, and Nara Milanich. "Money Talks: Narrator Compensation in Oral History," *Oral History Review*, 50:2 (2023): 148-68.

Gluck, Sherna Berger. "Reflecting on the Quantum Leap: Promises and Perils of Oral History on the Web," *Oral History Review*, 41 (summer/fall 2014).

Greenspan, Henry. "The Humanities of Contingency: Interviewing and Teaching Beyond 'Testimony' with Holocaust Survivors," *Oral History Review*, 46:2 (summer/fall 2019): 360-79.

Holmes, Katie. "Does It Matter If She Cried? Recording Emotion and the Australian Generations Oral History Project," *Oral History Review*, 44 (winter/spring 2017): 68.

Kerr, Daniel R. "Allan Nevins Is Not My Grandfather: The Roots of Radical Oral History Practice in the United States," *The Oral History Review*, 43:2 (summer/fall 2016): 367-91.

Lambert, Douglas. "Oral History Indexing," *The Oral History Review*, 50:2 (2023): 169-92.

Larson, Mary A. "Steering Clear of the Rocks: A Look at Oral History Ethics in the Digital Age," *Oral History Review*, 40:1 (winter/spring 2013): 36-49.

Larson, Mary A. "'The Medium is the Message': Oral History, Media, and Medication," *The Oral History Review*, 43:2 (summer/fall 2016): 318-37.

Morrissey, Charles T. "Why Call It 'Oral History'?" *The Oral History Review*, 8 (1980): 20-48.

Morrissey, Charles T. "Riding a Mule through the 'Terminological Jungle': Oral History and Problems of Nomenclature," *The Oral History Review*, 12 (1984): 13-28.

Reeves, Troy, and Caitlin Tyler-Richards, eds. "'Confessing Animals,' Redux: A Conversation between Alexander Freund and Erin Jessee," *Oral History Review*, 41 (summer/fall 2014).

Russell, Robyn. "Archival Considerations for Librarians and Oral Historians," *Oral History Association Newsletter* (spring 2004): 4-5.

Sheftel, Anna. "Talking and Not Talking About Violence: Challenges in Interviewing Survivors of Atrocity as Whole People," *Oral History Review*, 45:2 (summer/fall 2018): 288-303.

Sheftel, Anna, and Stacey Zembrzycki. "Who's Afraid of Oral History: Fifty Years of Debates and Anxiety about Ethics," *The Oral History Review*, 43:2 (summer/fall 2016): 338-66.

Sheftel, Anna, and Stacy Zembrzyciski. "Slowing Down to Listen in the Digital Age: How New Technology is Changing Oral History Practice," *The Oral History Review*, 44:1 (winter/spring 2017).

Shopes, Linda. "Mellon Project on Folklore, Musicology, and Oral History in the Academy—Background Paper: Oral History," unpublished paper, 2006.

Shopes, Linda. "Insights and Oversights: Reflections on the Documentary Tradition and the Theoretical Turn in Oral History," *The Oral History Review*, 41:2 (summer/fall 2014): 257-68.

Shopes, Linda. "After the Interview Ends: Moving Oral History Out of the Archives and into Publication," *Oral History Review*, 42 (summer/fall 2015).

Thomson, Alistair. "Four Paradigm Transformations in Oral History," *The Oral History Review* 34:1 (winter/spring 2007): 49-70.

Vickers, Emma L. "Unexpected Trauma in Oral History Interviewing," *Oral History Review*, 46:1 (winter/spring 2019): 134–41.

ORAL HISTORY ASSOCIATION PUBLICATIONS

A Guide to Oral History and the Law, second edition, John A. Neuenschwander for the Oral History Association, 2002 (see revised edition from Oxford University Press, 2014).

Doing Veterans Oral History, Barbara W. Sommer. A publication of the Oral History Association in collaboration with the Library of Congress American Folklife Center Veterans History Project, 2015.

Oral History for the Family Historian: A Basic Guide, Linda Barnickel, 2006.

Oral History Projects in Your Classroom, Linda P. Wood, with introduction by Marjorie L. McLellan, 2001.

Using Oral History in Community History Projects, Laurie Mercier and Madeline Buckendorf for the Oral History Association, 2007.

JOURNALS

Oral History Review. Oxford University Press. http://www.oralhistory.org/publications/oral-history-review/.

The Journal of the International Oral History Association. http://www.iohanet.org/the-journal-of-the-international-history-association-2017/.

The Journal of the Oral History Society. http://www.ohs.org.uk/journal/.

NEWSLETTERS

OHA Newsletter. Oral History Association. http://www.oralhistory.org/publications/oha-newsletter/.

ONLINE RESOURCES

Baylor University Institute for Oral History. *Oral History: Workshop on the Web*, http://www.baylor.edu/oralhistory/index.php?id=23560.

Baylor University Institute for Oral History. *Style Guide: A Quick Reference for Editing Oral Memoirs*, http://www.baylor.edu/oralhistory/index.php?id=23607.

"Capturing the Living Past: An Oral History Primer," Oral History Association, www.oralhistory.org/wp-content/uploads/2018/06/Capturing_the_Living_Past_-_An_Oral_History_Primer-3.pdf.

Making Sense of Oral History. History Matters: The U.S. Survey Course on the Web, http://historymatters.gmu.edu/mse/oral.

Minnesota Historical Society. *Oral History* (including *Resources*), https://www.mnhs.org/library/learn/collections/oral-history.

Oral History Association, "Archiving Oral History: Manual of Best Practices," https://oralhistory.org/archives-principles-and-best-practices-complete-manual.

Oral History Association, *Guidelines for Social Justice Oral History Work*, https://oralhistory.org/guidelines-for-social-justice-oral-history-work/.

Oral History Association, "Guidelines for Evaluation of Professional or Academic Oral Historians for Promotion, Tenure, or Other Review," https://oralhistory.org/oha-guidelines-for-the-evaluation-of-oral-historians/.

Oral History Association including its "Principles and Best Practices," www.oralhistory.org.

Oral History Association, *OHA Statement on Freelance, Independent, and Contract Oral History Labor*, https://oralhistory.org/oha-statement-on-freelance-independent-and-contract-oral-history-labor/.

Oral History in the Digital Age, https://oralhistory.org/oral-history-in-the-digital-age/.

Oral History Listserver. H-Oralhist is an international network for scholars and professionals active in studies related to oral history: http://www.h-net.msu.edu/~oralhist.

Shopes, Linda. "Questions to Ask," *History Matters: The Survey Course on the Web*, https://historymatters.gmu.edu/mse/oral/.

Vermont Folklife Center Field and Research Guides at the Vermont Folklife Center, https://www.vtfolklife.org/fieldwork-guides.

Voice of Witness, https://voiceofwitness.org/.

ORAL HISTORY ASSOCIATION

Oral History Association. Established in 1966, it provides professional guidance in a collegial atmosphere. Publishes the biannual *Oral History Review*, a digital *Newsletter*, a pamphlet series, and numerous other resources. For more information, see the Oral History Association website: http://www.oralhistory.org.

REGIONAL ORAL HISTORY ASSOCIATIONS

In addition to national oral history associations, many areas have regional oral history associations. Examples are the Michigan Oral History Association, Oral History in the Mid-Atlantic Region (http://www.ohmar.org), and the Southwest Oral History Association (http://www.southwestoralhistory.org). For details, see http://www.oralhistory.org/regional-and-international-organizations/.

INTERNATIONAL ORAL HISTORY ASSOCIATION

International Oral History Association. This is a world-wide network of oral history scholars, professionals, and researchers. For more information, see http://www.ioha.fgv.br.

ORAL HISTORY ASSOCIATIONS AROUND THE WORLD

Many countries have oral history associations that support the work of oral historians. Examples are the Oral History Society (Great Britain: http://www.ohs.org.uk/), Canadian Oral History Association (http://www.canoha.ca/), and the Oral History Association of Australia (http://www.ohaa.net.au/). Others include oral history organizations in Africa and the Middle East, the Americas, Asia and the Pacific, China, and Europe. For details, see http://www.oralhistory.org/regional-and-international-organizations/.

Index

About the Authors

Barbara W. Sommer, M.A., has over forty-five years of experience in the oral history field. She has been principal investigator and director of major community oral history projects and has taught oral history in post-secondary and community settings. She is a long-time member of the Oral History Association, where she has served in a number of volunteer positions. She is the author and co-author of *The Oral History Manual* (first through fourth editions), *Indigenous Oral History Manual: Canada and the United States* (2023, expanded second edition of *The American Indian Oral History Manual*), the *Community Oral History Toolkit* (2013), *Practicing Oral History in Historical Organizations* (2015), and *Doing Veterans Oral History* (2015). She also is the author of the award-winning book *Hard Work and a Good Deal: The Civilian Conservation Corps in Minnesota* (2008, reissued in 2022). She holds degrees from Carleton College and the University of Minnesota.

Mary Kay Quinlan, Ph.D., is associate dean emerita at the College of Journalism and Mass Communications at the University of Nebraska-Lincoln, where she taught for twenty years. Quinlan also has taught or team-taught journalism, oral history, and American history classes at University of Nebraska-Lincoln, the University of Maryland, Nebraska Wesleyan, and Doane University. Before turning to the classroom, Quinlan had a fifteen-year career as a newspaper reporter, primarily as a Washington correspondent for the *Omaha World-Herald* and Gannett News Service, during which time she served as president of the National Press Club. She has been active in regional and national oral history activities for many years and has served as editor of the *Oral History Association Newsletter* since 1993. Quinlan's oral history background includes conducting workshops, teaching, and co-authoring (with Barbara W. Sommer and others) several oral history publications, and she has presented at regional, national, and international conferences. Quinlan earned a bachelor's degree in journalism and French from University of Nebraska-Lincoln, a master's degree in journalism from the University of Maryland, and a Ph.D. in American studies, also from the University of Maryland. In 2022, she was inducted into the Nebraska Women Journalists Hall of Fame. In 2024, she received Oral History in the Mid-Atlantic Region's Forrest C. Pogue Award for Excellence in Oral History.